Strategy in War

For Tim, with thanks

Strategy in War and Peace

A Critical Introduction

Aaron Edwards

EDINBURGH
University Press

Edinburgh University Press is one of the leading university presses in the UK. We publish academic books and journals in our selected subject areas across the humanities and social sciences, combining cutting-edge scholarship with high editorial and production values to produce academic works of lasting importance. For more information visit our website: edinburghuniversitypress.com

Edinburgh University Press Ltd
The Tun – Holyrood Road, 12(2f) Jackson's Entry, Edinburgh EH8 8PJ

Typeset in 11/13 Sabon by
IDSUK (DataConnection) Ltd, and
printed and bound in Great Britain by
CPI Group (UK) Ltd, Croydon CR0 4YY

A CIP record for this book is available from the British Library

ISBN 978 0 7486 8397 0 (hardback)
ISBN 978 0 7486 8398 7 (paperback)
ISBN 978 0 7486 8399 4 (webready PDF)
ISBN 978 0 7486 8401 4 (epub)

Contents

Synopsis

Have you ever wondered why strategy remains a central concept in international security? Or why as a term it travels so well across the academic disciplines of history, politics and international relations? In providing the answers to these and other key questions, this book argues that strategists should aspire to conceptual sophistication, not sophistry, by exploiting the rich tapestry of history to understand strategic thought and action. It explores strategic episodes from world history and politics, dealing with themes ranging from the interplay between human nature and strategy-making to the organisational constraints facing states and non-state actors which seek to employ military and non-military instruments of power to implement their policy goals, as a way to help readers unpack the key scholarly and policy debates on strategy. The book's overarching focus is on assessing strategic theory as a practical intellectual approach to understanding the complex and uncertain international security environment in which we live today.

Preface

There was a jovial, if somewhat competitive, atmosphere as those gathered around the well-polished antique mahogany table in a prestigious room in one of the country's oldest military establishments contemplated their next moves against a determined enemy in the form of the Islamic State in Iraq and al-Sham (known in the West as ISIS and to Arab opponents as *Daesh*). Everyone was well aware of the high stakes involved in resolving the crisis in Iraq. After all, ISIS had seized over two-thirds of Syria before it turned its sights south and launched a lightning war across northern and western Iraq in the opening months of 2014. ISIS was indeed a ruthless opponent, laying waste to the paltry resistance displayed by Iraqi state security forces and executing prisoners as if international law and the Geneva Conventions were inconsequential. The room quietened as military officers and civil servants discussed their preferred strategies in hushed tones before making the next move. Then, emboldened in their single-mindedness to 'do the right thing' and rescue Iraq from the glowing furnace of Islamist extremism, they cast the die and began the fightback against ISIS.

This may sound like the kind of high-powered strategising that goes on behind closed doors in the corridors of power in Whitehall or Washington; however, on this occasion it was in fact a war game being played out by Directing Staff in the Le Marchant Room of Old College at the Royal Military Academy Sandhurst in March 2015. Even though I have taught on a security studies course at Sandhurst since 2008 – and have briefed senior policymakers and generals at home and abroad on everything from counter-terrorism to the challenge of future war – that spring evening introduced me to the uncertainty, chance and passion more readily known to those who have had the destinies of whole states in their hands. However, the opportunity to war-game some of what I have been writing and speaking about for many years was a worthwhile pursuit that evening. It also threw up some uncomfortable questions, such as: Who does strategy? How effective are they? What are states and non-state actors actually like at doing strategy? And, perhaps most importantly, why should we really care?

The American scholar of strategy Bernard Brodie was agnostic on the question of the utility of war games in preparing government officials and military commanders for the real business of strategy. He felt that the war game,

> even at its most elaborate, [was] an austere abstraction from the real thing. It is a way of eliminating one kind of bias, that is, it is a means of giving the enemy his full due, and also a way of constraining weak human beings to think through systematically a number of consecutive acts and stages in a conflict.[1]

If the war game is a process by which we can introduce probability and risk into our planning process then they are, he argued, 'marvellous ways of bringing informed, scientifically-trained minds intensively to bear on baffling problems'.[2] Nevertheless, what really mattered, ultimately, was the application of that knowledge of strategy to real world problems. As the Swiss soldier-strategist Baron Antoine-Henri de Jomini reflected in his posthumously published *The Art of War* (1862),

> The study of the principles of strategy can produce valuable practical results if we do nothing more than keep them in remembrance, never trying to apply them, with map in hand, to hypothetical wars, or to the brilliant operations of great captains.[3]

For someone who has been a participant, as well as a leader (albeit a junior one), in battlefield studies and military exercises over the years, it seems appropriate that strategy be, above all, a practical art. What I am always conscious to remind my students in my lectures and seminars is that strategy can be a guiding light, employed to illuminate the darker recesses of a complex and uncertain battle-space in which they ply their trade. Even if the problems these students may encounter appear insoluble or opaque at first glance, strategy can still offer them a way of making informed judgements, recommendations and, ultimately, as leaders, good decisions.

In this respect, strategy is fundamental to how we make sense of the world around us. It helps politicians, policymakers and military commanders to think practically about the ways they might achieve their stated ends with the means at their disposal. Whether in times of war or peace, boom or bust, strategy – and more specifically, grand strategy – has been vital in orientating peoples, governments and nations towards the future. From the Peloponnesian War of 431–404 BC to the Napoleonic battlegrounds of the nineteenth century, and beyond to the First and Second World Wars, the Cold War and the post-9/11 world, strategy has been an indispensable guide to action. Good strategy has meant victory on the battlefield, while bad strategy has been a recipe for crushing defeat and ruin. Importantly, the strategic implications of success and failure in war have far-reaching repercussions for peace. In peacemaking, for example, strategies of bargaining between belligerents can make or break negotiations, while staving off mistrust and fostering long-term reconciliation.

This book grounds discussion of modern strategy in its broader historical, geographical and intellectual context. It emphasises the political, social, cultural and, above all, the human dimensions of strategy. Although it assesses the contribution of important strategic theorists, from Thucydides and Carl von Clausewitz to Mao Tse-Tung, Thomas C. Schelling, Bernard Brodie and Colin S. Gray, as well as key strategic episodes, its main focus is on providing readers with a lively and concise introduction to the practical application of strategy in today's world. Adopting an interdisciplinary approach to analyse the under-explored concept of strategy, this volume seeks to appeal directly to students and scholars of history, political science and international relations, as well as those policymakers with an interest in the practical business of strategy-making in the twenty-first century.

It would be tempting to over-conceptualise strategy. Indeed, many books on strategy concentrate the reader's attention on highly abstract ideas, without linking them to real-world examples.

Moreover, there are indeed some strategists who have tended to avoid bridging the gap between academia and policy and practice. This book takes a different approach. It argues that strategists should aspire to conceptual sophistication, not sophistry, by exploiting the rich tapestry of history to understand over 2,000 years of strategic thought and action. The focus of the book, above all, is on familiarising readers with the military and non-military instruments of grand strategy. In this respect, it takes its cue from the work of strategists who believed in the utility of strategy as an intellectual approach to understanding war and peace. 'Conditions and weapons change,' wrote the naval strategist Captain A. T. Mahan in the late nineteenth century; 'but to cope with the one or successfully wield the others, respect must be had to these constant teachings of history in the tactics of the battlefield, or in those wider operations of war which are comprised under the name of strategy.'[4] This was something echoed by Sir Basil Liddell Hart, who thought fighting was 'a physical act', but 'its direction is a mental process'. Liddell Hart believed that the 'better your strategy, the easier you will gain the upper hand, and the less it will cost you'.[5]

Each chapter, therefore, explores practical examples of how strategy is applied, dealing with themes such as the interplay between human nature and strategy-making or the organisational constraints on using military power or diplomacy to implement policy. The chapters are organised in this way to illustrate the historical context in which strategy has been employed – and with what consequences – to enable readers to unpack the key academic and policy debates on strategy. The principal argument advanced is that the introduction of human factors into the strategy-making process makes it a much richer and varied body of universal theory than previously thought, opening up the possibility for exploiting other, non-lethal, options for politicians, policymakers and citizens. Here the book differs from others on strategy, both because of its analysis of grand strategy, a highly political concept that has utility in both war and peace, and its emphasis on the problem-solving attributes of strategic theory.

The US strategist Rear Admiral J. C. Wylie advocated a three-pronged approach to employing strategy as an intellectual framework. First, he recommended looking beyond battles to understand the general pattern of war, 'the whole of the thing'.[6] Second, he said that the basic patterns of strategic thought should not be looked on as any kind of secret. The more people who know about and understand these patterns, he wrote, the more healthy will be our democracy in strategic decisions. Finally, Wylie felt that strategy could be 'an intellectual discipline of the highest order and in evaluating it the strategist should prepare himself to manage ideas with precision and clarity'.[7]

As I have told general staff officers from a range of armies around the world, the main thrust of my role at Sandhurst is not only to give an intellectually honest appraisal of the political, legal and strategic context within which Britain's armed forces operate, but also to ensure my students are equipped with the conceptual skills to out-think their adversaries. It has become something of a truism to note that both the state and non-state adversaries facing Western militaries have turned increasingly to irregular or hybrid forms of warfare in the post-Cold War world. They may also be smarter, more ruthless and determined, and more willing to die for their cause than anything we have faced in the past. Moreover, I make no apology for thinking about security challenges in the international system from a strategic perspective grounded in the international relations theory of offensive realism.[8] Over the years I have had the opportunity to contribute to policy-making and discussion at a number of levels and remain convinced that developing conceptual thinking shaped by the intellectual tradition of strategy studies is key to grappling with the practical security issues frequently encountered by governments, militaries and communities around the world. Strategy, when practised properly and effectively, can, above all else, help in the unenviable task of improving national, regional and international security.

Acknowledgements

It is a privilege to thank a number of people who have contributed to my understanding and application of strategy over many years. First and foremost I am indebted to the work of Professor Colin S. Gray from the University of Reading, whose contribution to the scholarship on strategy is unparalleled. Without his pioneering work, the flame of strategy would be much dimmer. As with my previous books, I wish to thank my colleagues at the Royal Military Academy Sandhurst for supporting my ambitious programme of research over the years. In particular, I am grateful to Tim Bean for his generosity in taking the time to talk through many of the strategic conundrums detailed in this book. My colleagues Alan Ward, Dr Ed Flint, Lieutenant Colonel (Ret'd) Peter McCutcheon MBE and Dr Martin Smith have also been exceptional in encouraging me in my research and, therefore, deserve special mention here. The award of a research sabbatical in 2013 enabled me to get the book off the ground and permitted me some space and time to think through many of the issues and topics that eventually found their way into the finished product. Colleagues beyond Sandhurst, including Colonel (Ret'd) David Benest OBE and Major Crispin Coates, have been extremely generous with their time over the years and in permitting various opportunities to speak to a range of audiences about my research. My students, who bear the brunt of my meditations on strategy, have been excellent first responders when I have insisted upon road-testing some of my more unpolished ideas. The invaluable opportunities created by Colonel (Ret'd) Ronnie McCourt TD, in particular, have undoubtedly improved the quality of my analysis here and I owe my military and civilian colleagues at Sandhurst an immense debt of gratitude for the opportunity to interact with strategists from Santiago, Muscat and Riyadh to Khartoum, Dhaka and London and a host of other places in between on many of the ideas contained in this book.

As with other book projects, without the support of my family – my parents Jim and Barbara, my brother, Ryan, and sister Stephanie – and close friends, none of this would be possible. My friend and colleague Tim Bean has been first-rate in his practical assistance with reading lists and advice for an intellectual undertaking like this. I cannot thank him enough for his good humour in answering my many pedantic and precise questions about strategy and war over the years. This book is dedicated to him as a small token of my appreciation.

Introduction

Scope

What is strategy? How can strategy help to advance one's goals during times of war or peace? Who practises strategy, and with what consequences? Moreover, are they any good at it and if not, why not? These are just some of the questions posed and answered in this book. In this introduction we will consider some of the key issues in the study of strategy – from debates over the meaning of the concept through to how it has been applied by civilian and military leaders in the recent past, particularly in the United States, with what consequences, and whether we can learn from that experience – so as to face today's fast-changing international security environment with confidence.

Strategy and International Security

Strategists have been accused of focusing too much on conflict and the use, or threatened use, of armed force in human relationships. While it would be misguided to concentrate disproportionately on what Professor Sir Lawrence Freedman has called the 'dark side' of the strategic imagination, it is evident that the world has not become less violent, despite the arguments advanced by some commentators.[1] One has only to glance at the pressing security issues in the international system to see that there are clear benefits to be accrued from the practice of strategy. We are constantly reminded by governments that since the end of the Cold War in 1991 the world has become a much more uncertain, complex and unpredictable place.[2] For the forty-year duration of the Cold War between the late 1940s and the late 1980s governments looked to civilian and military strategists to provide certainty where none had existed before. Insofar as this strategic advice provided comfort, rather than certainty, those decision-makers in the front line of the confrontation between the two major power blocs of the United States and the Soviet Union had to contemplate the possible use of weapons of mass destruction. Should superpower rivalry escalate, then the threat from nuclear holocaust would become a distinct possibility and, as a consequence, governments looked to strategists to apply a robust intellectual approach to offset the likelihood of a nuclear war between East and West.[3]

However, the ending of this decades-long phase of confrontation between diametrically opposed power blocs did not automatically end great power rivalry. Indeed, there was little to suggest the prospect of long-term peace between the United States and Russia.[4] During the Cold War, renowned political scientist Kenneth N. Waltz made the case that a state became 'a great power not by military or economic capability alone but by combining political, social economic, military, and geographic assets in more effective ways than other states can'.[5] In doing so, great powers came to rely heavily on grand strategy to marshal these resources in the direction of their stated political objectives. Furthermore, despite its collapse and reconstitution as the Russian Federation, Russia was down, but not out. The truth was that new power vacuums had sprung up in regions such as South Asia, the Middle East and East Africa. Once places where nuclear war seemed like a distant possibility, they now became hotbeds for instability, genocide, ethnic cleansing and meddling by neighbouring states. After the drift towards unipolarity in the international system – with the US the predominant superpower in the post-Cold War world – the upsurge of ethnic conflict, terrorism and insurgency, to say nothing of the degeneration of weak states into failed states, disease pandemics and poor governance as new security challenges, made the international security environment a much more challenging and fragmented place.

Amidst the dissipation of superpower confrontation in the post-Cold War world, states nevertheless remained central but they have been joined in recent years by other non-state actors such as terrorist and insurgent groups, transnational criminal gangs, multinational corporations and non-governmental organisations, all of which have sought to embrace the practice of strategy. Just as power has continued to shift from West to East, it has also become more diffuse as it has filtered outwards from states to non-state actors.[6] In this context strategic thinking has been employed in a range of ways, from working out national security resources, foreign policy goals and the deployment of troops to the approach of businesses to the market. For example, the work of ancient Chinese general Sun Tzu has found a receptive audience amongst a new generation of business leaders. Unlike in war, however, in which military strategies 'were tested only occasionally in one-off encounters that might not always be as decisive as hoped', argues Freedman, in business, strategies 'were tested daily'.[7] Common to both business and warfare, therefore, we find that the application of strategy has ultimately required 'intelligence, imagination and nerve'.[8]

Nevertheless, it remains the case that more and more people have found the strategic approach useful as a guide for understanding complex challenges they are faced with in today's world. This is not a perspective accepted by all civilian and military strategists, many of whom have tended to over-militarise the concept of strategy, preferring to see it as only relevant for fighting wars, rather than enabling choices that may seek to prevent conflict from arising in the first place. As a way of avoiding adopting this narrow approach, this book defines strategy as a practical activity that can be employed by a wide range of individuals, groups and states in the linking of their stated end goals with the means at their disposal. In keeping with J. C. Wylie and Lawrence Freedman's flexible interpretation of strategy as having utility in *both* war *and* peace, this book regards strategy – and more specifically grand strategy – as being central to our understanding of how political actors get their way in the world.

As later chapters make clear, strategy is very much a practical process utilised by a range of actors in war and peace. It is not the preserve of military historians or defence planners, nor is it the preserve of those who concentrate their gaze on much broader geopolitical concerns. *Strategy in War and Peace* follows Freedman's lead in suggesting that 'Strategy is undertaken in the conviction that it is possible to manipulate and shape one's environment rather than simply become the victim of forces beyond one's control'.[9] There is, he argues, 'no reason in principle why the strategic imagination should not be directed towards improving the human condition through finding ways to restrict and progressively reduce the role of armed force'.[10] But one must nonetheless remain vigilant when faced with the prospect that turning swords into ploughshares might not close off the possibility that others, less affected by liberal sensibilities, find utility in force even if we do not. In the words of Prussian philosopher of war Carl von Clausewitz, one must be careful not to recoil too easily at the sight of slaughter, for it is indeed a serious business towards a serious end, but we should also 'not provide an excuse for gradually blunting our swords in the name of humanity'. If that is done, argued Clausewitz, 'sooner or later someone will come along with a sharp sword and hack off our arms'.[11] Despite its bloody-minded reputation, the application of strategy is, nonetheless, the measure of effective leadership by states, for the reasons outlined by Colin S. Gray:

> Those equipped with a Clausewitzian understanding of the nature of war and the function of strategy can turn their minds to the details of the problem of the hour, confident that they have in their intellectual armoury the necessary weapons to help them prevail over ignorance, confusion, friction, and stupidity.[12]

It is for this reason, ultimately, that strategy matters, though as a human endeavour we must be realistic about what it can achieve.

As stated above, strategy-making is, above all, a political activity that has been used by both civilian and military leaders during times of war and peace. It was the soldier-strategist Sir Basil Liddell Hart who distinguished between two principal forms of strategy: military strategy and grand strategy. As he argued in his influential book *Strategy: The Indirect Approach*, 'pure military strategy needs to be guided by the longer and wider view from the higher plane of "grand strategy"'.[13] In this respect, grand strategy refers to the utilisation of all of the instruments of national power – ranging from military, diplomatic, economic and, increasingly, soft power assets at the disposal of governments.[14] As Professor Paul Kennedy has written,

> [the] crux of grand strategy lies therefore in policy, that is, in the capacity of the nation's leaders to bring together all of the elements, both military and nonmilitary, for the preservation and enhancement of the nation's long-term (that is, in wartime and peacetime) best interests.[15]

Building on Kennedy's definition, this book departs from state-centric focused understandings of strategy to also ask how non-state actors use strategies to effect change that is favourable to their own agendas. In doing so it looks specifically at terrorist and insurgent groups, which are considered the most dangerous armed adversaries facing states, largely because of the political nature of the challenge they represent.

Strategy and National Security

One of the foremost practitioners of strategy in the world today is, of course, the President of the United States. Few US presidents, however, have been in a position to understand the process of strategy-making from the point of view of both a military practitioner and a policy agenda setter. The president may technically be the Commander-in-Chief of the US Armed Forces but it is rare for the office holder to have previously been a practitioner of strategy at the highest levels, especially in uniform. One president who did have first-hand experience of military strategy was Dwight D. Eisenhower. In his memoirs he recorded how a nation's 'global policy comprises the worldwide objectives of the government and the basic methods and programs developed for achieving them'.[16] As a career soldier, it might have been considered Eisenhower's prerogative to define strategy in purely military terms, though as president he did not do so and recognised how the US's principal adversary, Soviet Communism, had a sophisticated understanding of strategy too. 'The Communists know, as we do,' he wrote, 'that the security of a nation depends upon a balanced strength comprised of morale, economic productivity, and military power'.[17] By the late Cold War period there was a real danger that US strategists had become too narrowly focused on a military-based analysis of grand strategy. However, this did not automatically mean that they thought aggressively about how to meet security challenges and even under Republican President Ronald Reagan there was some consideration given to resolving the confrontation with the Soviet Union by more diplomatic means.

In 1984, Reagan's Secretary of Defense, Caspar W. Weinberger, outlined under what circumstances force should be employed by the US to protect its national interests. His six admonitions were later promulgated by the US Army officer who had served as his military adviser, Colin Powell, when he became Chairman of the US Joint Chiefs of Staff in 1989. In the 'Powell Doctrine', US forces were only to be used 'to achieve clear political objectives, which should be determined in advance, and that they should be deployed with overwhelming military force to achieve a quick victory'.[18] Professor Sir Hew Strachan informs us that Powell's logic effectively blocked US troop deployments in Bosnia in 1992–3.[19] Arguably, in the immediate post-Cold War period, US grand strategy was less suited to tackling problems that had become, in Robert D. Kaplan's emotive language, a consequence of 'the withering away of central governments, the rise of tribal and regional domains, the unchecked spread of disease, and the growing pervasiveness of war'.[20] Although this 'coming anarchy' may have been a natural consequence of the shifting balance of power in world politics, it was also thought to be part of a wider 'clash of civilisations'. In the words of political scientist Samuel P. Huntington:

> The local conflicts most likely to escalate into broader wars are those between groups and states from different civilisations. The predominant patterns of political and economic development differ from civilization to civilization. The key issues on the international agenda involve differences among civilizations. Power is shifting from the long predominant West to non-Western civilizations. Global politics has become multipolar and multicivilizational.[21]

In many ways Huntington may have overstated the degree to which the world had become multipolar in the immediate aftermath of the Cold War. By the 1990s the balance was further tipping away from unqualified allegiance to the nation state and towards particularist identities that operated both above and below the level of the state.

With the attacks by the al-Qaeda terrorist group on the US on 11 September 2001 the era of non-state actors appeared to have arrived, thereby, in the minds of some statesmen and soldiers, replacing the existential threat once posed by World Communism. Even if it did not rank in the same league as previous threats, suggested American political scientist Francis Fukuyama, 'The Islamo-fascist sea within which the terrorists swim constitutes an ideological challenge that is in some ways more basic than the one posed by communism'.[22] The challenge may have been basic but there was little basic about the solution, as the invasion of Afghanistan a matter of weeks after 9/11 would prove. The toppling of the Islamist Taliban regime in late 2001, however, signalled an end to the post-Cold War moratorium in US defence circles of using force in a more circumspect way, for, in President George W. Bush's words in the State of the Union address in January 2002, their enemies had come to 'view the entire world as the battlefield'. The time was now ripe to respond, Bush informed the American people. By remaining 'steadfast and patient and persistent in the pursuit of two great objectives', they would prevail over all enemies, including those who would come to be designated 'rogue states' by the US:

> First, we will shut down terrorist camps, disrupt terrorist plans, and bring terrorists to justice. And, second, we must prevent the terrorists and regimes who seek chemical, biological or nuclear weapons from threatening the United States and the world. (Applause.)[23]

Even though we might consider Bush's framing of the existential threat posed by a new asymmetric enemy, some strategic theorists have argued that the reality is somewhat different:

> The prime imperative of American grand strategy of the last twenty years has been to avoid another Cold War, that is, to avert the rise of

a hostile peer rival who could match the United States on key power dimensions and thus pose challenges to U.S. security interests across the globe.[24]

In taking action against the Taliban, the US was left with 'a choice amongst unattractive alternatives: tolerate a degree of terrorist violence against innocent American civilians, or invest enormous sums in blood and treasure to avoid this'.[25] The ready deployment of US hard power assets would send a clear message to states – as well as non-state actors – that wished to challenge the unrivalled power of the US: step aside or face the full frontal assault of the most powerful nation on earth.

The Weinberger Doctrine

First, the United States should not commit forces to *combat* overseas unless the particular engagement or occasion is deemed vital to our national interest or that of our allies.

Second, if we decide it *is* necessary to put *combat* troops into a given situation, we should do so wholeheartedly, and with the clear intention of winning. If we are unwilling to commit the forces or resources necessary to achieve our objectives, we should not commit them at all.

Third, if we *do* decide to commit forces to combat overseas, we should have clearly defined political and military objectives. And we should know precisely how our forces can accomplish those clearly defined objectives. And we should have and send the forces needed to do just that. As Clausewitz wrote, 'no one starts a war – or rather, no one in his senses ought to do so – without first being clear in his mind what he intends to achieve by that war, and how he intends to conduct it.' War may be different today than in Clausewitz's time, but the need for well-defined objectives and a consistent strategy is still essential. If we determine that a combat mission has become necessary for our vital national interests, then we must send forces capable to do the job – and not assign a combat mission to a force configured for peacekeeping.

Fourth, the relationship between our objectives and the forces we have committed – their size, composition and disposition – must be continually reassessed and adjusted if necessary. Conditions and objectives invariably change during the course of a conflict. When they do change, then so must our combat requirements. We must continuously keep as a beacon light before us the basic questions: 'is this conflict in our national interest?' 'Does our national interest require us to fight, to use force of arms?' If the answers are 'yes,' then we must win. If the answers are 'no,' then we should not be in combat.

Fifth, before the U.S. commits combat forces abroad, there must be some reasonable assurance we will have the support of the American people and their elected representatives in Congress. This support cannot be achieved unless we are candid in making clear the threats we face; the support cannot be sustained without continuing and close consultation. We cannot fight a battle with the Congress at home while asking our troops to win a war overseas or, as in the case of Vietnam, in effect asking our troops not to win, but just to be there.

Finally, the commitment of U.S. forces to combat should be a last resort.[26]

Although grand strategy is essentially about applying military and non-military instruments to accomplish the political objective being sought, it is also about lighting the path and guiding those who employ it towards a more favourable outcome. In other words, strategy has an explanatory function in helping us to understand why decisions were made in the way that they were and with what consequences. Theory is, if nothing else, an educated guess about how something works. In purely academic terms, strategic studies is a direct sub-discipline of security studies, which is itself a sub-discipline of international relations and all, ultimately, are branches of the field of political science. While strategic studies deals with many of the same concepts as the broader disciplines of which it is an integral part, it is much more about dealing with the practical application of knowledge in order to link political purposes with the means by which to accomplish these and is, therefore, more goal-orientated. There is no getting away from the conundrum of how one can achieve one's stated policy goal by applying the threat or actuality of force, even though strategy can also be considered a process aimed at preventing war and mitigating the effects of violent conflict. That one might choose to outsmart one's opponent both on and off the battlefield was fully explored in *The Art of War* by Sun Tzu (c.400–320 BC), which makes clear that 'what is of supreme importance in war is to attack the enemy's strategy'.[27] The way to defeat one's opponent, according to Sun Tzu, was to take advantage of their unpreparedness by exploiting weaknesses and vulnerabilities. Only by linking one's intended goals with the ends and means at one's disposal, though, can a level of success in war and peace be guaranteed.

Linking Ends and Means in Strategy

The sub-discipline of strategic studies has succeeded in focusing our attention on the utility of strategy in war and armed conflict, detailing the various courses of action that soldiers and statesmen have employed in order to get their way in the world. The emphasis has been on how good strategy can ensure victory on the battlefield. Even though strategy 'lies at the interface between operational capabilities and political objectives' and is 'the glue which binds each to the other and gives both sense', it is also based on 'a recognition of the nature of war itself'.[28] There has been a tendency amongst Western states to remain diffident to defining what that nature is. Consequently, we see an over-emphasis on change at the expense of continuity.

Throughout the second half of the twentieth century the world witnessed a marked decline in regular war, that is, an armed conflict between two fairly equally matched belligerents. By the 1970s it was becoming increasingly obvious that inter-state wars were being replaced by intra-state wars (or civil wars), where governments faced off against a variety of non-state actors in the form of terrorist and insurgent groups.[29] Most of these groups, in the words of Chinese guerrilla commander Mao Tse-Tung, recognised the strength of their opponents and sought to utilise guerrilla tactics to harrass and, in the cases of Cuba and Angola, overthrow the pre-existing order. As we know from recent history, they have chosen to do so by utilising kinetic and non-kinetic ways.[30] With the proliferation of intra-state wars, however, the idea of war did not suddenly dissipate from the minds of those military planners who continued to prepare for the eventuality of a Third World War between East and West. Many civil wars and wars of national liberation, such as Vietnam (1965–75) and Afghanistan (1978–88), drew in the superpowers and became vehicles for them to fight each other via proxies. With the end of the Cold War and the fragmentation of the Soviet Union and Former Republic of Yugoslavia, conflict over identity, rather than only territory or ideology, became endemic.

This has led to a switch in focus amongst military historians and other commentators from preoccupation with 'old wars' (i.e., conventional inter-state wars) to what Professor Mary Kaldor has called 'new wars'.[31] However, a note of caution is required before we accept this distinction wholesale. The Cold War itself witnessed a range of wars, from huge conventional conflicts, including the Korean War of 1950–3, the Arab–Israeli wars of 1949, 1967, 1973 and 1982, the war of independence between India and Pakistan, which led to the creation of Bangladesh in 1971, the protracted conflict between Ethiopia and Eritrea in the years 1974–91, the Falklands War of 1982, the Iran–Iraq War of the 1980s and the brief skirmish between Russia and Georgia in 1993. These wars have had far-reaching repercussions for the states involved and continue to fuel confrontation and conflict in the world today, particularly since they failed to decisively resolve the differences between belligerents. For Europeans, who spent much of the post-war period building up institutions to prevent a reoccurrence of war between Germany and France, this 'trepidation about war', writes Hew Strachan, is 'not just a matter of casualties, destructiveness and loss of life. It is an anxiety over political consequences.'[32]

For some strategists there is a tendency to forget the purpose of war and to concentrate only on the means employed to achieve it.

As British strategist Basil Liddell Hart informs us, nations 'do not wage war for war's sake, but in pursuance of policy'. Therefore, in Liddell Hart's view, 'any study of the problem ought to begin and end with the question of policy'. At the close of armed conflict, negotiations aimed at securing terms for the termination of war have relied heavily on strategy to ensure that the belligerents secure that peaceful outcome. In negotiating an end to hostilities, parties to a conflict must keep in mind the political objective which they originally aimed to accomplish. As Liddell Hart contends:

> The object in war is a better state of peace – even if only from your own point of view. Hence it is essential to conduct war with constant regard to the peace you desire. That applies both to aggressor nations who seek expansion and to peaceful nations who only fight for self-preservation – although their views of what is meant by a better state of peace are very different.[33]

Liddell Hart believed that war, even if it had been started contrary to reason, should be controlled by reason to ensure it was aimed at the rational object of war, that is, the stated policy goal.

Strategy as Art, not Science

As the preceding discussion has hinted at, strategy is a practical art not a science. With this in mind it ought to be relatively straightforward for practitioners to utilise the strategy process to obtain what they deem to be important to their interests. However, as we noted above, while strategy is simple to understand it does not necessarily follow that strategy is easy to do.[34] The unravelling of plans because of the miscalculations by states, such as the ill-thought-through invasion of Iraq in 2003 by the US-led 'coalition of the willing', which lacked a clear and coherent strategy, have been costly. And it is not just states who make mistakes. Al-Qaeda in Iraq, a non-state actor that later mutated into the organisation known as Islamic State in Iraq and al-Sham (ISIS, known to Arab opponents as *Daesh*), failed to circumvent the resilience of pre-Islamic tribal structures in the western Iraqi province of al-Anbar, thereby enabling the US to outmanoeuvre them. A similar miscalculation happened in Afghanistan, where the brutality of the Taliban in the Helmandi district of Marjah led to the spontaneous uprising of tribesmen against them and caused the insurgents to rethink their strategy.[35] In other words, the brutality meted out by these Islamist extremist groups in both Iraq and Afghanistan limited their appeal in places, even where there was some sympathy with their anti-government agendas. This was something that was learned by ISIS in 2014, a group that came to recognise the need to co-opt powerful tribes and other interest groups, such as Ba'athist party members (the old secular governing elite under Saddam Hussein), in order to put down firm roots and prevent an outmanoeuvring by the governments in Damascus and Baghdad. As we will discover in later chapters, the ability of non-state actors to interact, impact and, in some cases, dictate policy changes in the post-Cold War world has been consistently underestimated by states.

This book invites readers to consider what strategic studies can offer us in terms of insights into some of the most determined security challenges in the twenty-first century. As a practical intellectual approach, moreover, strategy offers us the opportunity to learn from three millennia of history to bring solutions to the most profound problems in the international system. In this respect, confining our analysis to military strategy alone would limit our understanding of how strategy is formulated and applied by political actors in the world today. In seeking to analyse the variety of instruments of grand strategy – military, political, diplomatic primarily – *Strategy in War and Peace* instead draws upon the close support of the most advanced historiography, as well as other disciplines most closely associated with a scholarly appraisal of these aspects of state power. By widening the scope of this book it is intended to go some way to addressing Sir Lawrence Freedman's observation that 'Practical problems can rarely be encapsulated in the terms of a single discipline', for 'Life is interdisciplinary'.[36] Given that it is rare for historians working in military academies to write history for its own sake, as luxurious and insipid a prospect as that might well be, it is important also to keep in sharp focus how strategy can equip us to deal with the challenges the future may well have in store.

Key Questions

1. Why is strategy important to states and non-state actors?
2. How does strategy differ when applied in the context of war and peace?
3. What is the difference between military strategy and grand strategy?
4. How can strategy help us to understand the world?
5. Why is it so difficult to link ends to means?

Further Reading

Baylis, John, James J. Wirtz and Colin S. Gray, *Strategy in the Contemporary World*, 4th edn (Oxford: Oxford University Press, 2013).

Burk, James (ed.), *How 9/11 Changed our Ways of War* (Stanford, CA: Stanford University Press, 2013).

Clausewitz, Carl von, *On War*, translated and edited by Michael Howard and Peter Paret (Princeton, NJ: Princeton University Press, 1976).

Eisenhower, Dwight D., *The Whitehouse Years: Waging Peace, 1956–1961* (London: Heinemann, 1966).

Freedman, Lawrence, *Strategy: A History* (Oxford: Oxford University Press, 2013).

Gray, Colin S., *Another Bloody Century: Future Warfare* (London: Weidenfeld and Nicolson, 2005).

Gray, Colin S., *Strategy and History: Essays on Theory and Practice* (Abingdon: Routledge, 2006).

Gray, Colin S., *The Strategy Bridge: Theory for Practice* (Oxford: Oxford University Press, 2010).

Huntington, Samuel P., *The Clash of Civilizations and the Remaking of World Order* (London: Simon and Schuster, 1996).

Kaldor, Mary, *New and Old Wars: Organized Violence in a Global Era*, 2nd edn (Cambridge: Polity, 2006).

Liddell Hart, Basil H., *Strategy: The Indirect Approach* (London: Faber, 1945).

Mackinlay, John, *The Insurgent Archipelago* (London: Hurst, 2009).

Mahan, Captain A. T., *The Influence of Sea Power upon History, 1660–1783* (London: Sampson Low, Marston, Searle and Rivington, 1889).

Nye, Joseph S., *Is the American Century Over?* (Cambridge: Polity, 2015).

Strachan, Hew, *The Direction of War: Contemporary Strategy in Historical Perspective* (Cambridge: Cambridge University Press, 2013).

Tse-Tung, Mao, *Selected Military Writings of Mao Tse-Tung* (Peking: Foreign Languages Press, 1963).

Tzu, Sun, *The Art of War*, translated and with an introduction by Samuel B. Griffith (Oxford: Oxford University Press, 1963).

Wylie, J.C. *Military Strategy: A General Theory of Power Control* (Annapolis, MD: Naval Institute Press, [1967], 2014).

1 What is Strategy?

Scope

Strategy is one of the most important concepts in the social sciences yet it remains ill-defined. Many definitions of strategy preferred in the Western world are generally confined to German, British or American sources. In asking the deceptively simple question 'what is strategy?', this chapter considers a broad spectrum of definitions from a diverse range of geographical perspectives, including under-explored Russian, Chinese and Arab sources. In doing so it makes the case that strategy is universal and timeless – it has infinite possible uses in times of war *and* peace – and, moreover, its defining feature is not only its explanatory value but also its utility as an intellectual approach for solving some of the world's most difficult security problems. This chapter also invites readers to consider whether it is strategically wise for states to run the risk of war in order to secure a better peace, which they often profess to aim to achieve, or whether they should avoid war altogether. It concludes by introducing a new strategic framework for application in security studies.

Introduction

The classic definition of strategy is 'the use of the engagement for the purpose of war' and was offered by perhaps one of the greatest philosophers of war, Carl von Clausewitz, a Prussian who lived between 1780 and 1831, and who formulated a general theory of war in his posthumously published classic *On War* (1832).

Yet, Clausewitz's concept of strategy was much more than a mere description of the use of force as a means of furthering a political end goal. Underpinning this illuminating concept is a powerful tool for thinking about war *and* peace in a way that was practically useful to those who would come to master it. And it is in this mastery of strategy that nation states, which by Clausewitz's time were becoming established as the principal political actors in international politics, seek to get their way in the world.[1] The utility of strategy envisaged by Clausewitz in *On War* was further promulgated a century later by the soldier-scholar Sir Basil Liddell Hart in his influential book *Strategy: The Indirect Approach* (1932), in which he reiterates the underpinning rationality of war found in the work of the Prussian master:

> For nations do not wage war for war's sake, but in pursuance of policy. The military objective is only the means to a political end. Hence the military objective should be governed by the political objective, subject to the basic condition that policy does not demand what is militarily – that is, practically – impossible.[2]

In more recent years, the meaning behind the interdependence – rather than the subordination – of war to policy has been refined by scholars who have made the case that *On War* ought to be read 'with greater care'[3] so as to exploit the opportunities Clausewitz affords us in '*how* to think about war'.[4]

Thomas Waldman has illustrated the complexity of Clausewitz's thought by employing the metaphor of a 'political web' which entangles policymakers and military commanders in the business of strategy. In his words:

> Wars, or events within war, are often utilized as political tools for interests that differ from proclaimed objectives. Whatever the form of such hidden motives and influences, these simply reflect the political web in which war takes place and from which it cannot be isolated. Policy-makers and commanders are inevitably entwined in this political web. The cynical reasons for which force is often employed may degrade the purity of policy, but it remains policy nonetheless and will invariably impact war, potentially to its detriment.[5]

Concurring with Waldman's political redefinition of Clausewitz's work, Colin S. Gray further informs us that, in practice, strategy is simple to understand but difficult to execute:

> Because strategy is hard to grasp as a concept and exceedingly difficult to do well, it is frequently the case that governments carry out policy (meaning politics), and they order fighting, but no one really connects the two with consistent purposeful direction; there is a vacuum where strategy ought to be.[6]

In short, as the international relations scholar Stanley Hoffman noted in his book *The State of War* (1965), 'force means little without the ability to use it well'.[7] It is in the conduct of its political and military affairs that the state has come to be regarded as the most proficient practitioner of strategy. Therefore, it is important to ask why this has come to be the case.

To illustrate this point about why it matters that states are proficient in the practice of strategy it is necessary to turn to a real world example. The choices facing Japanese political and military leaders in late 1941 were very stark. Japan's military was in good shape in the late 1930s. However, it was 'not free of weaknesses'.[8] Erratic government decision-making and shrinking stocks of foreign currency and raw materials guaranteed continuing US hegemony over markets in East Asia. As Professor H. P. Willmott would observe, 'every month that passed without her securing an alternative source of oil was one month that lessened Japan's capacity to resist an American military superiority that could only grow'.[9] In order to break the grip, the Japanese believed they had to launch a pre-emptive military assault on the US. It is clear that by launching an armed attack, the Japanese wished to inflict damage on US military power in the Asia-Pacific region, but in a way that would tip the balance economically as well. However, while the Japanese scored a tactical success by attacking Pearl Harbor on 7 December 1941 – an assault in which they crippled eighteen warships and killed scores of American sailors – they merely provoked a colossus, which would soon prove it had both the political will and the right strategy to match an opponent that relied heavily on its operational prowess.[10] Consequently, due to poor strategy and the heightened risks provided by armed conflict, the Japanese subsequently lost the war. The Second World War is replete with other examples of how political and military leaders failed to exploit battles for strategic gain. Several of these episodes will be covered in subsequent chapters of this book. Suffice to say at this stage that, although military commanders may like to think they take centre stage in war, in the business of strategy, politicians and policymakers do have an integral part to play in setting and managing the political ends as well as capitalising on the military successes during wartime. As Clausewitz reminds us, 'war cannot be divorced from political life'; or to put it another way, 'its grammar, indeed, may be its own, but not its logic'.[11]

Definitions of Strategy

'Strategy is the art of combining preparations for war and the grouping of operations for achieving the goal set by the war for the armed forces. Strategy decides issues associated with the employment of the armed forces and all the resources of a country for achieving ultimate war aims. While operational art must take into account the possibilities presented by the immediate rear (front logistics), the strategist must take into account the entire rear, both his own and his enemy's, represented by the state with all its economic and political capabilities. A strategist will be successful if he correctly evaluates the nature of a war, which depends on different economic, social, geographic, administrative and technical factors.'[12]

'"Each area, each level in the military domain, has this double aspect: the theoretical and the practical. All practical activity is conducted by reference to laws, principles, methods and processes established by theory and, in its turn, education draws from practical experience and constantly enriches the theory." There is a constant link between the two dimensions. Foch said, "You have to know a lot to have the power to do a little."'[13]

'Strategy is the science and art of improving military power in order to use it to increase the opportunities that will guarantee success for maximum delivery of force to achieve the goal of peace and war.'[14]

'Strategy is creating and orchestrating the instruments of power in support of long-term policy objectives . . . The UK's national strategy coordinates the instruments of national power in pursuit of national policy aims to secure our interests. The Prime Minister and Cabinet are responsible for the UK's national strategy. The government's political intentions are articulated as a national strategic aim or end-state, supported by strategic objectives. Our national strategy is contested globally within the diplomatic, economic, military and informational contexts. Therefore, formulating and executing strategy is dynamic and iterative. Unexpected events and crises may also radically change national strategy, requiring the military to operate outside of previous planning assumptions and Defence policy.'[15]

In his analysis of the role of states in war, Stanley Hoffman characterised these actors as 'the pied piper of death', but he was quiescent on the notion that they operated in a political vacuum. Pied pipers only succeeded, he argued, because of 'the bonds of affection and loyalty that tie their followers to them'. Even if we accept the hypothesis that the state remains the most dominant of all actors in the international system and, furthermore, the most accomplished practitioner of strategy, it would be wrong to see its actions in purely military terms. 'A certain moral blindness accompanies the assertion of solidarity that carries men to wars', asserts Hoffman, 'but denial of solidarity on behalf of peace or life has a certain moral arrogance.'[16] It is often thought that great power rivalry and war go hand in hand. Yale historian Paul Kennedy was one of the first to question the consensus that the decline in conventional wars between states after the Second World War and the technological development of nuclear weaponry necessarily spelt an end to the prospect of war. As he wrote in his magisterial *The Rise and Fall of the Great Powers* (1988), 'Those who assume that mankind would not be so foolish as to become involved in another ruinously expensive Great Power war perhaps need reminding that that belief was also widely held for much of the nineteenth century.'[17]

Although great power rivalry has dominated the international state system for hundreds of years, it was the First and Second World Wars that saw great powers clash in the most bloody and destructive global conflict ever seen. Even though they had echoed the equally bloody Thirty Years War (1618–48), the sheer appetite for fighting and genocide was unsurpassed. Even after the end of the Cold War, states have continued to determine the course international relations take. And they have been joined by a range of other non-state actors, from terrorist and insurgency groups to international organisations, such as the UN, NATO and the EU, and non-governmental organisations, including charities and human rights pressure groups, to say nothing of transnational actors such as criminal gangs, drug cartels and multinational corporations. As the world has become more globalised, a process spurred on by the development of new technologies, mass communications and increasing migration, states, and especially Western states, no longer command the authority and respect they once did. Power has become much more diffuse and newly emerging religious extremist movements have been undeterred in their single-mindedness to inform the West that their predominance is a relatively recent phenomenon. The erosion of the nation state, particularly in the West, to paraphrase Professor Sir Michael Howard, is well underway.[18]

Strategy: Levels of Analysis

Stephen Biddle has made the case that political scientists should pay more attention to the conduct and consequences of war, rather than simply its causes. He has argued that an appreciation of the different levels of war would lead to a more sophisticated understanding of war in the international system.[19] For our purposes, it is necessary to turn to an exploration of what these different levels are and how they interact in strategic terms.

Grand Strategy

Grand strategy is the subordination of all national instruments of power – military, economic, political, diplomatic, etc. – to the ends set by the government of a state. While the 'horizon of strategy is bounded by war,' writes Liddell Hart, 'grand strategy looks beyond the war to the subsequent peace.'[20] In theory, grand strategy is practised by those wishing to marshal all of the resources at their disposal to accomplish something deemed to be in their interests.

Military Strategy

Military strategy is the 'direction and use made of force and the threat of force for the purposes of policy as decided by politics'.[21] This category is narrowly focused on accomplishing effects in the military realm. General MacArthur's 'island-hopping strategy' in the Second World War would be one kind; the German invasion of France in 1940 would be another. As we will discover in Chapter 2, General Dwight Eisenhower's strategy of advancing on Germany along a broad front in late 1944 was a plan not without its flaws. Because it was to be achieved by a form of coalition warfare, involving not only the US but also militaries from Britain, Canada and Poland, it generated considerable heated discussion between him and his subordinate commanders about how he was to accomplish the objectives as laid down by political leaders back at home.

Operations

The operational level has come to feature in military campaigns since the late 1980s. Also known as the theatre level, it is the use of the engagement for strategic purposes. Britain's 'platoon house' strategy in Afghanistan in 2007 was the by-product of the operational level of war and 'capability-led planning' driving strategy.[22] Bad strategy led to British soldiers being put in harm's way without a coherent plan for

engaging in it.[31] Classical realists include historians E. H. Carr and Henry Kissinger, as well as political scientists Bernard Brodie and Hans Morgenthau. These theorists were concerned with describing and explaining international affairs as the product of rational behaviour. However, it is important to acknowledge Professor Michael Cox's caveat that we ought to 'take greater care when making sweeping generalizations about the relationship between a certain theoretical discourse and real world events'.[32]

Morgenthau on Realism, Strategy and Intervention

The work of Hans J. Morgenthau, the 'founding father of American realism', has enjoyed something of a renaissance lately. Morgenthau was an early advocate of the continuing relevance of rationality in the governance of state behaviour. Morgenthau defined 'politics' as 'a struggle for power over men, and, whatever its ultimate aim may be, power is its immediate goal and the modes of acquiring, maintaining, and demonstrating it determine the technique of political action'.[33] Although Morgenthau believed in interventionism as an option of last resort, particularly under conditions which favoured a state's national interests and the maintenance of the existing balance of power, he opposed the US's intervention in Vietnam on the grounds that it threatened to damage American prestige. He also held firm to the belief, intellectually at least, that such actions 'betrayed the fundamentals of realism'.[34]

In an influential article in *Foreign Affairs* in 1967, Morgenthau reminded his readers how intervention remained 'as ancient and well-established an instrument of foreign policy as are diplomatic pressure, negotiations and war',[35] but that the US's goals, in its 'misadventure in Vietnam' could not be achieved without 'unreasonable moral liabilities and military risks'.[36] Arguably, it was Morgenthau's 'calculus of power politics from a statist perspective' that defined later editions of his seminal work *Politics Amongst Nations* (1948).[37] It also informed his meditations on intervention during the Vietnam era, in which he argued strongly that 'All nations will continue to be guided in their decisions to intervene and their choice of the means of intervention by what they regard as their respective national interests'.[38] Morgenthau's work, which would later come to be known as 'human nature realism' or 'classical realism', would come to dominate the study of international relations in the 1940s and was based on the simple assertion that 'states are led by human beings who have a "will to power" hardwired into them at birth'.[39]

While guarded about why and when intervention should be undertaken for national interests, Morgenthau was forthright in advocating how this might be done. 'Intervention must either be brutally direct in order to overcome resistance', he wrote, 'or it must be surreptitious in order to be acceptable, or the two extremes may be combined.'[40] His theory of realism was fashioned according to a strategic conundrum, between the 'ends' of national 'interests involved' and the 'means' of national 'power available', which urged that balance ought to be a harbinger for success.[41] He argued – successfully as it later transpired – that the US should not overextend its reach for ideological reasons, for to make calculations based on anything other than hard-headed national interests invited failure in one's foreign policy. If nothing else, Morgenthau was demonstrating his consistency, reiterating the strategic view he first formulated 20 years earlier that 'the national power available determines the limits of foreign policy'.[42]

Fundamentally, Morgenthau believed that international politics could be defined as 'a continuing effort to maintain and to increase the power of one's own nation and to keep in check or reduce the power of other nations'.[43] Like most classical realists, he laid bare the zero-sum nature of power in the international system. However, he was sufficiently astute to know that 'the structure of the international system creates powerful incentives for states to pursue offense'.[44] His view of human nature, therefore, drove the competitiveness, selfishness and 'security dilemma' that saw the international system as an anarchic construct. Yet, even Morgenthau had a blind spot in his thinking, choosing to concentrate his gaze more on the interplay between national interests and domestic political opinion in the pursuance of policy, rather than on the symbiosis between these 'internal processes' and the 'very presence of other states as well as by interactions with them' prioritised by later defensive or 'structural realists' such as Kenneth N. Waltz.[45] Morgenthau, and realism more generally, forms an important strand in the intellectual genealogy of the strategic approach, especially when it gives consideration to issues of grand strategy, diplomacy and interventionism.

Unlike the US, where theory was more of a helpful handrail for understanding the shifts in power, in the Soviet Union, theory was more dogmatically the handmaiden of practice. Soviet strategists grounded their intellectual approach in a close reading of Marxism-Leninism, which stressed an adherence to dialectical materialism. Soviet theorists invested heavily in the belief that international relations was guided by what they perceived as the objective laws emerging out of Marxist theory. Theory fed policy and policy, in turn, guided action. As political scientist Margot Light put it, Soviet theory was 'a means of interpreting the past, a reliable guide to action in the present and an accurate method for forecasting future developments'.[46] Casting aspersions about the triggers of war was something Soviet leaders excelled at in the interwar period. Marxism told them that the underlying cause of war was always economic conflict. 'Although Lenin was firm about the economic bases of war, he was deeply impressed by Clausewitz's dictum that war is the continuation of politics by other means', argued Light, he also argued that the First World War was 'the continuation of the imperialist policies of two groups of Great Powers'.[47] As we will discover in Chapter 3, Lenin's disciple Leon Trotsky would embrace Clausewitz's more objective understanding of war, while Stalin would come to reject it,[48] believing Clausewitz to be part of the same Franco-Prussian militarism that would give birth to Nazism in Germany. Stalin did, however, share solidarity with the Clausewitzian analysis of the defence being much stronger than attack, and post-war Soviet strategy would play up the imminence of attack on the Soviet Union by capitalist powers and this would subsequently become a key component of Soviet strategy after the invention of the atomic bomb. Much later Soviet leaders would come to place considerable faith in the concept of deterrence, which stressed the need to signal to an opponent not only that you were *prepared* to attack but that you *would* attack.

There is a degree to which a thorough grasp of strategic theory is essential for those charged with wielding the instruments of state power. But that is not to downplay how strategists must be mindful of the role of chance or friction, as much as in their execution of a chosen strategy, in war. As Professor Cyril Falls informs us, to a 'very large extent strategy is shrewdness and common sense backed by experience, professional knowledge of weapons' and so on.[49] Without the technical competency, luck in strategy counts for very little. Sometimes the belief that one has inflicted a strategic blow against one's opponent can fool a belligerent into believing they have gained the upper hand. Rarely today do violent conflicts end with a clear-cut surrender or defeat and this can make it difficult for strategists to forecast the long-term effects of war on the ensuing peace. Nonetheless, what strategists can do, with a large degree of authority, is to explore the likely outcomes of pursuing various courses of action and advise on how best ends can be related to means in strategy-making. This is, ultimately, what strategists were able to provide for governments during the Cold War, even if they did not share a common understanding of the problems they faced. The end of the Cold War was thought to have heralded a 'peace dividend', particularly in the capital cities of the great powers caught up on the front line of the confrontation. Ironically, the fall of the Berlin Wall, when it came, would have much more far-reaching consequences for states, regions and the world than was ever thought possible in 1991. Rather than thinking about the Cold War as yet another set of strategic challenges, Western powers, especially, believed that it was the seductiveness of their liberal ideology that won the day, and not a superior handling of the strategic conundrums posed by the forty-year-long confrontation. This is important, for as Rear Admiral J. C. Wylie informs us, theory 'in any such slippery field as that of strategy is not itself something real and tangible; it is not something that actually has concrete existence'. It is simply an idea, a way to rationalise 'real or presumed patterns of events'. The real test is when the theory 'coincides with reality in any given situation'.[50] Rather than lose its utility with the end of the Cold War, then, strategic theory had new life blown into it as the prospect of nuclear holocaust was finally lifted from the world.

Strategy and the Changing Character of War

War is typically thought of as a process whereby uniformed armies oppose one another by force of arms across an open and predefined battlefield. This form of conventional warfare means that belligerents face one another in battle with near parity and are sustained by all of the central components of the state, from government, military and people through a mass mobilisation of the resources at their disposal. It is likely that that the state actor has taken the risky decision to commit troops to battle in order to seek a decisive settlement of its differences by bloodshed. Professor Mary Kaldor has challenged the basis of our conceptual thinking on the matter of both who fights wars and why they are fought. By categorising wars as either 'old' or 'new' she has attempted to point to the changing character of war from the 1990s onwards.[51] Stated very simply, 'new wars' are fought for a variety of reasons, including political, criminal and ethnically exclusivist reasons, and involve a myriad of belligerents. Rather than the principal rationale being to kill the enemy soldiers, Professor Kaldor highlights the rising number of civilian casualties in war as evidence that it has less to do with the resolution of differences between state forces and more to do with a deeply negative prosecution of war. For Kaldor, the darker recesses of modernity have given rise to the specific targeting of civilians, rather than combatants, in an attempt to reinforce the ethnic trappings of dominant groups within societies. Examples, including the fragmentation of the Former Republic of

Yugoslavia in the 1990s, serve to reinforce the uneasy ethnic equilibrium of these states and the consequences of pursuing war, in Clausewitzian terms, as the 'extension of political intercourse by other means'.

While many commentators have doubted the utility of Kaldor's prescription of the 'newness of new wars', it is interesting to note that she does not actually emphasise this aspect of her prognosis on the changes being wrought on warfare in the early twenty-first century.[52] Rather, her intention is not to undermine the Clausewitzian concept of political trappings of war – quite the opposite in fact – but rather to draw attention to how the character of war is changing and what policymakers might well do about it in the formulation of their strategies for managing armed conflict. If there is a criticism that can be levelled at Professor Kaldor it is not necessarily that, as her critics allege, she appears to overestimate the 'newness' of war, for mankind has demonstrated an insatiable appetite for settling disputes by violent means. In other words, the spear or machete may have given way to the drone and mobile phone but the delivery of death and destruction by bomb and bullet continues; it is the very art of duel, a wrestling match, in Clausewitz's metaphor, in which one opponent will try all he can to throw the other and, ultimately, to disarm him.[53]

Indeed, one cannot even criticise Professor Kaldor for her emphasis on civil wars, which are by no means new at all. British strategist J. F. C. Fuller made a prediction as far back as 1932 that 'War between nations will almost certainly be followed by war within nations; that is, civil war, in which the sufferings of the people will in most cases be beyond description'.[54] Where we can perhaps tackle Professor Kaldor's emphasis on 'new wars' is in those slow-burning conflicts that have evaded Western analysts, such as the genocide in Rwanda in 1994, or for that matter the two decades old series of armed conflicts in the Democratic Republic of Congo, where over 4 million people have perished by knife, gun, bomb and artillery shell, to say nothing of the structural deaths unleashed by disease, hunger and poverty.[55]

Christopher Daase has chastised those who, like Mary Kaldor and established scholars of war such as John Keegan and Martin van Creveld,[56] argue that Clausewitz's relevance has been lost along with the demise of 'old wars'. For Daase, 'Clausewitz provides the means for a superior conceptualization of political violence that allows us to describe historical and recent changes of war, including the emergence of guerrilla warfare and terrorism'.[57] This was earlier built on in an influential book, *The Utility of Force* (2005), written by retired British General Sir Rupert Smith. Smith made the compelling case that the old paradigm of industrial war was obsolete and that we must think of war as being 'amongst the people', which continuously stressed 'confrontation and conflict', rather than 'peace and war'.[58] The changing character of conflict has tended towards mass-casualty terrorism, resilient insurgencies, transnational links within and between armed groups, as well as the difficulty of mitigating risks and threats posed to state security. We know that 'the character of conflict evolves in close relation to changes in the broader strategic context'.[59] There are still those who doubt the accuracy of this conceptualisation of modern warfare. For instance, retired British General Sir Michael Rose has disputed whether war has actually undergone a paradigm shift at all:

> Indeed, there is little new in what is happening in Afghanistan today with regards to the nature of the war. As in all insurgency wars, winning the confidence and consent of the people of Afghanistan will always be more important than winning any particular tactical level military battle against the Taliban. It is this overriding factor that distinguishes the conflict in Afghanistan from conventional warfare in which the attitudes of the people are secondary to military imperatives.[60]

General Rose's view has been echoed by the former Chief of the General Staff, Sir Richard Dannatt, who countermanded Rupert Smith's articulation of a new paradigm by suggesting that 'we are in a continuum, not in a new paradigm'.[61]

Such disagreement on the changing character of war has been surpassed in more recent years by a recognition that what we should be debating is not whether the character of war is changing but how it has changed. David Kilcullen, a former advisor to US Secretary of State Condoleezza Rice, was among the first to advance the concept of 'hybrid warfare', which helps to explain how and why a myriad of armed actors operate in the way that they do:

> It is crystal clear that our traditional paradigms of industrial interstate war, elite-based diplomacy, and state-focused intelligence – the paradigms that were so shaken by 9/11 and the campaigns that followed it – can no longer explain the environment or provide conceptual keys to overcoming today's threats of hybrid warfare and a transnational enemy exploiting local, accidental guerrillas.[62]

Kilcullen's prescient analysis permits us a glimpse into the future at the types of threats emerging during the so-called 'global war on terrorism' that may well become the established pattern for future conflicts. In his view: 'Certainly in complex, multisided, hybrid conflicts like Iraq, conventional warfare has failed to produce decisive outcomes. We have instead adapted existing policing, nation-building, and counter-insurgency approaches – and developed new interagency tools "on the fly".'[63]

Kilcullen's point about 'hybrid wars' draws on the work of US defence specialist Lieutenant Colonel Frank Hoffman. 'The most distinctive change in the character of modern war is the blurred or blended nature of combat', argues Hoffman. 'We do not face a widening number of distinct challenges but their convergence into hybrid wars.'[64] This, of course, tallies with Rupert Smith's promulgation of most wars nowadays being 'wars amongst the people', in which, as Kilcullen points out, 'the utility of military force depends on their ability to adapt to complex political contexts and engage nonstate opponents under the critical gaze of global public opinion'. For Kilcullen, in these 'complex, multisided, hybrid conflicts like Iraq, conventional warfare has failed to produce decisive outcomes'.[65]

To be sure, the argument advanced by these commentators, of a twenty-first-century security environment more prone to fluctuations than it was during the Cold War (or even earlier), is certainly intuitively correct. However, we must be careful not to exaggerate this change. Strategy informs us that we must focus on both change and continuity and, for J. C. Wylie, it remains fundamentally a 'plan of action designed in order to achieve some end; a purpose together with a system of measures for its accomplishment'.[66] As we face an uncertain future it is instructive to consider broader strategic challenges, especially those that emanate

Franklin D. Roosevelt and Joseph Stalin, effectively determined the borders of post-war Europe. In 1989, the meeting between President George H. W. Bush and Mikhail Gorbachev on ships off the coast of Malta was meant to confirm Russia as a great power. That the US subsequently emerged triumphant in the wake of the collapse of the Soviet Union has remained a sore point for Russian leaders ever since. In Sakwa's view:

> The last straw was the perceived attempt to wrest Ukraine away from Moscow's economic and security sphere. The West regards Russian intervention in Ukraine, including the reunification with Crimea and support for the insurgency in the Donbass region, as a violent challenge to the system of international law. However, from the Kremlin's perspective – and, it must be said, from the point of view of the great majority of Russian citizens – the struggle over Ukraine is a desperate last stand to defend not only Russia's interests, but also that different vision of Europe's destiny enunciated by Gorbachev in the Cold War's dying days. Putin's Russia is a deeply conservative country at home, and in international affairs it claims to be defending a status quo threatened by the West's revisionism, manifested by the relentless urge to remodel regimes in its own likeness while pushing its security system to Russia's borders.[75]

Russia's goal of creating a more multipolar world, thereby reducing American global dominance, one might say, is being fulfilled by a grand strategy that aims to sow confusion and mistrust amongst the NATO allies. That it has stepped up its intelligence operations, including espionage, to levels not seen in over quarter of a century is further evidence of how Moscow is intent on rebalancing the geo-strategic calculus.

Notwithstanding its cynical interpretation of human nature, realism continues to have considerable purchase in influencing our understanding of international relations. Some states, wishing to accrue further power and influence in the world, continue to intervene in the internal affairs of other states, despite the norm of non-intervention encapsulated in Article 2(7) of the UN Charter. Indeed, this is done both directly and more surreptitiously, with state-based interventions being increasingly explained away under the rubric of the emerging international 'norm' of R2P

(Responsibility to Protect). The enduring relevance of national interests in affecting a state's decision to intervene in the internal affairs of another state is rarely acknowledged. For example, Uganda and Burundi's leadership of the African Union Mission in Somalia (AMISOM) is attributed to a series of principles that govern its mandate, none of which make any explicit mention of national interests. At the level of international politics as much as at the tactical military level power is the adhesive that enables actors, even weak non-state ones, to pack a punch whenever it comes to challenging states.

Strategy and the Rise of Non-State Actors

On the 11 September 2001, nineteen members of a relatively unknown terrorist organisation known as al-Qaeda ('the base') carried out a series of coordinated terrorist attacks on the United States which killed almost 3,000 people in the World Trade Centre, the Pentagon and on an airliner believed to have been bound for Washington before it was downed in a struggle between the terrorists and the passengers on board. By its actions al-Qaeda had begun to chart a course that would soon provoke Western powers into two costly wars in Afghanistan and Iraq and transform the international system in ways many did not think possible in the 1990s. Although the violent response to the 9/11 attacks included invasion of the sovereign states of Afghanistan and later Iraq, state and – more audaciously perhaps – the ensuing state-building projects, to say nothing of the dismantling of terror networks around the globe, there appeared to be a reluctance in the United States and Europe especially to deploy ground troops and large-scale interventions abroad.[76] This may be a consequence of war weariness, but it may also be a realisation that the problems 'over there' have their primary origins closer to home. It is something of a truism that al-Qaeda has been degraded both by Western efforts and, at times, in conjunction with more locally based state-based forces. Whatever the source of this aversion to risk-taking by states, there appears to be little to prevent non-state actors from seeking to strike at states whenever the opportunity presents itself.

Ordinarily, for terrorists to perpetrate an atrocity they require not only the intent and capability, but also the opportunity. Usually the opportunity can be found whenever states and their security forces drop their guard and expose their vulnerabilities. In simple terms this can manifest itself in the belief that the threat posed by terrorists is minimal in comparison to conventional war. It can also manifest itself in a lack of strategic imagination whenever it comes to permitting one's opponent the luxury of being as smart and resourceful, despite his or her inherent limitations. One way of thinking about the interaction of states and non-state actors is the belief in the rationality of the parties in conflict, as Nobel Prize-winning economist Thomas C. Schelling once wrote:

> To study the strategy of conflict is to take the view that most conflict situations are essentially bargaining situations. They are situations in which the ability of one participant to gain his ends is dependent to an important degree on the choices or decisions that the other participant will make. The bargaining may be explicit, as when one offers a concession; or it may be by tacit manoeuvre, as when one occupies or evacuates strategic territory. It may, as in the ordinary haggling of the market-place, take the status quo as its zero point and seek arrangements that yield positive gains to both sides; or it may involve threats of damage, including mutual damage, as in a strike, boycott, or price war, or in extortion.[77]

States and non-state actors have shown themselves willing and able to make credible threats to the safety and security of peoples across the world. That terrorism these days is a much more transnational phenomenon does not sit easily with international organisations, like the UN or EU, which were configured to manage inter-state conflict and confrontations. Nonetheless, it heralds a brave new world in which non-state actors have more of a say in international politics than they did in the past.

Those who look for a relatively peaceful transition in world affairs are continually surprised by the relevance of military conflict. We are frequently informed by self-deprecating academics that social scientists have never been any good at predicting the course of world events. After all, they failed to forecast the end of the Cold War, the al-Qaeda attacks on 9/11 and, more recently, the terrifyingly effective rise of *Daesh*. That academics have failed to predict the onset of the 'new face of terror' is an unfortunate outgrowth of the fixation politicians, policy makers and certain academics have for over-emphasising change at the expense of continuity.

Al-Qaeda's Dismal Strategic Vision

The following statement was issued by Osama bin Laden through the Qatari-based media company Al Jazeera in 2004:

All that we have mentioned has made it easy for us to provoke and bait this administration. All that we have to do is to send two mujahidin to the furthest point east to raise a piece of cloth on which is written al-Qaida, in order to make the generals race there to cause America to suffer human, economic, and political losses without their achieving for it anything of note other than some benefits for their private companies.

This is in addition to our having experience in using guerrilla warfare and the war of attrition to fight tyrannical superpowers, as we, alongside the mujahidin, bled Russia for 10 years, until it went bankrupt and was forced to withdraw in defeat.

All Praise is due to Allah.

So we are continuing this policy in bleeding America to the point of bankruptcy. Allah willing, and nothing is too great for Allah.

As we will discover in relation to al-Qaeda in the next chapter, terrorism is strategic in the sense that it uses force and the threat of force to communicate a message to a wider audience. Non-state actors like terrorists are able to strike at will and with impunity, as attacks in New York, Washington, Bali, Madrid, London and Paris attest. Their actions attract worldwide publicity, if not universal condemnation, but they are essentially limited in strategic terms. In the view of Colin S. Gray, 'Clausewitz's strictures on the subject of friction and the fog of war apply to irregular warfare, including terrorism and counter-terrorism, as much as they do to regular forms of conflict.'[78] Although terrorism cannot be decisively defeated, states continue to remain vigilant in the face of the increased risks – as defined by both likelihood and impact – so that they might reduce its strategic impact.

Conclusion

A leading authority on strategy and war, Professor Sir Hew Strachan, warns us that strategy 'has acquired a universality which has robbed it of meaning, and left it only with banalities'.[79] While strategy has indeed become an elastic concept, its meaning layered by 'confusion and ambiguity',[80] it nevertheless still remains the umbilical cord connecting policy with tactics. Defined by Clausewitz as 'the use of an engagement for the purpose of war', strategy has come to mean different things to different people. However, as this chapter has demonstrated, strategy may have become synonymous with the application of military power to achieve policy objectives, but it is by no means confined to this means. Strategy – and specifically grand strategy – has utility in both war and peace. Importantly, strategy, in this respect, enables politicians and world leaders to chart a path in international security flexibly enough to wage war successfully, or, to prevent war from arising. In line with Clausewitz's thinking on strategy, the ultimate purpose of war may be to disarm the enemy, but that does not automatically mean that bloodshed is required to accomplish this object. In his appraisal of the realm of strategy, Professor Cyril Falls reminds us that 'Strategy is not sorcery any more than it is geometry, though the skilful strategist sometimes seems to mesmerise his slower-witted opponent'.[81] Whether strategy is an art or a science remains an open question, but it is clear from the preceding discussion that it could be a little of both. The next two chapters ask how strategists have sought to reconcile the unequal balancing act of ends, ways and means that strategy demands of its practitioners when moving from its design to its execution.

Key Questions

1. How does strategy link policy to tactics and with what consequences?
2. What are the three general levels of war and how have they been blurred by the changing character of war in the early twenty-first century?
3. What contribution did social scientists make during the 'golden age of strategy'?
4. How have strong states, like Russia, applied grand strategy and with what consequences?
5. In what way do non-state actors, such as terrorists and insurgents, employ strategy and how does this differ from states?

Further Reading

Biddle, Stephen, 'Strategy in war', *PS, Political Science and Politics*, 40: 30, July 2007, pp. 461–6.

Brodie, Bernard, *Strategy in the Missile Age* (Washington, DC: RAND, [1959] 2008).

Brodie, Bernard, *War and Politics* (London: Macmillan, 1973).

Clausewitz, Carl von, *On War*, edited and translated by M. Howard and P. Paret (Princeton, NJ: Princeton University Press, 1976).

Freedman, Lawrence, *The Evolution of Nuclear Strategy*, 3rd edn (London: Palgrave Macmillan, 2003).

Gray, Colin S., *Explorations in Strategy* (Westport, CT: Greenwood Press, 1996).

Gray, Colin S., *Modern Strategy* (Oxford: Oxford University Press, 1999).

Gray, Colin S. *Another Bloody Century: Future Warfare* (London: Weidenfeld and Nicolson, 2005).

Gray, Colin, *The Strategy Bridge: Theory for Practice* (Oxford: Oxford University Press, 2010).

Heuser, Beatrice, *The Evolution of Strategy: Thinking War from Antiquity to the Present* (Cambridge: Cambridge University Press, 2010).

Howard, Michael, *Clausewitz* (Oxford: Oxford University Press, 1983).

Kaldor, Mary, *New and Old Wars: Organised Violence in a Global Era*, 2nd edn (Cambridge: Polity, 2006).

Keegan, John, *A History of War* (London: Pimlico, 1993).

Kennedy, Paul, *The Rise and Fall of the Great Powers: Economic Change and Military Conflict from 1500 to 2000* (London: Fontana Press, 1988).

Liddell Hart, Captain Sir Basil, *The British Way in Warfare* (London: Faber, 1932).

Light, Margot, *The Soviet Theory of International Relations* (Brighton: Wheatsheaf Books, 1988).

McChrystal, General Stanley, *My Share of the Task: A Memoir* (London: Portfolio, 2013).

Mearsheimer, John J., *The Tragedy of Great Power Politics*, updated edn (New York: W. W. Norton, 2014).

Schelling, Thomas C., *The Strategy of Conflict* (Cambridge, MA: Harvard University Press, [1960] 1980).

Smith, General Sir Rupert, *The Utility of Force: The Art of War in the Modern World* (London: Penguin, 2005).

Strachan, Hew, 'The lost meaning of strategy', *Survival*, 47: 3, 2005, pp. 33–54.

Strachan, Hew, 'Strategy and war', in Julian Lindley-French and Yves Boyer (eds), *The Oxford Handbook of War* (Oxford: Oxford University Press, 2012).

Sun Tzu, *The Art of War*, translated and with an introduction by Samuel B. Griffith (Oxford: Clarendon Press, 1963).

Thucydides, *History of the Peloponnesian War* (London: Penguin, 1972).

Willmott, H. P., *The Great Crusade: A New Complete History of the Second World War* (London: Pimlico, 1989).

Wylie, J. C., *Military Strategy: A General Theory of Power Control* (Annapolis, MD: Naval Institute Press, [1967], 2014).

2 Ends and Means in Strategy

Scope

Ends and means are theoretically linked by the umbilical cord of strategy. In practice, however, the business of linking the engagement to objectives is rarely straightforward. As we discovered in the previous chapter, each level of strategy is interdependent (but dependent nonetheless) upon the other, with the tactical battle linked to the wider operational campaign and the campaign to the overarching purpose of the war. However, at the level of grand strategy, there is much scope for disagreement between soldiers and politicians over the direction to be pursued. In assessing the challenges for military commanders in regular and irregular war, this chapter looks beyond capital cities to the 'ground truth' of operations. The difficulty of linking ends to means is a concern for both states and non-state actors, as the chapter makes clear. In order to get a more rounded picture of how ends and means are balanced in war it is necessary to look at the other side of the hill, at how terrorists and insurgents face similar challenges.

Introduction

In *On War* (1832), Clausewitz suggests that strategy is a process that seeks to link policy objectives to the tactics employed to win the war. The belief that this could be done by engagement with the enemy, however, predates Clausewitz's era and can be traced back to one of the oldest known accounts of men in battle. In Thucydides' *History of the Peloponnesian War* (431 BC), Pericles, the great Athenian general, makes an inspirational speech reminding his warriors of the need to make sacrifices to the gods for the glory of Athens. 'I could give you many other reasons why you should feel confident in ultimate victory', he tells them assertively, urging his people not to overreach in battle and reminding them to remain focused on the purpose of war. 'What I fear is not the enemy's strategy, but our own mistakes.'[1] We know that in more modern times, force has come to be more and more monopolised by the state. As responsibility for devising and executing strategy has widened to encompass political leaders, military officers, security chiefs, to say nothing of governmental, quasi-governmental and non-governmental bureaucracies, the scope for mistakes has also increased. Working from this starting point, Chapter 2 explores those instances when the modern state and its leaders and functionaries have had to prepare both intellectually and physically for war. In this it takes its cue from Niccolò Machiavelli's (1469–1527) celebrated work *The Prince* (1515), where we discover the Florentine consiglieri advising his master that:

> A wise prince must observe these rules, he must never take things easy in times of peace, but rather use the latter assiduously, in order to be able to reap the profit in times of adversity. Then, when his fortunes change, he will be found ready to resist adversity.[2]

For Machiavelli, studying war was central to the education of princes during times of peace and offered them a way of thinking about its consequences by attaining a rounded introduction to strategy. Much later, of course, Clausewitz would elucidate the key decisions of a strategic education in *On War*. Once it was established what war was meant to achieve it was easy to chart a course. However, while in tactics, strategy required 'more strength of will to make an important decision' and to press 'boldly on',[3] in strategy proper, war remains an intensely political activity, shaped by national interests and power. As we have already discovered, strategy is utilised by statesmen – working in concert with their subordinate military commanders and civil servants – as a way of employing force to achieve their policy goals. Ultimately, argued Clausewitz, while everything in strategy was 'very simple', it did not necessarily follow that everything was 'very easy'[4] and the more people involved in the strategy-making process the more likely became the prospect for its misapplication.

The conclusions one can draw from the intellectual antecedents of modern strategy are obvious. Successful strategy requires the participation of men and women with the conviction, experience and iron will to see it through, regardless of the resistance they encounter. However, it is important to address here the conundrum of how military power can be used in the service of the political object of war, that is, how ends can be reconciled with means. At the grand strategic level there is added pressure on strategists to utilise all available means at their disposal in order to accomplish their overriding objectives. As Professor Paul Kennedy informs us:

> It is because of the essentially political nature of grand strategy – what are this nation's larger aims in the world, and how best can they be secured – that there has to be such a heavy focus upon the issue of reconciling ends and means.[5]

At the lower levels of military strategy, at the level of operations and tactics, the sharper end of conflict tends to concentrate minds on the immediate task of fighting and killing the enemy. In his evocative tale of soldiers deployed to the harsh battlefields of Afghanistan, journalist Sebastian Junger paints a vivid portrait of life on the front line for US soldiers. He draws several pertinent points about combat from his time embedded with soldiers who saw the 'ground truth' reality of operations. 'Combat starts out as a fairly organized math problem involving trajectories and angles but quickly decays into a kind of violent farce, and the randomness of that farce can produce strange outcomes.'[6] The Korengal mountains held a foreboding, almost hypnotic allure for the American troops stationed there during the US-led intervention in 2001–14. But they were less demanding for in-theatre commanders and strategists back in Washington. Success in battle in an outpost like this could make a real difference in war only when it was worked into a wider narrative that sought to claim victory from Taliban forces at a strategic level. General Stanley McChrystal, the senior commander of all coalition troops in the country between 2009 and 2010, captured the essence of what the International Security Assistance Force (ISAF) was attempting to do in its strategy:

Not only was the Afghans' allegiance critical, but I did not think we would defeat the Taliban solely by depleting their ranks. We would win by making them irrelevant by limiting their ability to influence the lives of Afghans, positively or negatively. We needed to choke off their access – physical, psychological, economic – to the population.[7]

In this process, it became vital that the grand strategic plan to win the consent of the Afghan population dovetailed with the operational priority of protecting the local population and rendering the insurgents irrelevant, while also seeking to win every engagement at the tactical level. Without success at every level the possibility of strategic victory can remain elusive.

Linking Ends and Means

'In tactics the means are the fighting forces trained for combat; the end is victory ... Here, it is enough to say that the enemy's withdrawal from the battlefield is the sign of victory. Strategy thereby gains the end it had ascribed to the engagement, the end that constitutes its real significance. This significance admittedly will exert a certain influence on the kind of victory achieved. A victory aimed at weakening the enemy's fighting forces is different from the one that is only meant to seize a certain position. The significance of an engagement may therefore have a noticeable influence on its planning and conduct, and is therefore to be studied in connection with tactics.'[8]

'The original means of strategy is victory – that is, tactical success; its ends, in the final analysis, are those objects which will lead directly to peace. The application of these means for these ends will also be attended by factors that will influence it to a greater or lesser degree.'[9]

'Strategy depends for success, first and most, on a sound calculation and co-ordination of the end and the means. The end must be proportioned to the total means ...'[10]

Grand Strategy and Civil Military Relations

General Sir Peter Wall was head of the British Army between 2010 and 2014. He oversaw the transformation of the regular army from a standing strength of 102,000 soldiers to a small, agile and adaptable force structure of 82,500 troops. The remainder of the projected 112,000 standing army would be backfilled with reserves, all of which would be required to be in place by 2020. It was the biggest shake-up of the Army in a quarter of a century. In May 2014, General Wall addressed the Royal Military Academy Sandhurst on the theme of values-based leadership. Noted as being a somewhat cautious general, he told his audience that dealing with politicians on a daily basis meant he had to offer professional military advice, even if this risked giving government ministers the unvarnished truth. 'There must be one accepted version of the truth', he told those gathered to hear him speak. 'You have to be honest.'[11] This was particularly insightful, especially as General Wall's tenure as Chief of the General Staff (CGS) witnessed a 20 per cent reduction in the size of the armed forces and an overall decrease in the influence of the defence chiefs. General Wall saw this as an opportunity rather than a challenge, since he was 'freed up to run the Army'. By permanently relocating the Chiefs of Staff to their respective headquarters outside central London, the government was reducing their capacity to intervene in what Downing Street regarded as purely political matters. In a study of Britain's high command, Major General Christopher Elliott suggests that the reason why military commanders stray so readily into political matters is because of their lack of involvement in the making of grand strategy:

> The Chiefs, by contrast, trade in absolutes or in fine judgements of risk, forged from the binary 'win or lose' of the battlefield, and it is counter-intuitive for them to 'fly blind' or engage in a 'suck it and see' approach. They are not comfortable with loose discussions peppered with compromises, or the balancing between competing priorities which is the reality of the discussions in Whitehall. They like decisiveness, not deliberately weaving a web of ambiguity and spinning things out as the political classes inevitably find they have to do.[12]

concerned'. Churchill was adamant that such changes at the level of military operations should be approved at the highest grand strategic levels. 'What cannot possibly be allowed', said Churchill, 'is that the Governments concerned should not be consulted about changes so far-reaching in the high commands.' In a slight broadside fired at Alanbrooke, Churchill protested: 'You were perfectly justified in acquainting me when you did of the proceedings, but I do not think matters should have gone so far without my being informed. Happily we are agreed on what should actually be done.'[31] Later, the British Chiefs of Staff informed Churchill that they believed there needed to be a 'thrust':

> In our opinion the limited success which has so far attended the operations envisaged in General Eisenhower's directive of 28th October has been due to the dispersion of effort which has taken place and to the lack of concentration of force at the vital point. From what General Eisenhower has told us we are apprehensive that this will probably occur again.[32]

In a revision of the strategic military aim, Eisenhower reissued orders to his subordinate commanders: 'To destroy enemy forces WEST of the RHINE, NORTH of the MOSELLE and to prepare for crossing the RHINE in force with the main effort NORTH of the RUHR'. Yet, he refused to back down on Montgomery's insistence that the campaign was flagging, telling his subordinate:

> I am not quite sure I know exactly what you mean by strategic reverse; certainly to date we have failed to achieve all that we had hoped to by this time, which hopes and plans were based upon conditions as we knew them or estimated them when the plans were made. The Ruhr is an important place, but let us never forget for one second that our primary objective is to defeat the German forces that are barring our way into Germany. The Ruhr itself was always given as a geographical objective, not only for its importance to Germany, but because it was believed that in that region the German forces would be largely concentrated to meet our attacks.[33]

With the bruising encounter in Montgomery's headquarters fresh in his mind Eisenhower urged him 'not to continue to look upon the past performances of this great fighting force as a failure'.

The debate over military strategy in the North-West Europe campaign of 1944 demonstrates that friction can come from within as much as without. Human factors, such as arrogance, disagreement and the enemy's refusal to leave the field of battle, can coalesce to throw even the best strategies into sharp relief. It also reinforces how conventional war is fought by belligerents that are close to parity with one another in terms of military power, equipment and numbers. However, it is important to switch our attention to those asymmetric conflicts where that parity is non-existent and where the weaker belligerent resorts to tactics and strategies that seek to maximise their reach by exploiting the weaknesses of their enemies. This is especially the case in guerrilla warfare when the smaller force seeks to attack (usually) the state and its forces at the point where it is most vulnerable. In short, it seeks also to hit the enemy where it is weakest in much the same way as Montgomery's idea of 'colossal cracks'.

Ends and Means in Post-Maoist Guerrilla Warfare

According to the twentieth century's most famous guerrilla leader and strategist, Mao Tse-Tung, the question of linking ends and means was one of the most important questions in the planning and execution of military operations. Mao believed strongly that, as a strategy, guerrilla warfare gave the weak an ability to confront the strong on terms that exaggerated their differences while enabling the former the possibility of securing victory over the latter, even when the odds were stacked against them. It could be argued that this form of guerrilla warfare has put governments and occupying powers at something of a disadvantage, despite their advantageous command over military and non-military resources. It also suggests that everything that contributes to the maintenance of a functioning state – in terms of the monopoly over the legitimate use of force – hinges on a blended approach of consent and coercion being used in response to the challenge.

The post-war period would see a dramatic upsurge in armed groups resorting to guerrilla warfare. Although by no means a new set of tactics, guerrilla warfare became synonymous with

Communist movements that sought to play on emotional ties to ethnicity and nationalism to give sustenance to the anti-state message they were articulating. The concept of 'propaganda of the deed' enabled these groups to take the fight to much larger and better trained security forces because of the reliance on 'shoot-and-scoot' tactics. Ambushes and individual assassinations of high value targets came to define terrorism that grew out of a necessity to switch tactics whenever state forces discovered new ways of beating their irregular opponents. As a consequence states began to warm to the idea of special operations forces that could give them greater strategic reach in preventing and responding to surprise attacks by terrorists. While insurgents and classic guerrillas generally distinguished themselves on the battlefield by carrying their arms openly, identifying themselves according to an emblem or combat fatigues, groups such as ETA (the Basque nationalist group Euskadi Ta Askatasuna) and the IRA (Irish Republican Army) did not. They certainly did so in their propaganda videos and publications, but the reality was that they could not distinguish themselves from non-combatants for to do so would have sealed their fate in open engagements with the security forces.

The Strategic Utility of Special Operations Forces

The deployment of an SAS (Special Air Service) squadron to put down a rebellion in Muscat and Oman in 1958–9 demonstrated how modern states could call upon special operations forces to offer strategic options in service of political objectives. The Middle Eastern intervention proved that the tactics developed in Malaya could be successfully applied to operations elsewhere. In a sign of things to come, the SAS mission was to 'penetrate the JEBEL AKDAR to kill or capture the rebel leaders TALIB, GHALIB and SULEIMAN and their followers'.[34] Faced with a lack of intelligence, split loyalties amongst the civilian population, and an enemy that were masters at concealment from the air, the SAS developed a plan based on deception, reliable combat service support and aggressive patrolling. The enemy they faced was determined and well-armed and they succeeded in killing their first SAS casualty on 26 November 1958. In reports filed at the time, the SAS demonstrated great humility towards their opponents: 'As to the enemy they are a much tougher crowd than was thought – especially the hardcore whose minor tactics – fire and movement especially – are first class. I think it will take us some time [to defeat them].'[35]

Yet, the battle imposed constraints as it gained momentum and soon proved to be a very different environment from Malaya. SAS officer Major Johnny Watts filed an after action report in which he said that rest and retraining periods 'mean failure to ensure continuous pressure against enemy'.[36] In a private letter to his commanding officer, Anthony Deane-Drummond, Watts wrote: 'The squadron are all in very good heart and health though some are feeling the strain of this type of fighting – very different to Malaya – battles last for hours and some soldiers have a number of cut faces due to chips of rock kicked up by close bullets. We have been lucky on the casualty side to date but I fear the law of averages will award us some soon.'[37] SAS operations were ultimately designed to enable the British government to effect a strategic outcome to the insurgency. Deane-Drummond informed his boss back in London that, even 'if we do not kill Talib I think we should be able to give his followers really bloody noses. This should condition the rebels' frame of mind to the extent where negotiations will be successful.'[38] The lessons learned by the SAS in Oman would soon be re-applied in other theatres and would go some way to proving the utility of special operations forces.

In Algeria, a bloody campaign by the Algerian state forces against the Front de Libération Nationale (FLN, National Liberation Front) and its armed wing, the Armée de Libération Nationale (ALN) was marked by increasing brutality as the combatants slugged it out between 1954 and 1962. Deployments of French troops in response to the opening of the ALN insurgency were 'hesitant and misdirected' and a lack of intelligence meant that the initial 'reflex action was to aid, rather than hinder, the FLN'.[39] Large-scale arrests and an influx of an additional 20,000 troops could not camouflage the fact that the French lacked situational awareness and 'failed to appreciate the nature and potential scale of the insurgency they faced'.[40] The French response grew more heavy-handed as the insurgency wore on and by 1958 was showing a degree of success. There was even a threat from the French generals to march on Paris. Operation Resurrection would have entailed an airborne assault on the capital and in all probability secured 'significant support from commanders based in metropolitan France'.[41] Acting to prevent an escalation of the crisis, Charles de Gaulle demanded the resignation of left-wing president Pierre Pflimlin and, following endorsement by the socialists, contested an election in which he won 80 per cent of the popular vote. By the end of the year de Gaulle had been installed as French president and moved to end the insurgency in Algeria.

France was not the only former imperial power to face a determined insurgency in the mid-twentieth century. After 1969 Britain faced one of its most determined adversaries in the form of the Provisional IRA. IRA leaders learned much from the national liberation struggles affecting other parts of the world from Algeria to Vietnam and Rhodesia to South Africa and beyond to Cuba. Guerrilla warfare was deemed to have considerable utility in that it offered the weaker side strategic advantage if it could draw states into inflicting harsh penalties on the people from whom the guerrillas drew support and sympathy. By 1972 the IRA succeeded in placing the British government and its security forces on the back foot, particularly since they had not had to fight a guerrilla army on home soil since the Irish War of Independence in the second decade of the twentieth century. A decision by senior military strategists in the Army's headquarters in Lisburn, just outside Belfast, to take action based on previous intimate knowledge of campaigns in colonial hotspots in Malaya, Cyprus and Aden only served to make matters worse. In 1972 the total number of casualties reached 497 dead and ten times as many injured. After successful peace talks aimed at reaching political accommodation in Sunningdale, England, at the end of 1973, the resulting power-sharing executive was

brought down by a popular strike by the majority Protestant unionist community. By now 1,000 people had lost their lives, including
300 soldiers and 25 police officers, and the situation began to further deteriorate. The security forces were in turmoil, with their tactics called into question by the European Court of Human Rights
and the lack of a coherent strategy from London. The senior Army
general in the Province, Sir Frank King, wrote to the government
minister in charge of Northern Ireland, Merlyn Rees:

> I have become increasingly disturbed by the lack of intelligence forth-
> coming from the questioning of the many terrorists that we have
> arrested. In the remainder of the United Kingdom it would be true
> to say that police questioning is one of, if not the primary, source of
> operational intelligence against subversives. Whilst I fully understand
> the emotive issues that arise with Army involvement and also the
> problems for the RUC with Strasbourg still unresolved, it does appear
> that this is an area which is going by default and it is tying the hands
> of the Security Forces to a degree which makes no sense in what must
> be termed insurgency conditions.[42]

As far as the authorities in London were concerned, the Army was
playing an invaluable role in helping to restore security amidst
increasing intercommunal violence:

> Ever since the Army were called into Northern Ireland in 1969 it has
> performed the essential task of helping to maintain law and order and
> to protect the innocent majority of men, women and children in a part
> of the United Kingdom where the level of violence and terrorism is
> clearly beyond the capacity of normal police control. Everything pos-
> sible is done to provide our troops with the best support and equip-
> ment including protective equipment. They have had considerable
> success but have also suffered loss of life and injuries which the Gov-
> ernment deeply regrets. It must be remembered that Northern Ireland
> is part of the United Kingdom and as such its citizens are entitled to
> the same protection from terrorism as the people of any other part of
> the United Kingdom.[43]

Behind the scenes politicians groped around in the dark for a strategy, which saw the military take the lead between 1971 and 1976
until a more comprehensive plan could be put in place.

to be lucky always. Give Ireland peace and there will be no war.' The message being communicated, though in a very different political context, remains much the same. Withdraw your troops, submit to our demands or die. Although the maximalist demands of *Daesh* are unrealistic, it does provide a lightning rod around which disaffected individuals across the world can unite.

Conclusion

The state is regarded as the most important political actor in international relations. The rise of the modern state can be traced back to the Treaty of Westphalia in 1648, which drew to a close the devastating Thirty Years War. Although the concept of the state in fact dates back to the city states, principalities and other collective political units of ancient Greece, it has its modern roots in the industrial revolution of the nineteenth century. Nowadays the state is under increasing pressure to maintain its relevance in the lives of citizens across the world. As we have seen above, there has been a serious challenge levelled from Islamist extremism that rejects modernism and plays to a broader identity that is dictated by a religion that does not even pre-date the birth of Christ. In this sense it is not so much a challenge to the state as the disparate tribal identities of many states in the Middle East. The challenge for strategists is how to achieve policy goals in societies where the centralising authority of the state itself is under fire from non-state actors with a powerful narrative capable of rivalling the government in providing for its citizens.

Key Questions

1. Why is a unified vision in civil–military relations important in grand strategy?
2. Why is it important to link ends to means?
3. What effect do internal disagreements have on the implementation of military strategies?
4. Why is it difficult for states to respond to terrorists and insurgents?
5. What challenge does Islamist terrorism and insurgency pose to states?

Further Reading

Beevor, Antony, *The Second World War* (London: Weidenfeld and Nicolson, 2012).

Burke, Jason, *The 9/11 Wars* (London: Penguin, 2011).

Cohen, Eliot A., *Supreme Command: Soldiers, Statesmen, and Leadership in Wartime* (New York: Free Press, 2002).

Elliott, Christopher, *High Command: British Military Leadership in the Iraq and Afghanistan Wars* (London: C. Hurst and Co., 2015).

Handel, Michael (ed.), *Clausewitz and Modern Strategy* (London: Frank Cass, 1986).

Handel, Michael, *Masters of War: Classical Strategic Thought*, 3rd edn (London: Frank Cass, 2001).

Hart, Russell, *Clash of Arms: How the Allies Won in Normandy* (Oklahoma: University of Oklahoma Press, 2004).

Hart, Stephen, *Colossal Cracks: Montgomery's 21st Army Group in Northwest Europe, 1944–45* (Mechanicsburg, PA: Stackpole Books, 2007).

Hosken, Andrew, *Empire of Fear: Inside the Islamic State* (London: Oneworld, 2015).

Junger, Sebastian, *War* (London: Fourth Estate, 2010).

Kennedy, Paul (ed.), *Grand Strategies in War and Peace* (New Haven, CT: Yale University Press, 1991).

Machiavelli, Niccolò, *The Art of War*, revised edn (Indianapolis, IN: Bobbs-Merrill, [1521] 1965).

Mao Tse-Tung, *Selected Military Writings* (Peking: Foreign Languages Press, 1963).

Paret, Peter, *Makers of Modern Strategy: From Machiavelli to the Nuclear Age* (Oxford: Clarendon Press, 1986).

Urban, Mark, *Big Boys Rules: The SAS and the Struggle against the IRA* (London: Faber, 1992).

3 The Practical Application of Strategy

Scope

The utility of strategy stands or falls on the basis of a skilful balancing of ends, ways and means. Often, this is dependent on the ability of civilian and military leaders to reach an agreed position on what can most realistically be achieved in the process of strategy formulation and execution. By focusing on the decision-making process, this chapter introduces readers to how strategy has been practically applied from the early twentieth century to the present day. It presents a diverse array of cases, from Bolshevik strategy during the Russian Civil War, via American-led counter-insurgency strategy in the Vietnam War to Britain's application of a counter-terrorist strategy in the early twenty-first century. The key argument made here is that strategic thinking, regardless of the context in which it is applied, must effectively connect policy to the tactics being employed. If it does not do so it risks jeopardising the instrumentality of security responses, whether these appear in the form of regular war-fighting, countering insurgency or counter-terrorism operations.

Introduction

As we discovered in Chapter 2, statesmen and commanders may be the most visible figureheads in war, yet their orders rely heavily on the individual rank-and-file soldier for implementation. Whenever there is a lack of a shared understanding of why fighting is being employed to secure policy goals, there is a danger

69

that this can pollute the process by which these are achieved. This chapter explores the decision-making process before, during and after sustained armed conflict. From the capital cities, where the decisions to go to war are often made, to the remotest parts of the world, where these decisions are played out in mortal combat, Chapter 3 considers the human and organisational constraints on the application of strategy. It suggests that stovepiping the formulation of strategy – so as to leave politicians to exclusively decide on national policy, while expecting soldiers merely to implement it – creates a partial and disjointed understanding of strategy that can jeopardise political success. The chapter makes the case that it is in the blurring of boundaries between the individuals and interest groups involved in forging strategy where the most serious challenges to its successful application can be found.

Political Leaders and Strategy

As we saw briefly in the previous chapter, Winston Churchill had a special preoccupation with the business of military strategy. He had, after all, served as a commissioned officer in his younger days, prior to becoming prime minister. This insight, albeit brief and at a lower tactical and operational level, was invaluable in exposing Churchill to the demands of the practical implementation of strategy. However, after May 1940, he risked much by becoming too involved in military matters and his hands-on approach was only really curtailed with the appointment of Sir Alan Brooke (later Field Marshal Lord Alanbrooke) as Chief of the Imperial General Staff in 1941. Alanbrooke was so incensed by his clashes with Churchill on these matters that he wrote in his diary:

> I had another row with him [Churchill]. He is insisting on capturing the top of Sumatra Island irrespective of what our general plan for war against Japan may be! He refused to accept that any general plan was necessary, recommended a purely optimistic policy and behaved like a spoilt child that wants a toy in a shop irrespective of the fact

that its parents tell it that it is no good! Got nowhere with him, and settled nothing! This makes my arguments with the Americans practically impossible![1]

As far as Churchill was concerned, he was an energetic war leader, a warlord, who needed to know as much about the trivia of warfare as the strategies that made war possible. Few doubted Churchill's own personal bravery, particularly since he was a wartime leader who had actually gone to war before. The prime minister was a man, it was said, whose 'great love was war'. In his fascination with war, Churchill tended to see 'things in black and white, right or wrong', who had a 'respect for liberty and an intense dislike of tyranny'.[2] Nevertheless, he was also a man who knew his limitations and this meant he tended to fall into line, rather begrudgingly, once his Chiefs recommended a course of action.

Alanbrooke's ability to counter-balance his prime minister's involvement in military strategy lay in direct contrast to Adolf Hitler, himself a veteran of the First World War, who dismissed the commander-in-chief of the Wehrmacht, Walther von Brauchitsch, and made all operational decisions his own responsibility. It was to be a costly exercise in hubris, for Hitler's interference in the military decision-making process during the Battle of Stalingrad, for instance, may well have sped up Germany's strategic inertia and, ultimately, its defeat and ruin in 1945. In general terms, the interference of politicians in the business of war is all too apparent and can sometimes cloud the mission which soldiers are sent to achieve. However, that does not hold under all circumstances and, rather, it is perhaps best to think of strategy as a bridge by which all those involved in the business of national security may use the military and non-military instruments at their disposal to reach the other side of the bank and thereby accomplish their stated policy goals.[3] As this chapter will go on to demonstrate, even if rank-and-file soldiers do not give politics more than a passing – and in the author's experience, often derogatory – thought in the everyday business of 'combat', their actions are directed by and, in turn (by conversing with policy), help shape the political context of war. It is worth turning to the idea of politics in war in a little more detail.

Political Leaders as Strategists

'The military man tends to see himself as the perennial victim of civilian warmongering. It is the people and the politicians, public opinion and governments, who start wars. It is the military who have to fight them . . . Politics deals with the goals of state policy. Competence in this field consists in having a broad awareness of the elements and interests entering into a decision and in possessing the legitimate authority to make such a decision. Politics is beyond the scope of military competence, and the participation of military officers in politics undermines that professionalism, curtailing their professional competence, dividing the profession against itself, and substituting extraneous values for professional values. The military officer must remain neutral politically . . . The area of military science is subordinate to, and yet independent of, the area of politics. Just as war serves the ends of politics, the military profession serves the ends of the state. Yet the statesman must recognize the integrity of the profession and its subject matter. The military man has the right to expect political guidance from the statesman. Civilian control exists when there is this proper subordination of an autonomous profession to the ends of policy'.[4]

'All operations have political consequences. They can increase or diminish a nation's ability to achieve its goals; they can commit it unwisely to new and unforeseen objectives; they can, by failure of calculation or execution, discourage its allies or bring new support to the side of the enemy. If excessive meddling in operational planning and decision making by political leaders can have disruptive consequences, inability or unwillingness on their part to exercise critical control over such plans and decisions runs the risk of placing in military hands powers that can jeopardise the national security for which the political leadership has ultimate responsibility. Here too, then, it is difficult to frame a theoretical definition of appropriate roles that is not so general as to be meaningless.'[5]

Strategy and the Formation of the Red Army

As Thucydides wrote of Pericles, the Athenian general of repute, in his *History of the Peloponnesian War*, 'A man who has the knowledge but lacks the power clearly to express it is no better off than if he never had any ideas at all'. No strangers to advocating revolutionary change, the Soviets eventually thought practically about how best to link their chosen ends to the ways and means at their disposal. However, this did not come easily as many Soviet leaders vehemently disagreed about how strategic theory could be squared with an overbearing reliance on Marxist ideology. Even the most careful amongst Soviet strategists rejected the idea that war could be waged according to strict theoretical precepts. Leon Trotsky, the first Commissar for War in the Soviet Union, famously noted in his military writings that 'to play chess "according to Marx" is altogether impossible, just as it is impossible to wage war "according to Marx"'.[6] This led to disagreement with his fellow revolutionary leaders and also his subordinate commanders, many of whom articulated a vision of military strategy grounded more firmly in the proletarian method of war, which reflected a commitment to the position of the armed forces in relation to the means of production.

Despite opposition to his more objective reading of military matters, Trotsky nonetheless held firm to Clausewitz's interpretation of war as 'a continuation of political intercourse by other means'. As he famously remarked in an early address as War Commissar, 'war, too, is politics, realised through the harsh means of blood and iron . . . War is politics, and the army is the instrument of this politics'.[7] Trotsky's view of war as an art, rather than a science, did not prevent him from abandoning his belief that Marxism still had the potential to act as a guide to 'analyze the world situation, especially in our modern and exceptional epoch'.[8] In his view, Trotsky even suggested that a thorough understanding of Marxism might well give soldiers an edge in a battle, perhaps more vociferously than other branches of science. For Trotsky, 'it would be absurd to deny the great importance of materialism for disciplining the mind in all fields', going on to claim that:

Marxism, like Darwinism, is the highest school of human thought. Methods of warfare cannot be deduced from Darwin's theory, from the law of natural selection; but an army leader who studied Darwin would be, given other qualifications, better equipped. He would have a wider horizon and be more fertile in devices he would take note of those aspects of nature and man which previously had passed unnoticed. This applies to Marxism even to a greater extent.[9]

Although he was sceptical of the elevation of Marxist thinking on warfare to the same league as the natural sciences, he did seek to maintain an open mind on the continuity of experience and cultural tradition.[10] Yet, in many other intellectual interpretations of the world, Trotsky concurred with Marx that revolution was 'the locomotive of history' and, for example, shared Marx's view of the backwardness of the peasantry and their inability to provide the necessary raw material on which to build a new state. Even in this, however, he was prepared to support Lenin's policy of 'War Communism', which would see mass conscription introduced and the peasantry, along with other social classes, recruited into the Red Army.[11]

According to Clausewitz 'the aim of warfare is to disarm the enemy'. To leave the enemy utterly defenceless, in this respect, 'to overcome the enemy, or disarm him – call it what you will – must always be the aim of warfare'.[12] In order to effect this outcome it is necessary to create, equip, train and imbibe a fighting force with a fighting spirit and ethos that will carry it through even the most difficult and dangerous battles. General Sir Rupert Smith has commended Trotsky for his creation of a mass, industrial army that owed much to Clausewitz's Trinitarian view of war as involving the state, army and people. 'Without all three elements of the trinity – state, military and the people,' argued Smith, 'it is not possible to conduct a successful military operation, especially not over time'.[13] As Smith writes of Trotsky, his 'creation of the Red Army signalled the advent of an enormous war machine, which soon resembled the traditional armies of its enemies with its centralized staff structure and planning, its rigid adherence to orders and the paralleling of its chain of command with a political structure'.[14] Like Clausewitz, Trotsky also believed that the course of war could not be determined by universal laws. Trotsky accepted Clausewitz's argument that for 'war is to be fully consonant with political objectives, and policy suited to the means available for war',[15] the statesman and soldier should be concentrated in one individual with executive authority.[16] Yet he would come to see the need for military experts as long as they were aware of the demands of revolutionary policy. In this he further concurred with Clausewitz that:

> Subordinating the political point of view to the military would be absurd, for it is policy that has created war. Policy is the guiding intelligence and war only the instrument, not vice versa. No other possibility exists, then, than to subordinate the military point of view to the political.[17]

Trotsky also took Clausewitz's other pronouncements on war and politics more seriously, such as his contestation that 'Politics, moreover, is the womb in which war develops – where its outlines already exist in their hidden rudimentary form, like the characteristics of living creatures in their embryos'.[18]

For many Russians the 'decree on peace' was received with 'a gasp of relief'.[19] The Treaty of Brest-Litovsk in 1917 may have led to intense factionalism between those who advocated continued war and those who wished to grasp the nettle of peace, but the ratification of peace enabled Trotsky to 'arm the revolution'. In this Trotsky remained unrepentant. He also held firm to the belief that the Russian Army had been defeated in the war with Germany for three interconnected reasons: first, that the country was economically and technically 'backward', making the sustainment of war impossible; second, that the peasantry, who made up the vast bulk of the army, had been thoroughly oppressed by Tsardom, to such an extent that they were prone to falling in battle because of an absence of 'initiative and individual enterprise'. Finally, Trotsky argued that the officer corps was not up to the task of leading the army, chiefly because 'the commanding apparatus had throughout all its past been closely bound up with those ruling classes'. All of these elements contributed to the peace of Brest-Litovsk, and, as Ian D. Thatcher explains, the war remained key to understanding why Trotsky would make the choices he later did as War Commissar.[20]

Even though he personally remained sceptical of the Red Army's ability to transform itself into a revolutionary movement of its own volition, Trotsky refused to undertake a wholesale clear-out of the officers' corps and to replace them with the Red Guards and militia that made up Bolshevik forces. In this, as in much else, Trotsky had 'to contend against the old generals on the one hand, and against the young revolutionary officers on the other. To the former he spoke as an innovator attacking their conservative habits of thought. To the latter he appeared almost as an advocate of military orthodoxy'.[21] Nevertheless, Lenin's declaration of 'War Communism' meant that a process of mass conscription would have to be put in place, which would draw on people from all social classes. Like Clausewitz, Trotsky proposed the short-term use of militias, but thought their utility questionable. He also proposed that non-commissioned officers (NCOs) from within the ranks of the old Tsarist army be promoted to assume the mantle of the officer corps in the new Red Army. Trotsky took this decision in large part out of practical constraints, not ideological ones; and as he put it, 'whoever is engaged in current work on building the army . . . will not philosophise but will choose commanders from the material that is at hand'.[22] Many of those senior officers who commanded the Red Army at the time of the Battle of Stalingrad (and who had survived Stalin's purges) were products of Trotsky's earlier innovations. As he armed the revolution, Trotsky was also conscious of the privileged position the NCOs enjoyed in terms of their closeness to the working class:

> From the technical standpoint you do not possess the advantages that the officers had. You are military men who know the soldier's trade precisely because the old army brought you forward, and from private soldiers turned you into NCOs. But you have at the same time enormous advantages from the class standpoint. You belong, flesh and blood, to the working class and the peasantry.[23]

Trotsky believed that the military propensity to fight just as hard as those who laboured in the coal mines, in the factories and in the fields would spur on the revolutionary process in equal measure:

> For every army, discipline must be created by the army itself. An army must understand what it serves, what its purpose is, what it is that

obliges every honorable soldier to devote his strength and labour, and even his life and his blood, on behalf of these interests. And once an army has woken up, once the soldier's consciousness has spoken, then the old discipline and the old stories and catchphrases of the monarchy, the nobles and the bourgeoisie cease to be able to sustain this army.[24]

Many of Trotsky's fellow Communists recognized him as the lightning rod for the rebuilding of the new army out of the embers of the old Tsarist construct. It was his contemporary Karl Radek who observed how, 'We needed a man who was the embodiment of the war-cry, a man who became the tocsin sounding the alarm, the will demanding from one and all an unqualified subordination to the great bloody necessity'.[25] Trotsky was that man.

Leon Trotsky (1879–1940)

Leon Trotsky (1879–1940) was one of the pre-eminent Marxist thinkers of the twentieth century, yet his writings on war have been largely ignored by military theoreticians. Trotsky's theories on warfare were gained primarily from his close study of the work of Carl von Clausewitz and other writers on war but they were ultimately learned during the harsh reality of the civil war between Bolshevik 'Reds' and Menshevik 'Whites' (with their assortment of supporters, including former Tsarists and nationalists) which was fought in the wake of the Russian revolution of October 1917. In his autobiography, *My Life*, Trotsky notes how the entire 'fate of the revolution depended on the course of military operations', yet during the Civil War (1918–21) the Central Committee of the Bolshevik Party remained divided over military strategy.[26] On the one hand the key military command posts were filled by people who lacked an appreciation of social and political conditions and on the other the experienced revolutionary politicians who lacked military knowledge and experience. Trotsky's answer was to integrate the decision-making process but this inevitably led to dissent and conflict. One of the ways it was proposed to reconcile this friction was to form a cadre of political commissars who were on hand to 'approve all actions of the nominal commander'.[27]

Trotsky's reading of Clausewitz was to have profound implications for the direction taken by the Red Army after the civil war. Being a much more receptive student of Prussian military strategy than his contemporaries, Trotsky believed it was important for warrior-scholars to actively seek to unify their theories on war with the prevailing Hegelian philosophy of dialectical materialism. As Trotsky's pre-eminent biographer, Isaac Deutscher, put it so persuasively: 'When in the middle of March 1918 Trotsky was appointed Commissar of War and President of the Supreme War Council, he did not even put down his pen to take up his sword – he used both'.[28] This would have far-reaching consequences for later Marxist thinkers who sought to deal with the dominant issues of war, peace and strategy.

What these disputes within the Soviet Union ultimately exposed was that Marxism should be only one strand feeding into theories about how military means could be employed to serve political ends. They also illustrate how important it is to remain flexible in the face of the very practical challenges thrown up by the ever-changing context of war. This was not a view shared by everyone. Trotsky's longstanding rival, Joseph Stalin, who later oversaw his comrade's exile and murder, would come to take a more flexible and somewhat looser approach to strategy. He would soon prove this, perhaps in one of the most costly ways imaginable, during the Second World War, which he and his commanders referred to as the 'Great Patriotic War'.

As a theoretical approach, Marxism has lost much of its utility since the collapse of the Soviet Union in the early 1990s. Nevertheless, Trotsky's experience as War Commissar demonstrates that politicians, even revolutionary ones, must recognise the delicate balance to be struck between policy and war. As one notable scholar of the Red Army put it:

> The presence at the head of the armed forces of a man of such powerful charisma, notoriously prone to disregard party considerations and to draw ideas from currents of thought foreign to the Bolshevik tradition, fuelled fears regarding the political role that the Soviet military machine might eventually come to play. In 1921–2, it still seemed to many Bolsheviks that the ghost of 'Bonapartism' was threatening the country's prospects for socialist development.[29]

Even after Trotsky's fall from grace, the Red Army nonetheless continued to develop as a hub for sound and original theoretical and empirical thinking. However, by the 1930s, Stalin's purges would remove some of the most talented staff officers who had developed key strategies such as Deep Battle and Deep Operations, which were to be abandoned by 1942. Arguably, even with his removal and subsequent exile, Trotsky's more objective reading of war and strategy would influence other revolutionary Marxist thinkers, such as Mao Tse-Tung and Fidel Castro, who sought to apply Communist thinking on irregular warfare in more innovative ways so as to undermine their imperial enemies.

Guerrilla Armies and Maoist Strategy

By the mid-twentieth century, a range of Communist-inspired guerrilla movements had emerged to challenge what they saw as Western imperialism. In places as diverse as Latin America, the Middle East, North Africa and South-East Asia, national liberation forces grew in confidence and popularity. Attracting a range of highly educated middle class intellectuals and backed by the Soviet Union and China, these movements sought to blend guerrilla tactics with an exuberant repertoire of classical Marxism. Even though these tactics were elucidated in the pamphlets and speeches of Chinese Communist revolutionary Mao Tse-Tung, they effectively drew on a much longer tradition of guerrilla warfare dating back thousands of years. Experts agree that the defeat of the Romans had been set in motion when Julius Caesar led his legions in a huge raid on Germanic hordes along the Rhine. For it was the view of Roman officials that barbarian peoples were 'unchanging and unchangeable' that spelt disaster for the empire.[30] However, the Romans did adeptly handle the challenge of insurgents, as victories in Wales, Spain and Judea prove. The overriding strategic qualities – such as endurance and brutality – exhibited by the Romans were something that would become anathema to Western counter-insurgents by the early twenty-first century. Nonetheless, the application of principles by indigenous forces – tenacity, knowing the ground intimately and fighting with the support of the local people – were to become a feature of irregular warfare from early Roman times to the present day.

Perhaps one of the twentieth century's most proficient practitioners of irregular warfare was the famed leader of the 1917 Arab Revolt, T. E. Lawrence, known best by the sobriquet Lawrence of Arabia. One of his early biographers, Captain Basil Liddell Hart, wrote of Lawrence:

> Military history cannot dismiss him as merely a successful leader of irregulars. He is seen to be more than a guerrilla genius – rather does he appear a strategist of genius who had the vision to anticipate the guerrilla trend of the civilized warfare that arises from the growing dependence of nations on industrial resources.[31]

This over-dependence on industrial mass would come to typify regular war in the First World War and Second World War. In the post-war period, European governments, wishing to withdraw from their overseas empires, struggled to maintain their ability to coerce, deter and crush opponents when the situation demanded it. For instance, the French were to discover that their inter-war strategy of pacification in Algeria was losing its currency in terms of domestic public opinion by the mid-1950s, when the FLN began its ruthless and determined insurgency.

The French were not alone in facing this form of revolutionary warfare. Britain also faced determined guerrilla armies in a range of colonial hotspots, from Borneo and Malaya in Asia to Kenya in sub-Saharan Africa and Aden in the Middle East, to say nothing of EOKA terrorists in Cyprus and the Irish Republican Army in Northern Ireland. The 1950s were alive to the sound of the clatter of guns in colonial outposts around the world. Many of the armed groups ranging against the British may have held disparate political beliefs but they were united in drawing inspiration from Maoist guerrillas in 1930s and 1940s China. One of Britain's most revered counter-insurgency theorists, Frank Kitson, suggested in his influential book *Low Intensity Operations* (1971) that state security forces' 'first step should have been to prevent the enemy from gaining ascendancy over the civil population, and in particular to disrupt his efforts at establishing his political organization'.[32] It was to be those groups that retained a synergetic understanding of the political purpose of irregular war and its capacity to win the consent of sections of the population (and, occasionally, whole populations) that threatened to undermine regimes. This was something painfully learned by France in Algeria. As French counter-insurgency expert David Galula (who had observed the campaign in Algeria at close quarters) would argue in his influential book *Counter-insurgency Warfare* (1964), there was an urgent need for the military to be prepared to adapt to perform functions other than war-fighting. In his words:

> To confine soldiers to purely military functions while urgent and vital tasks have to be done, and nobody else is available to undertake them, would be senseless. The soldier must then be prepared to become the propagandist, a social worker, a civil engineer, a schoolteacher, a nurse, a boy scout. But only for as long as he cannot be replaced, for it is better to entrust civilian tasks to civilians.[33]

Implied in this extract from Galula's work is the danger of allowing the military to completely colonise civilian tasks:

> That the political power is the undisputed boss is a matter of both principle and practicality. What is at stake is the country's political regime, and to defend it is a political affair. Even if this requires military action, the action is constantly directed toward a political goal. Essential though it is, the military action is secondary to the political one, its primary purpose being to afford the political power enough freedom to work safely with the population.[34]

The idea that the military instrument should play second fiddle to the overriding political purpose of war was to remain lost on the United States as it became embroiled in Vietnam in the 1960s.

It was not without some reluctance that the United States became involved in the Vietnam War. 'American leaders did consider it vital not to lose Vietnam to a Communist-led insurgency directed and supported by North Vietnam', writes Guenter Lewy, and this view was 'widely shared by the Congress, the media and the articulate public'.[35] Vietnam, to paraphrase Lewy, was considered to be of sufficient strategic value to the non-Communist world that the United States should intervene on the side of the government of South Vietnam. As the fighting became more intense the need to alter the strategy – but to remain engaged in order to defeat the insurgency – took precedence. One of the important aspects of the war was to build a coalition of support so as to help deliver a re-energised South Vietnamese security forces who were later to take the lead in attempts to defeat the North Vietnamese Army (NVA) and the Viet Cong guerrillas. One of those nations that responded to American calls for assistance was Australia. In 1966 the first units from the 1st Australian Task Force (1ATF) landed in Vietnam. It was not long before they were in battle against the NVA and Viet Cong. A scroll presented to Brigadier General Jackson, the first commander of 1ATF, by Lieutenant Colonel Le Aie Dat, Chief of Phuoc Tuy Province, records the nature of the battles engaged in by the Australians:

> Your military activities within the Province have been outstanding, highlighted by the decisive defeat of the Viet Cong at Long Tan on 18 August 1966, and the numerous highly successful cordon and search operations, which netted many Viet Cong captives without sustaining a single friendly casualty . . . We, the people of Phuoc Tuy Province, extend to you our heartfelt thanks for your personal interest in our struggle for peace. You and your men together with other allied forces have shown the world your belief that freedom is of paramount importance to all people. You have done much to help Phuoc Tuy Province take a long stride toward a long sought after peace. Your personal drive, interest and sympathy for our people shall go down as a milestone in the history of the Province.[36]

Wishing to see for himself the real situation on the ground, the Australian Chief of the General Staff, Lieutenant General Thomas Daly, visited 1ATF in Phuoc Tuy, which was close to Phnom Penh, in November 1970. The scene that greeted him was one of utter chaos. GVN (Government of Vietnam) forces had virtually no fighting structures to speak of, no coherent training programme, an assortment of weapons and few professional qualified officers. He recalled a discussion with the South Vietnamese Divisional Commander, General Lon No. 1, who outlined his plans for taking on the Viet Cong. They were courageous and innovative, noted Daly, but lacked the sophistication he felt Australian forces could bring to the fight:

> Basically, he plans to stabilize the situation along a general line running from the vicinity of Siem Reap through Kompong Cham, endeavouring to eliminate the NVA south of this line, conducting a guerrilla type war throughout the countryside, aided by the villagers whom he claims have no doubts as to where their loyalties lie. He also plans to employ harassing tactics against NVA units in the North. The concept is an attractive one since it makes use of such assets as the Army possesses, strong legs, stout hearts, and the support of a loyal population. I would feel happier if the guerrilla groups had a little more professional skill of the kind common in our SAS squadrons.

Interestingly, General Daly considered the problem facing South Vietnamese forces to be one of a chronic shortage of 'the kind of military expertise needed to solve what is, at the present time, primarily a military problem'.[37] The confusion over whether the problem in Vietnam was a military or political one continued for much of the war. With the election of Richard Nixon to the presidency in 1969, preparations for Vietnamization were accelerated and US combat troop numbers began to fall. Withdrawal was in line with an agreement by the Government of Vietnam (GVN) to shoulder more of the burden of fighting.[38]

However, this was not without its problems. In the province of Long An, adjacent to Phuoc Tuy, the situation was precarious for the GVN. The Viet Cong had long since laid firm roots amongst the peasantry and formed a revolutionary fighting force that commanded the support of the people before the Americans had even deployed to the country. In contrast to GVN forces, the

Viet Cong would enter villages and homes by emphasising their politeness and leave the impression that they could be trusted to act in the best interests of the local people.[39] In practical terms, this meant developing popular policies that contrasted sharply with the Saigon government of President Diem. One of those policies was pacification, which often meant resettlement in 'new villages', something that had been tried by the British in Malaya a decade earlier. A civil affairs report recalled the reaction by locals to the prospect of resettlement: 'Initially the refugees were bewildered, but they quickly adapted themselves to their new environment.' Their reaction became most favourable, the report went on to suggest, after they were made aware that they were guaranteed sufficient food, accommodation, land and security. The report also noted how the process of resettlement was painfully slow and suffered from a chronic lack of interpreters.[40]

In a subsequent discussion on the civil affairs aspects of the campaign between General Daly and Jonathan Ladd, a former Colonel in the US Special Forces who had been placed in charge of the US aid programme (which had a budget of US$165 million), the Australian CGS left with a somewhat mixed impression of the state of GVN forces:

> He hoped that the mistakes made in Vietnam of producing an indigenous army to an appropriate US design would not be repeated. He would do all in his power to prevent Cambodians cluttering themselves up with masses of vehicles, headquarters paraphernalia, and a sophisticated logistic system which would inevitably cause them to become roadbound. Their natural strength lay in their ability to move freely through the countryside, supported by the civil population. Provided that they could be given the training necessary to enable them to meet the enemy with confidence and a logistic system and a simple command and control organization suited to their peculiar circumstances, they should, on their own territory, be more than a match for the NVA . . . I left in the evening for Singapore, per RAAF Dakota, with a strong impression of a brave, proud, and physically tough people, with high morale but pathetically short of basic military knowledge. I wondered how long the morale would survive in the face of the losses they must suffer should the NVA be able to assemble the resources to wage a really aggressive campaign.[41]

The ability to sustain and endure a campaign is a perennial problem in countering irregular adversaries. Ultimately, states rely upon a greater magnitude of firepower and technological superiority when confronted with an irregular adversary. The NVA and Viet Cong exuded masterful ability to outmanoeuvre the larger, clumsier forces of the US and their South Vietnamese and Australian allies. In all of this intelligence was vital. As one Australian officer noted in a lecture to the Army Staff College in Canberra,

> There is no doubt that successful operations against the VC requires accurate, detailed and timely intelligence. This can only be achieved if every officer and soldier [is] aware of the value of intelligence information, no matter how unimportant it may seem.[42]

Despite the optimistic tone of General Daly's appraisal of GVN fighting ability and military strategy, the VC and NVA proved more nimble and adaptable in their irregular approach to war. They also proved capable of turning the tide against the external presence to such an extent that the war was over by 1973. After a short-lived ceasefire between North and South Vietnam dissolved into a shooting war, GVN forces were forced to surrender in 1975.

Counter-Insurgency in Oman

The US was not the only state to have become embroiled in counter-insurgency operations in the 1970s. In a much simpler operation involving the British, Sultan Tahmir of Muscat and Oman was overthrown by his son, Qaboos, in a palace coup in July 1970. This prompted Britain to become more intimately involved in the war against Communist guerrillas who now ranged against Sultan Qaboos. In early 1971 the Communist-backed People's Front for the Liberation of the Arabian Gulf (PFLOAG) had cut Oman's only land link with the outside world. London exerted pressure on Qaboos to continue the work of development that had been begun under his father's reign.[43] As a result, the PFLOAG became entrenched in the southern region of Dhofar. An early intelligence summary remarked how: 'Enemy military strength now on the Jebel gives them freedom of movement and consequently they retain the initiative.' As the report continued, 'Tactically they can operate offensively and react energetically to SAF operations'.[44]

The solution, apart from redirecting forces to Salalah in the south-west, was to ensure the enemy were dislodged from their base. The British believed that like any insurgent force, the PFLOAG were determined to achieve their political aim of overthrowing the new Sultan by military means and their principal plan of action was to defeat his forces in battle. As one senior British officer involved in the campaign went on to write in an internal situation report at the time: 'The war is for the minds of men! The war is to win and control the people. By tactics designed to tie down the security forces in defence of static locations, the strength of the security forces can be effectively dissipated and all initiative lost . . . Only by offensive action into the guerrilla element to bring the hard core Adoo to battle, and more essentially, to re-establish contact and control over the people, can the Government win. Such is the nature of insurgent operations'.[45] Military success by itself could not defeat the Adoo. There was also a need to 'win the people'. In terms of ratio, 60 to 40 per cent had to be directed 'in favour of civic action'. Those behind the strategy to counter the insurgents in Oman knew that to do this successfully required the skilful application of military means to political ends. In this they could be assured that the Arabian Peninsula did not provide fertile ground for Communism, which, as the senior British commander at the time remarked, remained 'the foremost enemy of Islam'.[46]

Within a few months the British-backed Omani Armed Forces had inflicted heavy casualties on the insurgents in Dhofar and successfully captured rebel-held territory relatively quickly. The British believed that three factors had contributed to the defeat of the insurgents. The first was a marked increase in surrenders from enemy forces, the second that many Dhofaris were sickened by the violence and the cruelty meted out to them by PFLOAG forces, and, finally, that Oman's Armed Forces were becoming much more professional and successful in operations, thanks to the presence of British officers and NCOs.[47] By 1974, the insurgents were still strong in number. Interrogations undertaken by the British and Omanis at the time revealed a great deal about the planning, organisation and quality of PFLOAG fighters. They were able to glean, for example, that senior PFLOAG commanders met in a flat in Beirut to plan their attacks on Oman, that they intended to smuggle in weapons, munitions and explosives from supporters in Iraq, Libya and Syria, and that sabotage and political activity were designed to complement the military struggle. In terms of strategy, the Communists typically infiltrated Oman, contacted sympathisers and mounted a campaign of propaganda, followed by the formation of a special independent commando group, made up of Omanis and Palestinians. The PFLOAG's main training camps were in South Yemen and intelligence believed their intention was to carry out acts of terrorism, sabotage and subversion throughout the whole of the Gulf. Given intense pressure from British-backed forces, the PFLOAG's plans ultimately failed and they were defeated by 1975.

The United States emerged from the Vietnam War in the mid-1970s without a desire to ever repeat the mistakes of the past. To this extent they were to turn away from counter-insurgency and reconfigure their armed forces to fight only regular wars. This certainly made sense in the context of the Cold War, though it would become questionable after the fall of the Berlin Wall and the collapse of the Soviet Union in 1991. After the invasion of Iraq in 2003 and the descent into military competition with insurgents, it was felt that they needed to return to the lost art form of counter-insurgency. One of those who argued for a return to the 'golden age' of counter-insurgency was David Kilcullen, who suggested that 80 per cent of the international community's efforts in countering global insurgency must be political, diplomatic, development, intelligence and informational activity and that 20 per cent ought to be purely military effort.[48] Kilcullen was a key member of the writing team who produced the US Army's Counter-Insurgency Field Manual (3-24) that had such a huge strategic effect in reversing the losses of the United States and its allies in Iraq between 2003 and 2011.[49] By revisiting ideas first made fashionable by the likes of Frank Kitson and David Galula, Kilcullen and other counter-insurgency enthusiasts lobbied hard for the development of a military strategy that would shift the United States away from an over-reliance on conventional military hard power and its attendant mantra of 'shock and awe' towards what amounted to 'armed state-building'. However, not everyone was convinced that this was a good thing and some military officers, such as Colonel Gian Gentile, believed that this 'all in' approach constituted a dangerous threat to national security.[50] It is important, therefore, to ask whether this strategy was really able to offer a better appreciation of irregular security challenges than a more traditional understanding of grand strategy.

From Insurgency to Terrorism

As we noted in Chapter 2, the collapse of the Soviet Union in 1991 led to the creation of vacuums of power in those places where East and West had been locked in confrontation during the Cold War, each competing with the other for influence amongst indigenous social, political and military forces. Unsurprisingly, insurgent and terrorist groups sprung up in what would later become known as fragile, failing or failed states. Afghanistan, Pakistan and Yemen would be joined by those failed states that had been unaligned during the Cold War, such as Somalia, Iraq and Nigeria. In all these countries the growing proliferation of armed groups, ranging from those who wished to overthrow and replace governments to those seeking a more totalising agenda of establishing a religious caliphate, became commonplace, particularly after 9/11. From our discussion in Chapter 1, we know that it remains contestable just how 'new' this armed challenge actually was, for the myriad of security threats arising in the international system today exhibit traits of *both* change *and* continuity. Afghanistan, Pakistan and Yemen may seem, on the surface at least, relatively new hotbeds for Islamist extremism in the world, but that is not strictly true. Extremism in all three countries can be traced back to the years before the al-Qaeda attacks on the United States on 9/11 and have their medium term roots in the Cold War.

Indeed, they are also part of a long term religious revivalism that has reared its head a number of times since the onset of the Enlightenment. This Islamic reaction against modernity, according to journalist Jason Burke, has always centred on the two-pronged objective 'to reform their own societies, returning those Muslims who had departed in practice and belief to the true faith, and to battle outsiders, which from the late eighteenth century on usually meant non-believers, most often Europeans'.[51] In many respects the tendency to attribute the growing tide of Islamist extremism to root causes 'over there' is to ignore the incubation of extremism in Western states like Britain and France, which, as Gilles Kepel reminds us, in the late twentieth century, saw militants 'declare Britain a sanctuary'.[52] That Britain itself has provided a safe-haven for Islamist extremism is borne out by a quick glance at those who have perpetrated terrorist atrocities in the UK and elsewhere. The leader of the four suicide bombers who murdered 52 people on the London Underground on 7 July 2005, Mohammed Sidique Khan, may have trained in the 'ungoverned space' of the Pakistani Federally Administered Tribal Areas, but he became radicalised in the back streets of Beeston in Leeds, a city in northern England. Similarly, Michael Adebolajo and Michael Adebowale, two young British men who murdered soldier Lee Rigby in Woolwich in April 2013, were also radicalised in the UK.

The idea that extremism is nurtured closer to home than we think is controversial. In an article published in June 2007 entitled 'Londonistan Calling', the late liberal commentator Christopher Hitchens quotes an unnamed US counter-terrorism official as wryly observing how the UK's capital had become something akin to a 'Star Wars bar scene'. Just as killers, gangsters and other criminals frequent the fictional pirate city of Mos Eisley on the dodgy planet of Tatooine, a range of the world's most violent extremists seem to have flocked to London to plan, recruit and, in some cases, perpetrate heinous crimes in the name of a rather peculiar reading of the Koran. For Hitchens,

> It would still be the case that they belong to a movement that hates Jews and Indians and all kuffar, or 'unbelievers': a fanatical sect that believes itself entitled to use deadly violence at any time. The roots of violence, that is to say, are in the preaching of it, and the sanctification of it.[53]

In many ways the preaching of hate and the all-too-common articulation of one-dimensional religious soundbites has left government policy-makers and academics with a real challenge to adequately unpack the reasons why young men and women from Britain have turned to extremism and violence. In recognition of the flawed process by which previous governments tried to accommodate religious extremism, Home Secretary Theresa May unveiled a rebooted version of the government's counter-terrorism strategy (known as CONTEST – or 'CONTEST II' in policy circles) shortly after the Coalition government entered office in May 2010. CONTEST outlined in great detail how the government would seek to combat the rise of religious extremism and, perhaps more importantly, articulated a strategy for dealing with al-Qaeda and like-minded groups.

In a follow-up document entitled *Tackling Extremism in the UK* (2013), the government usefully defined extremism as

> vocal or active opposition to fundamental British values, including democracy, the rule of law, individual liberty and mutual respect and tolerance of different faiths and beliefs. We also include in our definition of extremism calls for the death of members of our armed forces, whether in this country or overseas.[54]

This was the first time that a thorough definition was advanced in a way that was consistent with new security powers of surveillance, arrest and detention. It also went some way towards recognising the phenomenon of young British men and women flocking to the cause of jihad overseas. As the Home Office stated in a document in June 2014, in which it gave reasons for the proscription of ISIS,

We are aware that a number of British nationals have travelled to Syria and some of these will inevitably be fighting with ISIL. It appears that ISIL is treating Iraq and Syria as one theatre of conflict and its potential ability to operate across the border must be a cause of concern for the whole international community.[55]

Unsurprisingly, those turning to violent extremism, government policy suggests, are disaffected in some way and vulnerable to the warped logic of a perverse ideology that misinterprets the teachings of the Koran.

Whether one accepts that the problem of Islamist extremism and terrorism has its source 'over there' or closer to home in the West, it is impossible to examine the escalation of violence by groups like al-Qaeda or *Daesh* as either relatively new creations or as in some ways ignorant of strategy. The truth is that the strategists in *Daesh* may be inspired by a noxious blend of Salafi, Wahhabi and Takfiri Islam, but they are entirely competent in how they wish to build their caliphate (ends) by way of waging violent jihad (ways and means). On the surface, *Daesh* are certainly committed to the literal, rather than a figurative, interpretation of the Koran and the implementation of Sharia Law. But beneath the surface they have been more pragmatic about the compromises they will have to make in order to make that happen. For instance, the leader of *Daesh*, Abu Bakr al-Baghdadi, appointed two former Ba'athist generals as his top lieutenants. And in seeking to develop a strategy that could take a more objective reading of war beyond a handful of Koranic verses, al-Baghdadi made Haji Bakr, a former Colonel in Saddam Hussein's Air Force, his chief strategist. Haji Bakr believed that the only way of building an effective state out of the embers of the two states they sought to destroy, Syria and Iraq, was to mimic how other non-democratic regimes had come to power.[56] In this planning he drew much inspiration from his days as a middle-ranking Ba'athist. Part of this strategy was also expeditionary and drew on al-Qaeda's decision to appeal to home-grown 'clean skins' in countries they wished to attack to deliver the terror right to the heart of the societies out of which they had emerged.

In order to meet the innovative threat posed by these groups the British government has sought to ensure it balances its commitment to enable people to go about their daily lives without hindrance or harm. The formulation of CONTEST emphasises the need to take robust action against extremists by placing them in detention or deporting them, if they are found to hold dual nationalities. For the UK, other important security threats have traditionally come from Northern Ireland, which is the site of one of Europe's most protracted ethnic conflicts that has lasted centuries and, in its current form, since the late 1960s. Although a peace deal was concluded in 1998 and power-sharing institutions established between the rival Protestant unionists and Catholic nationalists in 2007, there nevertheless remains a residual threat from terrorism, particularly amongst splinter groups from the Provisional Irish Republican Army, which had once posed one of the greatest security challenges to the UK from 1970 until its cessation of its armed campaign in 2005. By 2009–10, however, violence had re-emerged. The wounding of a police officer in 2007 and the murder of two soldiers and a police officer in 2009 by republican terrorists tipped the scales temporarily away from the threat posed by Islamist terrorism in the direction of Northern Ireland-related terrorism.

The Police Service of Northern Ireland (PSNI) is now leading operations against dissident Irish republican terrorists who posed a clear and present threat to the UK's national security. Yet, even though this fight takes place at the operational level, senior counter-terrorism officers admit that even though they have a full repertoire of assets at their disposal – from a sophisticated range of cameras, air support in the form of three helicopters and two planes, unmanned aerial vehicles, and limited assistance from the Ministry of Defence – they have other threats to public safety to manage. Up until 2015, those officers charged with fighting terrorism in Northern Ireland were also responsible for leading the fight against burglars, drug-dealers, organised crime gangs and human traffickers.[57] Following the establishment of the National Crime Agency and its extension of operations to Northern Ireland, there is more scope for the Special Operations Branch to focus on countering the most serious threats to Northern Irish security. However, senior counter-terrorism officers acknowledge that, given the legacy of the 'Troubles', the use of lethal force by police officers could jeopardise the brittle nature of the 'peace process'.

UK Counter-Terrorism Strategy: The Four Ps

The UK has had a national UK counter-terrorism strategy since 2010. It recognises the dangers posed by Islamist extremism, Northern Ireland-related terrorism and other forms of terrorism. Interestingly, however, the latest version of CONTEST (2011) only deals with the measures that have been taken to deal with Islamist-inspired terrorism. It has reduced a comprehensive strategy to a four-pronged strategy:

Pursue: to stop terrorist attacks;
Prevent: to stop people becoming terrorists or supporting terrorism;
Protect: to strengthen our protection against a terrorist attack; and
Prepare: to mitigate the impact of a terrorist attack.

The Four Ps have focused the minds of policymakers and those officials and members of the intelligence and law enforcement agencies and the military charged with implementing the strategy from the highest policy-making circles to the lowest tactical level.

The UK, like most other states with finite resources, prefers to take a more balanced approach to its national strategy. This has been done largely because it has always faced a challenge on two fronts. On the one hand it has been a hub for Islamist extremism for the past quarter of a century, something that has resulted in one successful terrorist attack on 7/7 and over thirty-four serious plots between 2001 and 2014. On the other hand, however, the UK has faced a challenge from Irish republican extremists who, in their more limited goals, wish to see Ireland free of British interference. Other states have faced wars on two fronts as well, of course. In Pakistan, the presence of an existential threat in the form of its neighbour India is joined by the lesser threat from Islamist extremism. In strategic terms Pakistan has always marshalled its resources in the direction of the one that poses the greatest threat, that is,

India. In Ukraine, Russian-based separatists and Russian forces amassed along the border pose a two-fold threat to the territorial integrity and political independence of the government in Kiev. Given that the UK has claimed that no other state threatens it, it is only natural that strategists should look to prioritise those security challenges that pose the greatest risk to its national security. In this states must choose what threats are more pressing.

Conclusion

As this chapter has illustrated with several diverse case-studies, strategy has practical utility in both regular and irregular war. However, in order to maximise this utility it is vital that those formulating policy – as much as those charged with implementing it further down the line – should be aware of how to balance the ends, ways and means in the strategy they choose to connect the two. As we saw with Trotsky's plan for the Red Army, the essence of war was such that it could not be fought in a wholly Marxist way. In a significant departure from other Bolsheviks, including Stalin, Trotsky lobbied hard for the Commissars to play second fiddle to military commanders and specialists charged with doing the fighting, which, like Clausewitz, he recognised as the central organising principle in war. However, as we saw in relation to Vietnam and in the British approach to British counter-terrorism, there is a need for those involved in the operationalisation of strategy to subordinate their actions to the political point of view in order to be ultimately successful. Each of these case studies, nevertheless, proves that there remains a tendency for civilians and military leaders to stray into each other's respective professional areas of expertise in ways that are not always unifying, nor reflective of a shared understanding of the context in which they are formulating and implementing strategy. In this sense, one must emphasise Clausewitz's point that a dialogue must be maintained between statesmen and soldiers in the fashion of one mastering a foreign language so as to express oneself more clearly and lucidly.[58] When this happens it can be disastrous. Although it is more common to note Sun Tzu's remark in *The Art of War* regarding this dichotomy – 'He whose generals are able and not interfered with by the sovereign will be victorious'[59] – it is important also to weigh this up with Clemenceau's riposte that 'war is too important to be left to the generals'.

Key Questions

1. Why must politicians and military commanders 'know their place' in the formulation and application of strategy?
2. How effectively did the Soviets blend Marxism with a more objective reading of strategy?
3. How have non-state actors applied strategy in challenging the power and legitimacy of states?
4. In the case studies of Dhofar and Northern Ireland, how effective was a knowledge of the wider security strategy in focusing the minds of those implementing policy at the sharp end?
5. What role should politics play in the application of strategy?

Further Reading

Benvenuti, Francesco, *The Bolsheviks and the Red Army, 1918–1922* (Cambridge: Cambridge University Press, 1988).

Burke, Jason, *The New Threat from Islamic Militancy* (London: Bodley Head, 2015).

Clausewitz, Carl von, *On War*, translated by Michael Howard and Peter Paret (Princeton, NJ: Princeton University Press, 1976).

Craig, Gordon A., 'The Political Leader as Strategist', in Peter Paret (ed.), *Makers of Modern Strategy: From Machiavelli to the Nuclear Age* (Oxford: Oxford University Press, 1986), pp. 481–509.

Danchev, Alex and Dan Todman (eds), *War Diaries, 1939–1945: Field Marshal Lord Alanbrooke* (London: Weidenfeld and Nicholson: 2001).

Deutscher, Isaac, *The Prophet Armed: Trotsky: 1879–1921* (London: Verso, 2003).

Galula, David, *Counter-insurgency Warfare: Theory and Practice* (London: Praeger Security International, [1964] 2006).

Gray, Colin, *The Strategy Bridge: Theory for Practice* (Oxford: Oxford University Press, 2010).

Huntingdon, Samuel P., *The Soldier and the State: The Theory and Politics of Civil-Military Relations* (Cambridge, MA: Harvard University Press, 1957).

Kepel, Gilles, *Jihad: The Trail of Political Islam* (London: I. B. Tauris, 2003).

Kilcullen, David, *The Accidental Guerrilla: Fighting a Big War amidst Small Wars* (London: Hurst and Company, 2009).

Kitson, Frank, *Low Intensity Operations: Subversion, Insurgency, Peacekeeping* (London: Faber and Faber, 1971).

Lewy, Guenter, *America in Vietnam* (New York: Oxford University Press, 1978).

Smith, Rupert, *The Utility of Force: The Art of War in the Modern World* (London: Penguin, 2006).

Sun Tzu, *The Art of War*, translated and with an introduction by Samuel B. Griffith (Oxford: Oxford University Press, 1963).

Thatcher, Ian D., *Leon Trotsky and World War One, August 1914 – February 1917* (Basingstoke: Palgrave Macmillan, 2000).

Trotsky, Leon, *My Life: The Rise and Fall of a Dictator* (London: Thornton Butterworth Limited, 1930).

Trotsky, Leon, *The Military Writings and Speeches of Leon Trotsky* (London: Pathfinder Press, 1969).

Trotsky, Leon *The Military Writings and Speeches of Leon Trotsky: How the Revolution Armed, Vol. 1: The Year 1918*, translated and annotated by Brian Pearce (London: New Park Publications, 1979).

United States Department of Defense, *Field Manual 3-24* (2006).

Wells, Peter S., *The Battle that Stopped Rome: Emperor Augustus, Arminius, and the Slaughter of the Legions in the Teutoburg Forest* (New York: W. W. Norton, 2003).

Worrall, James, *Statebuilding and Counterinsurgency in Oman: Political, Military and Diplomatic Relations at the End of Empire* (London: I. B. Tauris, 2014).

4   Strategy, Ethics and Restraint in War

Scope

It is sometimes argued that international rules and norms have very little impact on strategy because Realism's preoccupation with material interest makes the proposition of restraint in war an unworkable concept. Indeed, the very idea of restraint in war is regarded with considerable suspicion by those who do not accept that there is any utility in engaging in organised violence for a political end. As this chapter makes clear, one need only take a cursory glance at violence in parts of the Middle East to find evidence to support this proposition, though it is important to also analyse those instances where restraint has paid dividends in the longer term. For instance, after a series of civilian deaths in hostilities in Afghanistan, British and American operational commanders believed that their troops should exercise 'courageous restraint' in order to reduce the number of non-combatant casualties. Arguably, this should have been the strategic aim all along – that is, protecting the civilian population – so that the government of Afghanistan could win over the consent of the population and thereby combat the insurgency more effectively. In addressing well-known cases where restraint has been both present and absent in war, this chapter makes the case that moral behaviour can bring with it strategic advantages.

Introduction

'Air attack has reduced German morale to an unprecedentedly low level', reads a Royal Air Force report on the strategic bombing

97

carried out by Allied aircraft over German cities and towns in 1944. The 'prevailing nervous strain has been manifested in a state of general apathy which has seriously prejudiced the German war effort and it is causing the German authorities the gravest concern', it concluded.[1] The Germans had already dropped several thousand tonnes of ordnance on British cities in 1940 and 1941. London, Coventry, Liverpool and Manchester were all badly hit by the Luftwaffe as Germany set out to damage Britain's industrial heartlands. Air raid sirens, raging fires and broken bodies were common sights along with the mass evacuation of thousands of families to the countryside. As the war wore on RAF Bomber Command, headed by Air Chief Marshal Sir Arthur Harris between 1942 and 1945, flew thousands of sorties over the European mainland and into the heart of Germany, dropping over 850,000 tonnes of bombs at the cost of 40,000 aircrew casualties. Berlin, Hamburg and Dresden were hit by huge incendiary bombs which consumed medieval cities in raging infernos, all in an attempt to cripple the German war effort and break the will of the German people.

With a huge trail of destruction like this it is no surprise to find criticism of the Allied bombing strategy. However, much of the critical literature tends to assume that the strategists who planned these large-scale reprisals were in some respects morally insipid. If we take the example of Bomber Command, it is not difficult to make the case that bombing civilian targets in order to break the will of the German government is lacking an appreciation of the suffering of ordinary citizens, but that would be to side-step the fact that it had the additional purpose of destroying Germany's industrial production, which formed the basis of its continued resistance to Allied forces. If one wished to hold fast to the merits of moral equivalence, one could easily place Hamburg in May 1943 alongside the German bombing of British cities in 1941 as two examples where thousands of non-combatants were killed and many tens of thousands more rendered homeless. However, this does not in and of itself prove that the strategy was either faulty or wrong. Although it may be judged immoral by some to do so, it is important for us to give at least some consideration to the reasons why such destructive strategies were pursued, for ultimately they were aimed at resetting the balance that the Germans had ignored in the war by their large-scale industrialised slaughter of prisoners of war and social and racial groups they had designated 'unter-mensch'. Germans, as 'Bomber' Harris noted at the time, 'have sown the wind; now they shall reap the whirlwind'.

The Second World War saw an estimated 60–80 million people perish in the most destructive armed conflict ever witnessed up until that point. It proved that the strategy of escalating force to such a degree that it would sap the target population's morale and will to resist could act as a force multiplier in armed conflict, even if it did not always 'yield strategic advantage'.[2] This was taken to its most logical conclusion in August 1945 when the United States dropped atomic bombs on Hiroshima and Nagasaki, thereby precipitating the end of the war. Hundreds of thousands of Japanese civilians were killed and wounded in the attacks. Yet, to see these actions in war as merely the manifestation of violence is to ignore why they became both possible and necessary in the eyes of the Truman administration. The reality was that the Truman administration did not believe their population would tolerate the 'butcher's bill' that would be required in order to break the will of the Japanese and, thereby, win the war by conventional means. By seeking to analyse the political context in which strategy occurs – while also giving consideration to the moral and ethical questions it throws up – we can enhance our understanding of war as the discretionary (as opposed to the totalising) use of force in a clash of wills between belligerents seeking a more decisive resolution to their differences.

Regulating the Use of Force

It was in the context of avoiding another total war and dissuading states from escalating their disagreements to aggression and armed conflict that the UN Charter of 1945 was agreed as an important means for preventing future war. In fact, under the Charter, there are only two justifications for states wishing to engage in military action against other states. The first is whenever states are acting in self-defence (enshrined in Article 51) and the second whenever states are authorised by the UN Security Council to take action under a Chapter VII resolution. The justification for authorising intervention is typically fashioned along the lines of a *jus ad bellum* rationale (i.e., the questions surrounding the legitimacy of a war) and is limited to the most serious of situations. In considering whether to authorize or endorse the use of military force, the UN Security Council considers the following five criteria essential in order to provide legitimacy for armed action: (1) seriousness of threat, (2) proper purpose, (3) last resort, (4) proportional means, and (5) balance of consequences.[3] As we will discover in this chapter, it is important to keep in mind that modern warfare, if it is to be waged at all, is subject to rules and norms fashioned in the international *political* system. For this primary reason, therefore, war is directly influenced by policy, which, as we learned in the previous chapters, permeates 'all military operations, and, in so far as their violent nature will admit, it will have a continuous influence on them'.[4] However, that does not mean that everyone is in agreement that war is a necessary evil, no matter how logical, legal or legitimate it may be.

UN Charter, Chapter VII, Article 51

'Nothing in the present Charter shall impair the inherent right of individual or collective self-defence if an armed attack occurs against a Member of the United Nations, until the Security Council has taken measures necessary to maintain international peace and security. Measures taken by Members in the exercise of this right of self-defence shall be immediately reported to the Security Council and shall not in any way affect the authority and responsibility of the Security Council under the present Charter to take at any time such action as it deems necessary in order to maintain or restore international peace and security.'

As we discovered in Chapter 1, Realist scholars believe that the international system rests on the existence of order only within states and the presence of anarchy (the absence of a higher authority) beyond their territorial boundaries. Therefore, they view it as imperative in the absence of a central authority that states should be able to establish their own rules and laws in a search for order. Power is the lubricant by which this is exercised and the power of states to make and enforce laws, in particular, is seen as one of the key distinguishing features of sovereignty. In the international system it is states (as sovereign actors) that confer upon their armed forces the legal right to use lethal force against their enemies. This poses an interesting conundrum for modern states, especially for those who argue that their behaviour should be subject to international law and IHL (international humanitarian law). As Carsten Stahn has observed:

> One of the main achievements of the modern law of armed force is that it provides more than a mere framework outlawing armed violence or setting limitations on the conduct of armed forces. Contemporary rules of armed force do not contain only prohibitions for states and armed forces; they channel armed violence and regulate the relations between different actors (military forces, civilians, ousted government) in situations of armed conflict.[5]

Modern law on the use of force dates back to the Kellogg–Briand Pact signed in Paris in 1928, which was an attempt to limit aggression between states and render war illegal. In many ways it was an extension of other laws that have their genesis in the work of Grotius, who was writing at the time of the devastating Thirty Years War in the seventeenth century. Indeed, it was the much later eighteenth-century philosopher Jean-Jacques Rousseau who has been most persuasive in terms of affirming the influence of rationality on warfare. 'War is in no way a relationship of man with man but a relationship between States', argued Rousseau, 'in which individuals are enemies only by accident; not as men, nor even as citizens, but as soldiers.' This is important, for it attributes legality and legitimacy on the act of killing in war and recognises that force may, under certain circumstances, be seen as the primary currency by which policy is implemented at the sharp end and it has been judged necessary in order to achieve an objective such as forcing one's enemy to do something they would not do peacefully. From the earliest of wars to the most contemporaneous, war has been seen as an important instrument by which states and other political entities have sought to get their way in the world when non-lethal options have proved ineffective.

The role of force in achieving stated policy goals has a long history. Examples abound of political ultimatums being issued and then ignored, thereby paving the way for war. In the Battle of Hastings (1066), for instance, the refusal of King Harold to cede his throne to William, Duke of Normandy, led to an invasion of England. It was said that English soldiers stood shoulder to shoulder with one another as they were continually bludgeoned to death by Norman cavalry swinging heavy maces.[6] In the end the Normans prevailed because they rallied against their opponents, broke through a wall of shields and killed their leader, King Harold. It was a tactical defeat that allowed William to resolve a political crisis by force and settle the question over the legitimacy of the throne of England by crowning himself king.

Much later, in recent history, the policy of ethnic cleansing followed by Slobodan Milošević in Kosovo, a province of the Former Republic of Yugoslavia, meant that allies from the North Atlantic Treaty Organization (NATO) presented him with an ultimatum (which he would ignore) – either desist from his campaign against Kosovar Albanians or face the prospect of overwhelming force being used against his regime. NATO was left with no other choice in strategic terms than to follow through on their threats to bomb military targets in Kosovo. The extension of Operation Allied Force to bombing Belgrade eventually forced Milošević's hand and he withdrew his forces back to Serbia. However, not all states were supportive of the NATO campaign and the Russians and Chinese, as permanent members of the UN Security Council, led the chorus of opposition to it, thereby ensuring that the UN would not pass a resolution authorising the use of force. Nevertheless, the air campaign was considered to be morally right and, therefore, legitimate in the eyes of a majority of NATO leaders because it led to the reversal of the Serbian policy of ethnic cleansing in Kosovo.

It would be wrong to insist that war is only about violence. American strategist Bernard Brodie informs us that it is 'something else besides, something with a distinctive and quite special configuration'.[7] Regardless of what we personally think of war it would seem that it is regarded as having utility in the world. 'The fact that slaughter is a horrifying spectacle must make us take war more seriously, but not provide an excuse for gradually blunting our swords in the name of humanity', wrote Clausewitz. 'Sooner or later someone will come along with a sharp sword and hack off our arms.'[8] This was illustrated in dramatic terms by the attacks perpetrated by the al-Qaeda terrorist network on the United States on 11 September 2001 when commercial airliners were flown into the Twin Towers and Pentagon. The shock of the attack and the fact that anyone would dare to challenge the United States led to the reformulation of a more coercive national security policy. In the so-called 'Global War on Terror', President George W. Bush set out to revise how the US would respond to new and emerging threats:

> For centuries, international law recognized that nations need not suffer an attack before they can lawfully take action to defend themselves against forces that present an imminent danger of attack . . . We must adapt the concept of imminent threat to the capabilities and objectives of today's adversaries. The United States has long maintained the option of preemptive actions to counter a sufficient threat to our national security. The greater the threat, the greater is the risk of inaction – and the more compelling the case for taking anticipatory action to defend ourselves, even if uncertainty remains as to the time and place of the enemy's attack. To forestall or prevent such hostile acts by our adversaries, the United States will, if necessary, act preemptively.[9]

In terms of international law, this interpretation of self-defence to encompass preventive action was technically illegal and would lead to a precedent being set that would soon be followed by Russia in respect to its intervention in Georgia.

The 2008 war between Russia and Georgia is evidence of how Moscow, like Washington, used a loose reading of international law to undermine it. Russian forces intervened in the internal affairs of Georgia under the pretext of 'protecting its citizens' by deploying a 'peacekeeping force' to South Ossetia. The crippling of much of the state's military infrastructure sent a clear signal to

Georgian leaders about moving too far outside the Russian sphere of influence and towards a greater alliance with Western powers, such as the United States. Even though there was a risk of escalation in the week-long war, given that the Russian prime minister at the time, Vladimir Putin, expressed a desire to want to hang the Georgian President Mikheil Saakashvili, it nonetheless remained somewhat restrained. Although the same could not be said for Russian intervention in Ukraine a few years later, what the Russia–Georgia case illustrates is that, ultimately, it is rational policy that determines the logic of war and, as such, ensures that it does not degenerate into something, to paraphrase Clausewitz, 'pointless and devoid of sense'. Russia, in undertaking limited intervention in Georgia, was pursuing a deliberate strategy to link its policy of exerting its hegemony in the region through a mixture of limited military operations, striking up alliances with local sympathisers and undermining the attempts by governments in the 'near abroad' from pulling away from Russia's sphere of influence in the post-Cold War world. As these cases illustrate, law and its regulation have often taken a back seat whenever the national interests of states are much sharper in focus. In the words of Thucydides, 'if one follows one's self-interest one wants to be safe, whereas the path of justice and honour involves one in danger'.[10]

Applying Force on the Battlefield

While the balancing of ends, ways and means in war, discussed in detail in the previous chapter, may appear, on the face of it, a logical activity, it would be remiss of our study of strategy not to query the role played by morality that prevents it from descending into barbarism. As argued in earlier chapters, war is much more than the sum total of a bloody resolution of disputes between mortal enemies and has far-reaching political significance. For Professor Colin S. Gray:

> Strategic studies typically have no obvious moral content. Furthermore, it is rare indeed for strategic debate, even when inclusively

defined, to be conducted even in minor key with explicitly moral argument. But, because strategy is a human enterprise, albeit one conducted with many non-human and inhumane means, and because we humans are hard-wired to be moral animals, strategy is impregnated with moral content.[11]

If we follow Gray's argument to its logical conclusion, it may be more appropriate to talk about the 'moral impulse' behind strategic decisions rather than explicitly 'moral strategies'. It is important to separate the two while recognising that both are complementary to each other.

Regardless of whether they are part of a state's armed forces or a guerrilla group, lawful combatants must all adhere to the law of armed conflict (terrorists and mercenaries, for example, are not considered lawful combatants), which consists of four basic principles for the application of armed force. The first is distinction, which places an onus on those engaged in armed conflict to distinguish between combatants and non-combatants. Both groups have rights but the latter are afforded special provisions to prevent attack. The second principle is humanity, which means that combatants must not inflict unnecessary suffering. The third principle is military necessity, meaning that force, if it is used, is only used against military objectives and not civilian objects. Lastly, the fourth principle is proportionality, which is designed to ensure combatants only use that degree of force that is necessary to secure their military objectives. There is a limit of exploitation (to borrow a military phrase) placed on the use of armed force to ensure that combatants do not commit atrocities. All of these principles are meant to be observed by armed groups in conflict in order to comply with the legal application of force and also to alleviate the calamity of war befalling belligerents engaged in armed conflict. However, as we know from the reality of war, not all combatants (or unlawful combatants for that matter) adhere to these principles and many have been guilty of committing gross violations of IHL. In doing so they do still remain amenable to the law, which does not place a statute of limitations on war crimes.

Protection for Combatants and Non-Combatants

The Geneva Conventions of 1949 give protection to four categories of person.

Geneva Convention 1
  The wounded and sick on land

Geneva Convention 2
  The wounded and sick at sea

Geneva Convention 3
  Prisoners of war

Geneva Convention 4
  Civilians, including those living under occupation

Additional Protocol I (1977)
International Armed Conflict
Additional Protocol II (1977)
Non-International Armed Conflict
Additional Protocol III (2005)
Protection of the Distinctive Symbol – the Red Crystal

In order to adhere to these laws, discipline and morale are essential prerequisites for those troops charged with taking life by lethal force, should the situation demand it. Discipline has remained the glue that binds together the disparate traits needed in fighting men and women since ancient times. In the Battle of Mantinea (418–417 BC), in which the Spartans clashed with their old Athenian foes, discipline was necessary to make the army function effectively:

> The Spartans on their side spoke their words of encouragement to each other man to man, singing their war songs, and calling on their comrades, as brave men, to remember what each knew so well, realizing that the long discipline of action is a more effective safeguard than hurried speeches, however well they may be delivered.[12]

Professional soldiers are a unique breed of people who are conditioned to accept and adjust their behaviour patterns to the military ethos and way of life. In this respect they are expected to obey orders, but only up to the point where they are considered lawful. With the advent of the Geneva Conventions, orders to 'leave no quarter' are prohibited and, thus, by their very nature illegal orders that soldiers are not expected to obey. However, in practice, many combatants are faced with both a moral and ethical dilemma that they must resolve before necessarily taking into account the legality of their actions.

Why do Men (and Women) Kill in War?

Sigmund Freud was of the opinion that men were driven to action by two impulses. The desire to create (love), expressed most readily through sexual desire, and the innate desire to destroy (hate), which he attributed to animal instincts. In a famous exchange with the physicist Albert Einstein, Freud wrote: 'In the case of men, no doubt, conflicts of opinion occur as well which may reach the highest pitch of abstraction and which seem to demand some other technique for their settlement. That, however, is a later complication. To begin with, in a small human horde, it was superior muscular strength which decided who owned things or whose will should prevail. Muscular strength was soon supplemented and replaced by the use of tools: the winner was the one who had the better weapons or who used them the more skilfully. From the moment at which weapons were introduced, intellectual superiority already began to replace brute muscular strength; but the final purpose of the fight remained the same – one side or the other was to be compelled to abandon his claim or his objection by the damage inflicted on him and by the crippling of his strength. That purpose was most completely achieved if the victor's violence eliminated his opponent permanently – that is to say, killed him.'[13] Freud would share much in common with his fellow psychologists on the matter of man's aversion towards destructiveness. Yet it was Erich Fromm who informed us that 'man differs from the animal by the fact that he is a killer; he is the only primate that kills and tortures members of his own species without any reason, either biological or economic, and who feels satisfaction in doing so'.[14] We know from the work of later psychologists, such as Stanley Milgram, that this turn to destructiveness, even in war, may be attributable mainly to obedience to authority rather than necessarily to innate aggression.[15]

Ethics go to the heart of war in the modern world. However, it was not always the case. Up until the late eighteenth century it was far more likely that injured combatants lying on the battlefield would be dispatched with a swift sword or shot that hastened their demise. The Hague Convention of 1899 limited the types of ammunition one could use against an enemy so as to limit the killing of other human beings to more humane means and methods. In the opening decades of the twentieth century this moved onto the prohibition on the use of chemical weapons, such as mustard gas, on the battlefield. Ethics, in their simplest form, are about behaviour. Today we expect soldiers to abide by IHL and human rights law so that we might avoid the descent into barbarism. Yet, at a much higher level of government, strategy becomes a game of two halves – defeating the enemy and ensuring that the way this is done is designed to prevent a further outbreak of violence in the future. By wishing to understand war we do not have to compromise our moral standpoint that war is wrong or unjustifiable. We can critique it for its excesses, its ability to murder on a large scale and its seemingly incessant commitment to disproportionately affecting the weakest and most vulnerable. Political philosopher Judith Butler suggests 'It is as much a matter of wrestling infinitely the justifications for war. It is as much a matter of wrestling ethically with one's own murderous impulses, impulses that seek to quell an overwhelming fear, as it is a matter of apprehending the suffering of others and taking stock of the suffering one has inflicted.'[16]

The appreciation of having inflicted pain and suffering on others rarely drifts across the frame of patriotic framing of armed conflicts in the same way, identified by Butler, that 'shock and awe' in the 2003 invasion of Iraq was stage-managed for a Western audience used to resolving its problems from a great distance. Interventionism, if it was needed, would be short, sharp and quick and accomplished by brawn, not brain, for the Revolution in Military Affairs (RMA) was based on the premise of overwhelming firepower and precision-guided weapons. Of course, the onset of asymmetric adversaries in the form of terrorists and insurgents soon put paid to the Western penchant for the imposition of first world order on third world chaos from 30,000 feet. It was the inability to see the enemy as anything other than weak that led Western states, such as the US and UK, to believe in the infallibility of RMA. As they would soon find out to their cost – in both blood and treasure – the enemy does get a vote and one cannot predict with any certainty how he or she might react once drawn into the arena of conflict. Butler has called this 'vulnerability' and outlines how it can both, paradoxically, 'become the basis of claims for non-military political solutions' and, 'through a fantasy of mastery (and institutionalized fantasy of mastery) can fuel the instruments of war'.[17] In this sense war could not be wished away, though it could be controlled by making better decisions. The other problem Western states faced, of course, was that technology could not easily replace the need for coherent strategy based on an appreciation of the human terrain in a given battlespace. And in this it was necessary for troops to dismount from their heavily armed vehicles and interact with the local population, something that would bring both opportunities and challenges.

Observing Restraint in War

The moral philosopher Michael Waltzer reminds us that the saying '*War is hell* is doctrine, not description: it is a moral argument, an attempt at self-justification. Even in hell, it is possible to be more or less humane, to fight with or without restraint.'[18] Yet even if restraint in war is based on the customary acceptance of laws relating to armed force it is still dependent on the human conscience for individual compliance. Due to the enormous cost in lives and property inflicted during the First World War, attempts were made to limit the scope for unnecessary suffering due to the means and methods of war inflicting inhumane suffering on combatants and non-combatants alike and preventing states from going to war too readily. Furthermore, the Second World War would prove that, 'while the conduct of hostilities, particularly with regard to civilians in occupied territory, emphasised that existing treaties were not as effective as had been hoped in introducing principles of humanitarianism into the law of armed conflict'.[19] However, this misses the point that in reality wars have been regulated much more by the nature of the combatants fighting in them than by heavily regulated paper principles. As some noted authorities have informed us, those definitions 'that focus simply on body count are simplistic to the point of absurdity, ignoring the political and legal implications of defining war, in addition to saying nothing about the actual conduct of military operations'.[20]

Colin S. Gray has gone further, positing the idea that moral and ethical considerations ought to be a key consideration of professional strategists:

> The effectiveness with which strategies are prosecuted overall, operationally and tactically, always is affected by the attitudes to the conflict and to the conduct of behaviour of the belligerent parties, and sometimes of neutral, but candidate belligerent, observers. Rarely are these attitudes the product strictly of cold rationality alone. Rather they are shaped, in greater or lesser degree, by people's feelings and preferences, factors that have an unalienable moral, certainly ethical content. When strategists are neglectful of the moral aspect, they are riding for a painful fall.[21]

Examples are not hard to come by with respect to this point. For example, in its war in Afghanistan between 2001 and 2014, the British military operated a policy of courageous restraint after the deaths of a number of non-combatants. Senior commanders were at pains to convince their subordinates that the consequences of their actions in driving up the butcher's bill of collateral damage was not only morally unsustainable but also injurious to the overall campaign strategy of 'winning the hearts and minds' of the Afghan people. The policy was driven by an awareness also of the political effects of mounting casualties caused by indirect fire and the pressure that was being exerted by Hamid Karzai's government in Kabul. As we know, restraint takes many forms in war. It can denote the restraint of the individual soldier not to escalate force too rapidly if there is no overriding tactical, operational or strategic rationale for doing so. The level of operations is vitally important here because it links policy to tactics and it also helps reconcile the strategic application of force by ministers and senior commanders far removed from the battlefields to those directly affected by their decisions. And so it was that the idea of 'courageous restraint' was introduced. It is a curious term that one might well associate with an age of chivalry but it defies all evidence of experience in battle prior to the nineteenth century, which was often brutal, vicious and overly dependent on the opponent's goodwill rather than on the slavish following of rules. In practice unrestrained actions meant putting the wounded to death or leaving them without alleviation of the calamities that had befallen them on the battlefield. As the smoke lifted, the hacked off limbs, lifeless bodies and rotting flesh gave off a stench that few could bear. In this kind of environment strategy retained its utility and indeed could accentuate the decisiveness of a victory in battle.

Common Article 3

The Geneva Conventions marked a breakthrough, as it covered, for the first time, situations of non-international armed conflicts. These types of conflicts vary greatly. They include traditional civil wars, internal armed conflicts that spill over into other states or internal conflicts in which third states or a multinational force intervenes alongside the government. Common Article 3 establishes fundamental rules from which no derogation is permitted. It is like a mini-Convention within the Conventions as it contains the essential rules of the Geneva Conventions in a condensed format and makes them applicable to conflicts not of an international character: .

It requires humane treatment for all persons in enemy hands, without any adverse distinction. It specifically prohibits murder, mutilation, torture, cruel, humiliating and degrading treatment, the taking of hostages and unfair trial.

It requires that the wounded, sick and shipwrecked be collected and cared for.

It grants the International Committee of the Red Cross (ICRC) the right to offer its services to the parties to the conflict.

It calls on the parties to the conflict to bring all or parts of the Geneva Conventions into force through so-called special agreements.

It recognizes that the application of these rules does not affect the legal status of the parties to the conflict.

Given that most armed conflicts today are non-international, applying Common Article 3 is of the utmost importance. Its full respect is required.

One controversial form of strategic rebalance where states have committed large-scale violations of IHL is reprisals. Reprisals are perhaps the most serious attempts to escalate armed conflict in a way that seeks to rebalance the equilibrium but only in order to enforce compliance of IHL. The ICRC makes clear that states are less likely to advocate reprisals today and more likely to observe IHL:

> The reticence to approve of the resort to belligerent reprisals, together with the stringent conditions found in official practice, indicates that the international community is increasingly opposed to the use of violations of international humanitarian law as a method of trying to enforce the law. It is also relevant that there is much more support these days for the notion of ensuring respect for international

humanitarian law through diplomatic channels than there was in the 19th and early 20th centuries, when the doctrine of belligerent reprisals as a method of enforcement was developed. In interpreting the condition that reprisal action may only be taken as a measure of last resort, when no other possibility is available, States must take into account the possibility of appealing to other States and international organizations to help put a stop to the violations.[22]

Indeed, reprisals may only be undertaken with the express intent of making an adversary comply with IHL, as a measure of last resort, proportionate to the violation it is trying to stop, may only be authorised by the highest legal authority in a state, and must be terminated once the violation of IHL has ceased. Reprisals were heavily criticised by the UN in the case of the Iraq–Iraq War of the 1980s and are generally not considered a strategically advantageous course of action to address today's violations of IHL, which are largely based on the ruthless objective of coercing the enemy to give in, preferably without a fight. At this stage it is worth noting that the actions undertaken by non-state actors, such as *Daesh* in Iraq and Syria, are grave violations of IHL and not considered reprisals and are, therefore, prohibited.

Abandoning Restraint in Internal Conflicts

On 30 January 1972 troops from the British airborne unit, the 1st Battalion Parachute Regiment, were deployed to Northern Ireland's second city, Londonderry, with the express mission of arresting ringleaders taking part in civil unrest that frequently accompanied large-scale civil rights demonstrations. Military intelligence reports had anticipated the presence of armed members of the Irish Republican Army (they were indeed present and armed but were under orders not to provoke the Army) and a deterioration of events on the ground. In the afternoon the troops were ordered to deploy over their makeshift barricades in pursuit of rioters. However, one of the soldiers opened fire and caused a chain of events that would lead to the shooting dead of thirteen unarmed protestors and the wounding of fourteen others. The day would subsequently go down in history as 'Bloody Sunday'. The actions of the British Army on Bloody Sunday are an example of how the failure to restrain armed forces is as much a challenge in internal conflicts as in international and non-international armed conflicts.

In internal armed conflicts, where terrorism has become a major security problem, the failure to restrain military power can have significant negative impact on the legitimacy of the states attempting to bring intensive violence under control. Democratic states face the same challenges as non-democratic ones when it comes to terrorism. However, how they deal with it is inherently different. Michael Ignatieff delineates between the two:

> We should remember, in fact, that liberal democracy has been crafted over centuries precisely in order to combat the temptations of nihilism, to prevent violence from becoming an end in itself. Thus terrorism does not present us with a distinctively new temptation. This is what our institutions were designed for, back in the seventeenth century: to regulate evil means and control evil people. The chief ethical challenge with relation to terrorism is relatively simple – to discharge duties to those who have violated their duties to us. We have to do this because we are fighting a war whose essential prize is preserving the identity of liberal society itself and preventing it from becoming what terrorists believe it to be. Terrorists seek to strip off the mask of law to reveal the nihilist heart of coercion within, and we have to show ourselves and the populations whose loyalty we seek that the rule of law is not a mask but the true image of our nature.[23]

Non-democratic states, however, are less constrained in their responses and perhaps rely more on brute force to do the talking for them.

Thus, in 1994, the Russian Army pushed into Chechnya to put down an uprising that had led to self-proclaimed independence. They were defeated in 1996 by Chechnya separatists, who had overcome considerable odds to inflict huge losses on Russian forces. By 1999 the war resumed and just two months into Putin's term as prime minister the Russian military had retaken key areas, including Grozny.[24] An estimated 50,000 people lost their lives in these three years at the cost of transforming a nationalist rebellion into an Islamist one.[25] By the opening decade of the twenty-first century a Moscow-backed regime had installed a system of state repression, including arbitrary detention, disappearances and unattributable kidnappings and murders of prominent human rights advocates and journalists. Suicide attacks are on the rise. The number of insurgent attacks doubled between 2009 and 2010. As Human Rights Watch has revealed: 'The authorities' use of torture, abduction-style detentions, enforced disappearances, and extrajudicial killings in the course of their counterinsurgency campaign, coupled with impunity for these abuses, antagonized the population of the North Caucasus.'[26] Little is known about Russia's official strategy for dealing with Islamist separatism beyond the alleged activities its state forces and agencies have been engaged in.

Case Study: The My Lai Massacre, Vietnam, 16 March 1968

Situation: The My Lai massacre has gone down in US military history as one of the worst atrocities ever perpetrated by soldiers during wartime. On 16 March 1968 troops from Charlie Company were deployed forward in a 'search and destroy mission' to the village of My Lai in south-western Vietnam. They were briefed to expect stiff opposition from forces attached to the 48 NVA Regiment. When they reached their objective they found no resistance and set about 'neutralising' the village by murdering women and children in cold blood. One of those officers responsible for ordering the murders was Lieutenant William Calley, a troop commander. When some of his men refused his orders he opened fire on the civilians himself. Over 200 men, women and children were massacred.

Role of strategy: The US military authorities initially set about covering up the massacre at My Lai in order to prevent news of the atrocity from leaking out into the public arena.

They failed. Strategically the US administration moved to contain the effects of the story but it had come to symbolise the bankruptcy of American policy and strategy towards Vietnam. It was an indictment of the reliance on massive firepower and inhumane tactics in pacifying the civilian population and it scored the NVA and Viet Cong forces a massive media coup against their more powerful rival. My Lai became the turning point in the war.

The Russians are not alone in facing the challenge from powerful terrorist groups that have proven both brazen in their attitudes towards international law and resilient in their challenges to the sovereign basis of states. *Daesh* launched its blitzkrieg across Iraq in a military offensive that had not been seen in the Middle East since Israel undertook brief ground operations against militants in Gaza in 2014. *Daesh* victories in predominately Sunni parts of Iraq, however, were stopped in their tracks in the northern and southern parts of the country by the Kurdish resistance and Shia militias. In the fighting that ensued thousands of Iraqi soldiers and civilians from a range of religious sects and ethnic groups were to perish at the hands of an organisation that sought to raise the bar on the threshold of killing the like of which had not been seen since the *Einsatzgruppen* atrocities amidst Germany's invasion of the Soviet Union in 1941. In scenes redolent of Eastern Europe during the Second World War, *Daesh* have been seen to casually shoot prisoners in the head and dump their bodies into rivers, throw homosexuals from high-rise buildings and shoot women in the street because they were found to be wearing the wrong colour of abya.

Case Study: ISIS and the Capture of Mosul, June 2014

Situation: Terrorist groups are not known for their adherence to international laws governing the conduct of warfare. In fact some scholars have even suggested that terrorism is essentially the perpetration of war crimes in peace time. With that in mind it is perhaps worth examining the case of the Islamic State in Iraq and al-Sham for signs of where restraint is not uppermost in the minds of combatants. When they stormed Iraqi cities in early 2014 *Daesh* depended on the classic terrorist tactic of spreading fear through brutality in order to communicate a message to an audience (Iraqi government and security forces) that no quarter would be given to men, women or children who did not conform to their outlook. Consequently over 1,700 Iraqi soldiers who had fled the battlefield were promptly captured and paraded in front of the cameras where they were shot and their bodies dumped in the Tigris.

Role of strategy: The ruthlessness of ISIS has called into question whether IHL is still extant or relevant whenever non-state actors such as this blatantly disregard rules and norms to gain military advantage over their enemies. However, it is important to understand that there have been abuses perpetrated by all sides in this conflict since the invasion of Iraq in 2003. Strategy has sometimes played a role in advocating a heavy-handed approach to achieving a decisive consolidation or defeat of *Daesh* to such an extent that the Iraqi security forces were banished from key western cities such as Fallujah and Ramadi. The inability to link ends of providing security from the Iraqi people, regardless of tribal, religious or ethnic markings, has undermined the campaign to retake key cities from *Daesh*.

Today's battlefield has witnessed some of the most wide-ranging abuses of the rights afforded to combatants and non-combatants. In this it is merely a continuation of violence witnessed in a range of wars since 1945, including the Chinese Civil War of 1947–9, the many African civil wars of the 1950s and 1960s, right up to the Second Gulf War, the Yemen civil wars and the Balkans conflicts. The infringements on civilian immunity from attack are just a tip of the iceberg in terms of these abuses. There is an urgent need to reset the balance of international law in order to hold fighters accountable for their individual and collective responsibilities during armed conflict. However, it is important to understand that these abuses have been perpetrated before in recent history. The announcement that sarin gas, a particularly nasty chemical weapon that causes suffocation, involuntary muscle spasms, dizziness, blurred vision and, eventually, death in human beings, was deployed in the Eastern and Western Ghouta, a suburb of the Syrian capital Damascus, on 21 August 2013,[27] caused Western politicians to demand intervention on the part of the UN. However, this was not the first time that chemical weapons had been used in armed conflict in the Middle East. They had been used before in the Iran–Iraq War and much earlier by the Egyptians in the Yemeni civil war in the 1960s.

As violence intensified in South Yemen between British forces and Egyptian proxies in the form of the National Liberation Front and the Front for the Liberation of South Yemen, northern Yemen was in the grip of a civil war between republican forces that had ousted the ruling Imam, Muhammad al-Badr, in 1962 and his royalist tribesmen who were backed by covert support from the British and French.[28] Egyptian aircraft were mounting almost daily bomb runs on royalist villages and towns. The ICRC were quick to lodge a report with the UN highlighting one such attack on the villages of Gadafa and Gahar in the Wadi Herran, south-west of Jauf. What made this attack different, however, was that chemical weapons, rather than conventional bombs, were used. The attack was the latest in a long line of such outrages that 'forced events in Yemen back onto the conscience of the world'.

Egyptian planes buzzed their target, dropping three bombs into the wind 300 yards east of the village but no apparent damage had been sustained by the houses. Indeed the blast was minor and left only a small crater, 8 feet by 20 inches. Naturally inquisitive, the villagers came out to see what had happened. Panic ensued when some of the people began to choke and vomit. Others knelt down, holding their heads as their tear ducts opened and their eyes streamed fluid. Shortly afterwards the planes returned, dropping four more high explosive bombs. This time a handful of houses were damaged but seventy-five people died. Survivors complained of pain in the eyes, followed by blindness, and all of them experienced considerably difficulty breathing. A number of women and children died where they lay down in their homes. About 200 animals, including livestock, were also killed in the raid. All of the villagers who died were buried in four large communal graves.

A week later the Egyptian bombers returned to the vicinity of the villages, this time killing 243 civilians. When the ICRC arrived on the scene with it its own doctors they set about performing autopsies on the bodies. They were able to determine that the people died of pulmonary oedema, with the head of mission stating, 'The doctors cannot testify to an air raid with gas bombs of which they were not personally witness. On the other hand, they stress that all the evidence leads to the conclusion that edema was caused by the breathing of poison gas.' Imam Muhammad al-Badr lost no time in lodging a complaint with the UN Secretary General: 'On 2 July 1967 six Egyptian Ilyushin planes dropped 56 poison gas bombs on village of Darb 30 kms east of Sana'a. Similar poison gas bombings were dropped also on villages of Alhajrah and Shawkam 16 kms east of Sana'a. As a result 45 people including women children and old people died apart from another 100 people who died from their heavy injuries.' Militarily a stalemate soon developed in Yemen. Nasser's forces were moving in on royalist positions, ramping up cross-border raids and sponsoring terrorism on the streets of the southern port city of Aden and throughout the hinterland of southern Yemen. They were moving their forces close to the border with Israel.

Half a century on from the first civil war, Yemen remains a state engulfed by internal war. Yet, it is by no means alone. Like Iraq, Syria, Saudi Arabia and Kuwait, the challenge posed by Islamist inspired groups has not diminished by the use of force. In fact, the robust nature of military operations may even have contributed to the continuation of groups that capitalise on the over-reaction of states, as we have seen from Western involvement in Iraq and Afghanistan. However, a more balanced analysis would contend that Western states recognised how coercive strategies aimed at destroying violent non-state groups had to be matched with a more enticing offer to protect the people of the states affected. We must also consider what role strategy plays in resolving these crises and confrontations, with the case studies considered above reinforcing the requirement for strategists to factor the historical record into their decision-making.

Extract from a Letter from President Hadi of Yemen to Arab States

Dear brothers, I write this letter to you with great sadness and sorrow in my heart owing to the serious and extremely dangerous decline in security in the Republic of Yemen, a decline caused by the ongoing acts of aggression and the incessant attacks against the country's sovereignty that are being committed by the Houthi coup orchestrators, with the aim of dismembering Yemen and undermining its security and stability . . .

. . . In the light of those momentous events, it is vital to preserve the security and stability of Yemen and the region, not to mention international peace and security. Our brave Yemeni people, which has paid such a heavy price for the Houthi coup, must be kept safe. My constitutional responsibilities require me to protect the people and safeguard the unity, independence and territorial integrity of the nation. The Houthi militias have committed several acts of aggression, most recently deploying military columns to attack and take control of Aden and the rest of the south. The criminal militias have announced that they intend to move against the south, and the most recent report of the Special Adviser of the Secretary-General to the Security Council confirms that intention. It states that the Houthis' so-called Revolutionary Committee has instructed the military units under its control in the north to mobilize in preparation for an attack on the south. The report also states that the Houthis have continued to occupy Government buildings and have expanded to new areas, despite the repeated appeals of the Security Council. It indicates that, in a serious and unprecedented escalation, Air

Force aircraft seized by the Houthis have continued to circle and bombard Aden . . .

. . . I therefore appeal to you, and to the allied States that you represent, to stand by the Yemeni people as you have always done and come to the country's aid. I urge you, in accordance with the right of self-defence set forth in Article 51 of the Charter of the United Nations, and with the Charter of the League of Arab States and the Treaty on Joint Defence, to provide immediate support in every form and take the necessary measures, including military intervention, to protect Yemen and its people from the ongoing Houthi aggression, repel the attack that is expected at any moment on Aden and the other cities of the South, and help Yemen to confront Al-Qaida and Islamic State in Iraq and the Levant.

The Yemeni people will never forget how its allies stood by it at this tense and perilous time.

The Yemeni people will never let its trust in God Almighty be shaken. It will remain true to its national values, and will do everything in its power to safeguard the pride, dignity and sovereignty of the nation.

Abdrabuh Mansour Hadi, 24 March 2015

Ethical questions have inevitably been raised in relation to the conduct of hostilities in the Middle East. States may have a premium placed on their actions by international law; however, it is important to remember that the law remains anathema to many non-state actors employing armed force. For terrorist and insurgent groups, the strategic problems under which they labour sometimes mean that compliance with the law is secondary to the pursuit of victory over their state-based enemies. International law is reciprocal between states, though this reciprocity appears to be at an end whenever one considers the behaviour of non-state actors such as al-Qaeda and *Daesh*. The future evolution of international law must remain conscious of the importance of holding all combatants to account, both individually and collectively, for their actions. The *jus post bellum* phase will come increasingly into play once hostilities subside and peace (or a variation of it) descends on cities like Mosul, Gaza and Sana'a. Some legal scholars have lobbied for a tripartite conception of law which looks to enforce international law after conflict so as to ensure a fair and just peace.[29] There is much to commend this argument; however, the history of troubled regions such as the Middle East suggests that this is by no means the most likely outcome. Deep-seated hatreds and a particularist reading of the historical record will continue to feed the insatiable appetite of settling old scores. Strategists must be prepared for this eventuality.

Conclusion

As this chapter has sought to demonstrate, war has a rational purpose, even if we may deplore the decisions that lead to bloodshed. It is a serious means to a serious end. The end, as Liddell Hart informs us, may be a subjective one insofar as it is designed to secure a better peace than what went before. However, in order to get to this point it is necessary to shed blood (for that is the business of war) but in a way that is proportionate to the end sought. It is now well-established that the laws relating to armed force have a long lineage, stretching back to the time of Grotius and the Thirty Years War. However, *jus ad bellum* and *jus in bello* have found their most cogent adaptation and observance in the contemporary international state system. As we have noted above, this not without its challenges. We know that the dualist laws of war, even though they are enshrined in customary international law, are still not yet adhered to by non-state actors, many of whom are guilty of committing atrocities on non-combatants in times of peace as well as in times of war. Nevertheless, the universal call to restraint in war leaves a challenge that everyone involved in armed conflict must rise to confront, especially since war is destined to remain with us long into the future. In responding to the challenge we might profitably keep in mind the words of Clausewitz, who reminds us that the 'first, the supreme, the most far-reaching act of judgment that the statesman and commander have to make is to establish . . . the kind of war on which they are embarking; neither mistaking it for, nor trying to turn it into, something that is alien to its nature'.[30] In this respect we might concur with legal scholar Mark J. Osiel who informs us that 'the gesture of humanitarianism sends a signal' that the state adhering to it is worthy of emulation and, 'with regard to the rule of law. It still practices what it preaches.'[31] There is an urgent need also to examine the blurring of boundaries between war and peace as well as in the application of IHL, human rights law and enforcement action, when considering the employment of armed force.[32]

Key Questions

1. What are the strategic advantages for states adhering to international law?
2. What are the four key principles from IHL combatants must adhere to when they engage in fighting?
3. Why is it more accurate to talk of moral impulse and compulsion in strategy, rather than its moral logic?
4. Why should state and non-state military forces practice restraint in war?
5. What are the strategic disadvantages attached to those combatants that do not adhere to restraint in war?

Further Reading

Brodie, Bernard, *War and Politics* (London: Cassell, 1973).

Butler, Judith, *Precarious Life: The Powers of Mourning and Violence* (London: Verso, 2004).

Clausewitz, Carl von, *On War* (Princeton, NJ: Princeton University Press, 1976).

Gray, Colin S., 'Moral advantage, strategic advantage?', *Journal of Strategic Studies*, 33: 3, 2010, pp. 333–65.

Gray, Colin S., *The Strategy Bridge: Theory for Practice* (Oxford: Oxford University Press, 2010).

Green, Leslie C., *The Contemporary Law of Armed Conflict*, 3rd edn (Manchester: Manchester University Press, 2008).

Ignatieff, Michael, *The Lesser Evil: Political Ethics in an Age of Terror* (Edinburgh: Edinburgh University Press, 2005).

Jones, Clive, *Britain and the Yemen Civil War, 1962–1965* (Brighton: Sussex Academic Press, 2004).

Kennedy, David, *Of War and Law* (Princeton, NJ: Princeton University Press, 2006).

Osiel, Mark J., *Obeying Orders: Atrocity, Military Discipline, and the Law of War* (New Brunswick, NJ: Transaction Publishers, 1999).

Osiel, Mark J., *Making Sense of Mass Atrocity* (Cambridge: Cambridge University Press, 2009).

Osiel, Mark J., *The End of Reciprocity: Terror, Torture and the Law of War* (Cambridge: Cambridge University Press, 2009).

Stahn, Carsten, '"Jus ad bellum", "jus in bello" . . . "jus post bellum"? Rethinking the conception of the law of armed force', *European Journal of International Law*, 17: 5, 2007, pp. 921–43.

Thucydides, *History of the Peloponnesian War* (London: Penguin, [1954] 1972).

5 Strategy and the Utility of Force

Scope

A deeper understanding of strategy and war has certainly sharpened the intellectual focus of civilian and military leaders faced with the unenviable prospect of employing force to attain policy objectives. This chapter invites readers to think about the ways in which strategies have been employed by Britain and the United States in the Cold War and beyond. Historically, success in war has only come about when strategists understand the nature of the wars that they fight and fully reconcile their policy goals to the means at their disposal. This has been crucial on the battlefield from the time of the Peloponnesian War to more recent wars in Nigeria, Iraq, Syria and Ukraine. Today, it must also be understood that force is only one of several instruments of power at the state's disposal and may lack utility unless it is used more intelligently in conjunction with other means. To that end this chapter examines the successful application of strategic theory in the case of the nuclear stand off during the Cold War, the mixed success of strategy in Britain's decolonisation efforts in Palestine, Malaya and Kenya, and, finally, the uncertainty that has accompanied the application of strategy in conflicts since the end of the Cold War.

Introduction

This chapter is concerned with the business of employing force to secure policy objectives. Raymond Aron once wrote that 'force

125

without the will to use it, without a motivating idea, is sterile'.[1] If we assume from our preceding discussion in earlier chapters the presence of a motivating idea, then we might also contend that in the case studies consulted the employment of force was considered to be one of the best ways to achieve that end. Moreover, as we also learned, flexibility is vitally important to ensure the successful application of strategy in regular and irregular forms of warfare. As Chapters 3 and 4 illustrated, the practice of strategy has helped to sharpen the conceptual thinking of those civilian and military leaders grappling with the prospect of using force to attain policy objectives. In seeking to build on previous chapters, readers are invited to think about the ways in which strategies employed by the United States and its allies in recent conflicts in Iraq and Afghanistan have their origins in earlier strategic episodes. The central hypothesis explored here is whether the commitment to applying the experience gleaned in specific contexts has been a more costly enterprise than applying principles that are, arguably, more generic and useful in a myriad of new and challenging circumstances.

Strategy and the Use of Force

It is important at the outset of our discussion that we once again draw a clear distinction between grand strategy and military strategy. For the purposes of this chapter we will focus on the latter, which seeks to employ the military instrument in the service of stated end goals. Typically, in grand strategy, states seek to accomplish these goals by drawing upon a range of political, economic, military and diplomatic instruments. They might employ all of these during a total war, for example, which requires that all of the resources of the state are brought to bear on one's enemies in order to secure victory. At other times states might employ soft power, which includes social or cultural resources, in order to elicit consent from potential competitors, rather than rely disproportionately on coercion.[2] Ultimately, however, it is the use of force that is turned to in order to secure a more decisive policy outcome. This is not without profound risk, as Stanley Hoffman informs us:

> A state will use force to attain its goals if, after assessing the prospects for success, it values those goals more than it values the pleasures of peace. Because each state is the final judge of its own cause, any state may at any time use force to implement its policies. Because any state may at any time use force, all states must constantly be ready either to counter force with force or to pay the cost of weakness. The requirements of state action are, in this view, imposed by the circumstances in which all states exist.[3]

The sobering outlook articulated by Realists such as Hoffman is nevertheless a useful starting point for any analysis of the utility of force for it highlights how competition and the 'will to power' forms a natural component of the international system. It is this structural bias that may, in some cases, lead to confrontation and, perhaps even, conflict.

Historically, of course, there are a variety of case studies one can draw upon to illustrate the centrality of fighting in war and how military strategy can accentuate victories and defeats. The German '*Blitzkrieg*' in the closing months of 1939 and into the first half of 1940, when German forces paralysed Poland and France, was an ambitiously successful military plan executed by Hitler's generals. Although the Führer had originally planned to follow up the subjugation of an entire country with the invasion of another, France, the weather intervened and ensured it was postponed until the following year. Politically, it was said that French resistance to the German onslaught failed because of a faulty military strategy and domestic political divisions. There is some truth to this. The belief that the construction of an impregnable defensive wall (the 'Maginot Line') stretching to the border with Belgium would spare France the ignominy of having to fight another inter-state war on its own soil convinced the generals that they did not necessarily have to plan for a long-drawn-out offensive operation. This was short-sighted, for, in the words of historian Tony Judt, a 'rotting, divided polity collapsed unprotesting when its incompetent military caste caved in before a magnificent German war machine'.[4]

The French belief that its defences were somewhat impregnable may have convinced the generals of the literal interpretation of Clausewitz's view that 'defence was the stronger form of attack'. Yet the Germans capitalised on this overconfidence and the mass mobilisation of its resources to reinforce military successes on the battlefield.

British Army officer Major General J. F. C. Fuller was convinced that blitzkrieg heralded a new and more frightening kind of warfare that took most European leaders by surprise. He defined blitzkrieg in his book *The Conduct of War, 1789–1961* (1961) along the following lines:

> It was to employ mobility as a psychological weapon: not to kill but to move; not to move to kill but to move to terrify, to bewilder, to perplex, to cause consternation, doubt and confusion in the rear of the enemy, which rumour would magnify until panic became monstrous. In short, its aim was to paralyse not only the enemy's command but also its government, and paralysation would be in direct proportion to velocity.[5]

Blitzkrieg was indeed to prove useful as a military strategy in the opening years of the war but as we noted in an earlier chapter in relation to Pearl Harbor, winning the battle did not necessarily mean winning the war. In the post-Cold War era we have discovered that a lack of strategy connecting what happens on the battlefield to what is expected in political capitals can be fatal. As General Sir Rupert Smith has argued, the paradigm shift from understanding industrial war progressing in linear fashion, from peace to crisis to war, and finally, to its resolution and 'peace again', is misplaced and we are more likely to be moving towards a continuous criss-crossing of armed conflict from crisis to confrontation and to war or peace proves that force may lack utility in some respects but not in others.[6] War is not always necessarily the best way to ensure a decisive outcome, as recent complex conflicts in Nigeria, Iraq, Syria and Ukraine attest. Regardless of whether force has utility in and of itself, however, it is important to understand that wielding it without a proper strategy can mean defeat and ruin more quickly than anticipated.

Defining War

'[W]ar is simply a continuation of political intercourse, with the addition of other means.'[7]

'War in its *ensemble* is not a science, but an art. Strategy, particularly, may indeed be regulated by fixed laws resembling those of the positive sciences, but this is not true of war viewed as a whole.'[8]

'War rests on many sciences, but war itself is not a science – it is a practical art, a skill.'[9]

'It is a general principle, then, that conflicts of interest between men are settled by the use of violence. This is true of the whole animal kingdom, from which men have no business to exclude themselves.'[10]

'War no longer exists. Confrontation, conflict and combat undoubtedly exist all around the world – most noticeably, but not only, in Iraq, Afghanistan, the Democratic Republic of the Congo and the Palestinian Territories – and states still have armed forces which they use as a symbol of power. None the less, war as cognitively known to most non-combatants, war as battle in a field between men and machinery, war as a massive deciding event in a dispute in international affairs: such war no longer exists.'[11]

To return to the Realist interpretation of international relations once more, we note how states – as well as individuals – are inherently self-interested and this can lead, unavoidably, to conflict. As Kenneth Waltz writes: 'Force is a means of achieving the external ends of states because there exists no consistent, reliable process of reconciling the conflicts of interests that arise among similar units in a condition of anarchy.'[12] Realists, of course, stress the lack of an overarching mechanism for reconciling the differences between states. In doing so they are dismissive of the drive by liberals and idealists to create a forum where states could at least expect some formal arbitration of disputes. In the aftermath of the First World

War that came in the form of the League of Nations, which was a product of Woodrow Wilson's Fourteen Points programme. Despite its good intentions, the League did not survive American disengagement from its structures, Italian aggression in Abyssinia (now Ethiopia), German annexation of Czechoslovakia or Austria or, for that matter, Japanese invasion of Manchuria. After the devastation caused by the Second World War, the formation of the United Nations promised a new, more robust mechanism, with full US involvement that would ensure at least a preventative measure for mediating in disputes between states and as a way to offset aggression so that it did not spill over into all-out war. There was evidence that the UN could not hope to eradicate aggression in all of its forms when the US and Soviet Union became openly hostile towards each other in a large-scale Cold War confrontation that threatened world peace and, with the acquisition and deployment of nuclear weapons by both great powers, the possibility of the extinction of all life on earth.

US Nuclear Strategy in the Cold War

As we noted earlier in this book, the United States sought to outflank its opponents throughout the Cold War. The grand strategy that followed was aimed at containing the threat posed by the Soviet Union, which Washington sought to do by consolidating economic resources at home while building a nuclear armed alliance in the North Atlantic area (establishing the North Atlantic Treaty Organization (NATO) in 1949) and wider security guarantees in other regions. Containment, in the sense that it was first employed as a strategy, was about 'the adroit and vigilant application of counter-force at a series of constantly shifting geographical and political points, corresponding to the shifts and maneuvers of Soviet policy', but which could not be 'charmed or talked out of existence'.[13] Containment was by no means accepted as the prevailing view of the West during the four decades of Cold War and there were frequent debates between those who preferred containment to the idea of rolling back Soviet expansionism. With the increasing stockpiling of nuclear weapons and the formation of the Warsaw Pact in 1955, the US military called upon eminent scholars to assist them in anticipating the next move of Soviet Communist leaders in the Kremlin.

To this end, Tom Schelling, a Nobel Prize-winning economist, became one of two influential figures in the development of US strategy in the Cold War. His models were based on abstract formulation that took their cue from game theory and a belief in the inherent rationality of the human species. In Schelling's view,

> When one threatens to fight if attacked or to cut his price if his competitor does, the threat is no more than a communication of one's own incentives, designed to impress on the other the automatic consequences of his act. And, incidentally, if it succeeds in deterring, it benefits both parties.[14]

Schelling's ideas about the threat of force, the dynamics of bargaining, tacit agreements and restraints, and the manipulation of risk were so far-reaching, according to Hedley Bull, that they greatly 'affected thinking about international relations'.[15] In a similar vein, a noted contemporary of Schelling's, Herman Kahn, believed that not only could nuclear conflict be rationalised according to certain strategic principles but that it could also be 'conducted in a controlled, discriminating manner'.[16] In his impressive *On Thermonuclear War* (1961), Kahn parted ways with Schelling in remaining sceptical about the much adulated strategy of deterrence, which he considered to be in serious need of reappraisal:

> If the balance of terror were totally reliable we would be as likely to be deterred from striking the Soviets as they would be from striking us. We must still be able to fight and survive wars just as long as it is possible to have such a capability. Not only is it prudent to take out insurance against a war occurring unintentionally, but we must also be able to stand up to the threat of fighting or, credibly, to threaten to initiate a war ourselves – unpleasant though this sounds and is. We must make it risky for the enemy to force us into situations in which we must choose between fighting and appeasing.[17]

Kahn believed that in the absence of a world government – provided it was technologically and economically prudent – the West must have an alternative to peace that included a 'general war capability as well as a limited war capability'. As earlier chapters have illustrated, the concept of deterrence, as elucidated by Schelling and others, was believed to encompass both the capability and intent to act, rather than as some kind of preventative measure, that is, to prevent a threat from arising in the first place.[18]

Schelling's Conundrum

One of the most practical examples of strategic thinking employed by the economist Thomas C. Schelling was in relation to self-defence. It runs something like this:

You are disturbed in the night by an intruder and go downstairs to investigate. Upon discovering the individual, who has no right to be in your home, you challenge him. He is armed, you are armed. You might scare him off by brandishing your weapon. However, if he too is carrying a firearm, he might use it against you. What do you do? Do you shoot him first to gain the upper hand or does he act first to prevent you from cutting short his career as a burglar? While in most circumstances you may use your weapon in self-defence, you can only do so when you are in serious danger of attack. If you attack him when he is not brandishing a weapon of any kind and you shoot him down callously you may be seizing the upper hand but you are acting preventatively. If we were to play this out in a real world example, there are a range of strategic possible courses of actions you may take here. However, the important thing to work out very quickly – even in the heat of battle – is what do you want to do, how are you going to do it and what resources do you have at your disposal? These are strategic problems.

The possibility of nuclear war loomed large in the minds of political leaders and military commanders in Washington and Moscow during the so-called 'golden age of strategy'. In facing the prospect of imminent nuclear Armageddon, they nonetheless found comfort in the belief that their opponent was too rational to push the button that would lead to mutually assured destruction (MAD). As the preceding discussion has emphasised, the ability of either side to escalate the conflict in lesser terms did not mean, therefore, that force lacked utility. In many respects the Cold War concepts of escalation and de-escalation, for instance, could be translated into the grand strategic efforts of states locked in a struggle with a non-state opponent. As Kahn famously wrote:

> In international relations, escalation is used to facilitate negotiations or to put pressure on one side or both to settle a dispute without war. If either side wanted a war, it would simply go to war and not bother to negotiate. For this reason, the common observation that 'neither side wants war' is not particularly startling, even though it is often delivered with an air of revealed truth. Neither side is willing to back down, precisely because it believes or hopes it can achieve its objectives without war. It may be willing to run some risk of war to achieve its objective, but it feels that the other side will back down or compromise before the risk becomes very large.[19]

Kahn's metaphor for this game was 'chicken' – imagine two cars travelling some distance apart from one another towards one another; the first to swerve would lose. In the case of escalation towards nuclear war, however, Kahn believed that both players would wish to create rules for the adjudication of the game. In any case, he concluded, 'the balance of terror is likely to work well enough to induce some degree of restraint and prudent behaviour on each side'.[20] Moreover, the system of deterrence, argued Kahn, would only be viable if precedents had been set first. In this, he inadvertently made clear that, unlike escalation, it is much harder to force a suitable response in de-escalation: 'It is not really true that it takes two to make a quarrel; only one side need be aggressive in order to generate some certainty of a quarrel. But it usually does take two to make an argument (barring total surrender by one side).[21] For Kahn and other game theorists the belief in an established pattern and the playing for high stakes was the only way to guarantee stability of the system. With a fixation on balancing, there was less concern given over to the vacuum that would be created in other parts of the world as the superpowers recalibrated, subverted and called into question the strategy being pursued by their opponent. One of the ways to undermine one's opponents was to build up enough of a profile of the weaponry and intelligence capability at their disposal in order to offset their advances in the realms of military and industrial output.

In order to balance successfully the US built up a number of important strategic alliances with partners in Europe, considered by many to be the central front in any war that might break out with the Soviet Union. One of the key bilateral relationships during the Cold War was the transatlantic alliance between London and Washington. With their common bonds of language, culture and a shared belief in the merits of liberal democracy, both states came to build up a close partnership on security matters from 1941 onwards. Although Britain has come to be regarded as the junior partner in the 'special relationship',[22] it nevertheless did offer strategic advantage to its ally. Former US Secretary of State Dean Acheson characterised the reluctant yet vital role to be played by the US when he said:

> The United States does not want military power in order to take what belongs to others, or to make anyone accept its overlordship. We have no dreams of conquest or pax Americana. But, unhappily, the possibility always exists that force may be used against us and our interests, or against the interests of our allies, or the interests of other nations whose independence is important to us. Military power is necessary to deter these interferences or, if they do occur, to stop them.[23]

The special relationship between Britain and the US remained an asymmetric one born as much out of the coalescence of Anglo-American self-interest as through Churchill's 'fraternal association of English-speaking peoples'.

However, there was a more strategic dimension to the positions adopted by both sides in the Cold War, shaped as it was by the development of intelligence machinery to combat threats to national security. As Christopher Andrew has remarked, 'Intelligence is probably the least understood aspect of the Cold War, sometimes sensationalised, often ignored'. And those historians studying policy-making in East and West who 'fail to take intelligence into account are at best incomplete, at worst distorted'.[24] The quintessential Realist scholar-diplomat Henry Kissinger once wrote in respect to American foreign policy that '[o]ur challenge is to overcome an atmosphere in which all sense of reverence for the unique and therefore the capacity for real innovation stands in danger of being lost'.[25] As an intellectual – and later as a policymaker – Kissinger was well-placed to offer this sobering view of US foreign policy, especially in an era when the Cold War became a game with the strategy of conflict between rival superpowers and their allies now very much managed by deterrence. The maintenance of the nuclear alliance, therefore, became a defining feature of the West's strategy in dealing with the Soviet Empire and would, in many respects, survive long after the end of the Cold War.

British Strategy and the End of Empire

There were practical reasons why the United Kingdom's position as a great power began to slip by the middle of the twentieth century, not least because of the impact of the Second World War and the decline of its empire. It is now recognised that at one time the British had one the largest empires the world has ever seen. Stretching from the prairies of Canada to the vast Hadhramaut region in Yemen and beyond to the arid plains of the Australian outback, it underwent a rapid expansion in the nineteenth century. Within a century it would begin to decline as the central coffers in London ran dry and indigenous peoples set about throwing off the yoke of colonial rule. By the late 1940s politicians in London were calling for an 'orderly withdrawal' as a means of protecting British prestige as they moved to 'cut the knot' of colonial commitments around the world.

Palestine
The three-pronged Jewish insurgency waged at the close of the Second World War in Palestine – involving the Irgun, Haganah and Stern Gang – was so successful in harassing the British mandatory power that it challenged senior commanders to come up with innovative tactics to counter the violence. For the most part the military believed they were engaged in what they regarded as 'police work'. In a letter to the General Officer Commanding of

135

British troops, Sir Evelyn Barker, the Commander of Middle East Land Forces, General Miles Dempsey, wrote that the military's role had become civilianised:

> The maintenance of law and order in a friendly country: the guarding of public utilities and stocks and stores left over from the war: and so on. These and kindred duties are not properly the function of the soldier at all.[26]

What soldiers understood best, argued Dempsey, was the exercise of force, and this was certainly much in evidence in the late 1940s.[27] Having served in Ireland during the second decade of the twentieth century, the CIGS Field Marshal Montgomery had direct experience of Britain's use of disproportionate force in a particularly vicious small war involving insurgents. Writing in his memoirs he recalled how:

> In many ways this was worse than the Great War which had ended in 1918. It developed into a murder campaign in which, in the end, the soldiers became very skilful and more than held their own. But such a war is thoroughly bad for officers and men; it tends to lower their standards of decency and chivalry, and I was glad when it was over.[28]

However, while Britain's willingness to apply coercive military pressure on its enemies is perhaps one of the most remarkable features of all of its post-war small wars, it must not be forgotten that dialogue was also seen as holding strategic utility for bringing insurgents to the negotiating table. In the lead up to Britain's withdrawal from Palestine, the officer in charge of military intelligence, wrote candidly:

> The situation here is nothing like as bad as it sounds really. In fact, Jerusalem has been quite quiet the last three days or so. However, I've just heard that a train has been blown up on the coast and it looks as if there'll be a lot of casualties. We simply can't cope with maniacs. I've spent hours in the last few weeks in complicated negotiations with all sorts of people trying to keep things peaceful, and I might just as well have not wasted my time.[29]

Indeed, much of the internal military correspondence points to the need to maintain impartiality and restraint in the face of armed challenges in local areas such as Haifa, where Jews and Arabs wrought bloody attacks on one another and the British Army. As one directive clearly stated, the Army's role was twofold:

> [To] check the spread of lawlessness on the one hand and refrain from any action that is likely to create increased anti-British hostility among either community and thereby increase the difficulties in the near future of withdrawing our forces to the Haifa enclave.[30]

Interestingly, just as they had done in the North-West Frontier of India in the late nineteenth century, British forces placed great value on co-operating with the local tribal leaders (or mukhtars) through colonial administrative structures. This was done for largely practical aims: to deter villages from taking the law into their own hands and to augment military activity such as recovering stolen weapons and property. In all but exceptional circumstances, the Rules of Engagement (i.e., the directives issued under which British soldiers could open fire) were tightly controlled, though this did not prevent heavy-handed responses. By 1947 the political decision to withdraw had been taken and a military solution to the Palestine crisis was deemed to be an unlikely prospect:

> Although the maintenance of law and order is an important part of the Army's task, the main anxiety of GOC at the present time is the lives of the troops under his command. Punitive action against ARAB or JEW must therefore wherever possible be avoided if it is likely to lead to a situation making the withdrawal of our forces costly or unnecessarily difficult.[31]

The evacuation of British forces from India in 1947 and Palestine in 1948 did much to emphasise the reality that Britain's power and influence was fast declining on the world stage. Yet, Britain was down but not out, as events in South-East Asia were to prove.

Malaya

States take enormous risks whenever they decide to exercise force against irregular adversaries such as terrorists and insurgents. Lieutenant General Hughie Stockwell was appointed as GOC

(General Officer Commanding) Malaya in 1952 at a crucial time in the Army's campaign in the country. He was directly responsible to the Governor of Malaya, General Sir Gerald Templer, who was appointed by Prime Minister Winston Churchill to tackle the Communist insurgency. In a cover story on Templer, *Time* magazine said he had been given 'such military and political powers in his kit bag as no British soldier had had since Cromwell'.[32] He immediately set about formulating a plan to neutralise the insurgency and Stockwell was to play a key role in executing Templer's plan. As GOC, Stockwell inherited a post at a difficult time for British forces. A close confidant of Templer's, he believed wholeheartedly in winning the 'hearts and minds' of the Malayan people. And he had a very deliberate view on how this could best be done. In Stockwell's view, 'The Army's task can be a very potent factor in the Cold War and it must give all the help to Government that it can, morally, physically and materially'. This was reflected in his dealings with Templer but, arguably, it had been accepted by Templer's predecessor as High Commissioner, Henry Gurney. In a letter to the CIGS, Sir John Harding, Gurney declared:

> Nobody could have been more understanding and helpful in the task that I know runs counter to much of what the Army want to be doing. This has meant a continuous sacrifice and so a constant temptation to impatience, and I am therefore the more grateful for your always constructive approach and your own continuation to the best of military-civil relationships.[33]

Harding, Templer and Stockwell were well aware of the guiding principles of the British approach to combating insurgency, which favoured civilian primacy. In Stockwell's opinion:

> You will see then at all levels the Army Officer is working with Police and Civil Authorities and that he is supported by Naval and Air Forces. Officers must know the organisation and function of the Civil Government and must approach all problems with patience. The officer who sees everything from the purely military angle will often conflict with a political or civil one and unless the officer understands the whole pattern he will feel frustrated, and may well upset the smooth running of operations in his area.[34]

Stockwell also laid the foundations for the much lauded counter-insurgency practices which saw the Army assist in welfare activities in the local villages, training of the 'Home Guard', medical aid, and loan of transport and engineering equipment. Yet, he was at pains to stress: 'Don't let it be thought that, in Malaya, the State cannot and does not try to do all these things. The State does all it can, but everything cannot be done at once, though an awakening people will demand everything at once.' In Stockwell's opinion the Army 'must therefore do all it can to help'. Between 1952 and 1954 the British Army was responsible for formalising and disseminating the harsh lessons learned in the jungle, which proved an invaluable tool in defeating the long-running insurgency.[35]

In the battle to win over the consent of the Malayan people Stockwell shared with Montgomery and other leading figures back in Whitehall the view that this was a symptom of a wider confrontation with World Communism. And so it was in Malaya, where every plan formulated under the military commander, General Sir Rawdon Briggs, and his civilian counterpart High Commissioner Henry Gurney proved impenetrable to Malayan Communism; that was until Templer assumed overall military and political control. Nevertheless, he could not have executed a successful strategy without the invaluable leadership and example provided by Stockwell, who proved he was ahead of the curve in a number of ways, not least in cementing the civil–military partnership which would eventually end the Communist insurgency. Undoubtedly, he had learned invaluable lessons in Palestine, where his greatest challenge was ensuring the steady and orderly withdrawal of British forces from Haifa and in protecting both communities from the excessive violent actions of both Jewish and Arab terrorist groups. Stockwell's emphasis on inculcating a sense of steely resolve in his subordinates won him the admiration of all ranks. His attitude towards working in partnership with local Arab and Jewish leaders earned him much respect on the ground. In Malaya, Stockwell built on his reputation as a tough but fair commander and knew better than anyone the challenges posed by locating and contacting the enemy, the lack of a battle 'front', and in the high degree of initiative which tends to favour the guerrilla. In both these contexts he championed new ways of tackling old problems and in

Malaya, especially, he emphasised the utility of small unit patrols, intelligence and all round defence: tactical alterations which soon won strategic gains.

Above all, Stockwell was a consummate professional when it came to the art of strategy and excelled in positions that called for a rounded understanding of how force ought to be used alongside other instruments of power. 'There must be good direction from the summit, teamwork down the scale and professional competence at all levels', he would later write. Stockwell was an effective communicator and remained conscious of the utility of force in waging war against irregular adversaries. Although Stockwell's command during the Suez Crisis in 1956 overshadowed his previous accomplishments, he always maintained that military operations were doomed to failure without a clear political purpose. Yet he recognised as much as any other soldier that the military entered combat operations in order to fulfil the policy ends of the government.[36]

Kenya

By the early 1950s trouble in Britain's colonies had spread to Kenya in East Africa. The main source of grievances was the treatment of the Kikuyu tribal grouping, which gave birth to both a constitutional nationalism under Jomo Kenyatta and an extremist armed group known as Mau Mau. Responding to the crisis, Prime Minister Winston Churchill dispatched a senior general who had seen action in North Africa and north-western Europe during the Second World War and in the Canal Zone in 1951. Regarded as perhaps one of the most seasoned practitioners of brute force in the British Army, General Sir George Erskine believed that, in small wars at least, the police should take the lead role against insurgents. For Erskine – as with most senior British military commanders like Hughie Stockwell – the armed forces were mainly a support mechanism for dealing with situations that the civilian authorities proved incapable of handling with the meagre resources at their disposal. As he admitted in a press conference several months after being appointed Commander-in-Chief East Africa in June 1953, 'I do not believe bullets will finish the problem, although forceful measures are necessary to obtain respect for law and order'. In Erskine's view, the problem was 'not military, and there was no military solution'.[37] Achieving a non-military solution to the problem of nationalist rebellion in the colonies only became a reality for Britain when they realised detention without trial and more repressive measures could not bring about the kind of decisive victory demanded by London.

As with the British approach to countering insurgency in Palestine and Malaya, intelligence-led policing was seen as the most effective way to reduce the violence in the long term:

> The Commissioner of Police and the Government here are doing their best to increase the police force, but it would certainly help if the Colonial Secretary would give his support – particularly to the speedy recruitment of good young European police officers. I am pressing hard at this end and the Governor is giving full support. I have called for a comprehensive plan to show how KENYA is to be policed on a permanent basis, plus any emergency addition for say the next three years. Unless this is pressed hard at both ends we shall have the Army tied up on police duties for far too long.[38]

Ironically, as with other desperate situations in which irregular adversaries refused to play by the 'rules' governing state actions, Britain also resorted to twisting the law in more repressive ways that would come to characterise its campaign.

Critics of Britain's role in the post-war world flag up the coercive edge of military operations in Malaya, Kenya and Cyprus in the 1950s. Yet by articulating a case that academics are wont to take what policymakers and politicians say about their view of Britain in the world too seriously, they overlook the realpolitik motivating London at the time.[39] Britain's armed forces have maintained something of a schizophrenic view on the use of force. Despite a tendency to adhere to the policy of 'minimum force', more often than not the degree of force to be used was to be decided by the (often junior) commander on the ground. In Palestine the Rules of Engagement were altered to take into consideration the Army's role as a peacekeeping force but in Malaya and Kenya the concept of winning 'hearts and minds' had a double-edged meaning. Often the British embarked upon counter-insurgency on the wrong foot, eventually, after a process of trial and error, adjusting their strategy towards more successful operations.

Yet, coercion was an integral part of the business of British counter-insurgency.[40] Far from advocating a deterrent effect, the only enticement the military were likely to consider giving the insurgent was the stark choice of peacefully surrendering or being defeated. As Erskine wrote at the time:

> We may also have succeeded in driving a number of the gangs out of these areas. I intend that we shall hunt down and destroy those that remain, and that the prohibited areas should never again become main bases for terrorist activity.[41]

Kenya may have been regarded as 'a sideshow amongst side-shows',[42] given the fact that a more widespread insurgency was tying down British troops in Malaya and against the backdrop of the conventional Korean War, yet it absorbed a considerable amount of Britain's resources in one of its last colonies. Erskine was given overall operational control for fighting the Mau Mau insurgents, with all colonial, auxiliary, police and security forces at his disposal. And he enjoyed directing offensive military operations against the Mau Mau, liking nothing more than to report to the British military hierarchy in London that the 'large gangs do not show themselves because I think they realise they would be cracked on the head if they did so'.[43]

Even though he may have preferred wielding a big stick at the Mau Mau, Erskine knew he had to take a more co-ordinated approach to the problem. In forming a War Cabinet, which included the High Commissioner, the Chief Minister and GOC, he brought together a civil–military team that could apply repression on the Mau Mau organisation, in the form of the indiscriminate use of bombers that killed many insurgents but also alienated the local population, while equally seeking to parley with their enemies. What tends to be underappreciated though are the lengths to which he had gone to encourage the Mau Mau gangs to surrender, along similar lines to what had been tried in Malaya. Indeed, after a visit by Erskine to his old friend General Gerald 'Fred' Templer at the height of the Malayan Communist Party's insurgency, newspapers were remarking how he was keen to implement 'the Malaya Plan'.[44] Erskine was greatly helped in the exploration of secret channels by the surrender of 'General China', a leading Mau Mau commander in the region. In a letter to his wife at the time, Erskine remarked how he had ordered that China be 'very thoroughly interrogated', during which it was discovered that 'he has been very depressed about the fighting and did not think violence was going to get them anywhere'. Erskine continued:

> I therefore decided, with the agreement of H.E., to find out if China was willing to try and bring about a surrender of the gangs. We found he was not only willing but most enthusiastic. So on the 14th February I had him moved secretly to a house in his own area. He . . . saw a number of people and has been working for the last 3 weeks to bring about a surrender . . . Without being optimistic the thing has a fair chance of success but it may only be fairly local – unfortunately'.[45]

Erskine knew his actions taken to effect large-scale surrenders would be unpopular with the European settlers. 'The local European reaction will be terrific – negotiating with the filthy Mau Mau.' Erskine was nevertheless dismissive of their opinion. 'I don't care a damn – if it stops this stupid fighting or part of it we have a definite gain. I can't see British or World opinion being against [us?]' he charged. 'It was lucky we had Oliver Lyttelton and the C.I.G.S. here. H.E.'s feet were getting very cold. Oliver Lyttelton and the C.I.G.S. were strongly in favour – so we shall see!'[46]

British imperialism may have been motivated by the desire to leave its former colonial possessions because of the upsurge in popular support for nationalist movements, yet it would be wrong to see that as the only reason. In a stinging critique of British coercive measures in Kenya, historian Professor David French argued that:

> The notion that the British conducted their post-war counter-insurgency campaigns by employing kindness, and by trying to secure the 'hearts and minds' of the civilians among whom the security forces were operating, has gained wide currency in the literature. It has done so because it supported a Whiggish view of decolonisation that portrayed the way in which the British left their empire as having been an orderly and dignified process of planned withdrawal. But it is misleading. It rested

upon a highly selective range of sources, the accounts of senior officers and officials who were intent on sanitising the experience of fighting wars of decolonisation. It failed to take account of the many and varied forms of coercion that the British employed. The foundations of British counter-insurgency doctrine and practice were coercion not kindness. They sought to intimidate the population into supporting the government rather than the insurgents.[47]

Although some authors, like French, have created a binary understanding of the use of force in the prosecution of Britain's 'small wars', it is important to gain a more rounded perspective on how the British state applied all of the instruments at its disposal to achieve what it wanted in each of its colonial hotspots. The truth of the matter is that the British were prepared to do whatever it took to ensure the transition away from direct rule and the abdication of its imperial responsibilities as they had become costly to maintain. That sometimes meant using brute force, but equally it also meant using bribery, coercion and political incentives.

The Cold War had profound and far-reaching consequences for Britain's standing in the world. Having survived the turmoil of the Second World War, Britain now declined economically, politically and militarily in the face of Soviet aggression and American expansionism. Britain's powerlessness to inflict strategic defeat on its enemies during the immediate post-war period was nowhere better captured than in the political loss of nerve during the Suez Crisis of 1956. British, French and Israeli forces failed in their bid to repel President Nasser's attempt to nationalise the Suez Canal. Humiliating strategic defeat flagged up Britain's impotence in military operations and led to a strategic rethink within the War Office about power projection. And so Britain's empire began to disappear from the world stage until it became fixed in central Europe. By the time it withdrew from east of Suez, a conflict with mild colonial overtones had bubbled to the surface in Northern Ireland, It was a conflict that would come to define Britain's counter-insurgency interregnum and have longstanding repercussions for its defence posture in perhaps a more far-reaching way than Palestine and later Aden had done for withdrawal from the Middle East.

The Utility of Force in the Post-Cold War World

The fall of the Berlin Wall and the collapse of the Soviet Empire between 1989 and 1991 had profound effects for the international system. Not since the ending of the Second World War has a year been described as a watershed in modern history. Respected historian of the Cold War John Lewis Gaddis informs us that between the attack on Pearl Harbor and the dissolution of the Soviet Union in 1991, the US was in possession of a grand strategy. And with a few adjustments, it had a clear vision for securing its homeland from threats emanating from an 'evil empire' that jeopardised the very existence of its state, citizens and way of life. To borrow a phrase from more recent times, the West was entering an age of uncertainty where integration and fragmentation would come to characterise the post-Cold War order, rather than a straight clash of the ideological power blocs which had defined the post-war period. In Gaddis's words:

> The end of the Cold War, therefore, brings not an end to threats, but rather a diffusion of them: one can no longer plausibly point to a single source of danger, as one could throughout most of that conflict, but dangers there still will be. The architects of containment, when they confronted the struggle between democracy and totalitarianism in 1947, knew which side they were on; the post-Cold War geopolitical cartography, however, provides no comparative cartography. In one sense, this represents progress. The very absence of clear and present danger testifies to American success in so balancing power during the past four and a half decades that totalitarianism, at least in its forms we have considered threatening throughout most of this century, is now defunct. But, in another sense, the new competition between the forces of integration and fragmentation presents us with difficult choices, precisely because it is by no means as clear as it was during the Cold War which tendency we should want to see prevail.[48]

The collapse of this certainty brought with it both challenges and opportunities, argued Gaddis, but it was imperative that the 'long peace' – a peace reinforced more by fear than logic – survived the demise of the Cold War.

Extracts from a Statement on Iraq by Prime Minister John Major, 17 January 1991

With permission, Mr. Speaker, I shall make a statement on the start of hostilities in the Gulf in the small hours of this morning.

Aircraft of the multinational force began attacks on military targets in Iraq from around midnight Greenwich mean time. Several hundred aircraft were involved in the action, including a substantial number of RAF aircraft. The action was taken under the authority of United Nations Security Council resolution 678 which authorises use of all necessary means, including force, after 15 January to bring about Iraq's withdrawal from Kuwait.

The action was taken after extensive consultation with the principal Governments represented in the multinational force and following direct discussions between President Bush and myself over a period of weeks. It was taken only after exhaustive diplomatic efforts through the UN, the European Community, Arab Governments and others to persuade Saddam Hussein to withdraw peacefully.

The action is continuing. Attacks have been directed at Iraq's military capability, in particular airfields, aircraft, missile sites, nuclear and chemical facilities and other military targets. Reports so far received suggest that they have been successful. Allied aircraft losses have been low. I regret to inform the House that one RAF Tornado from later raids is reported missing.

The instructions issued to our pilots and those of other forces are to avoid causing civilian casualties so far as possible.

Our aims are clear and limited. They are those set out in the United Nations Security Council resolutions: to get Iraq out of Kuwait – all of Kuwait; to restore the legitimate Government; to re-establish peace and security in the area; and to uphold the authority of the United Nations.

As I explained in the debate in the House of Commons on Tuesday, it is only with the greatest reluctance that we have come to the point of using force as authorised by the Security Council. We did so only after all peaceful means had failed and Saddam Hussein's intransigence left us no other course. We have no quarrel with the people of Iraq. We hope very much for a speedy end to hostilities. That will come about when Saddam Hussein withdraws totally and unconditionally from Kuwait. Our military action will continue until he comes to his senses and does so.[49]

The roots of Soviet collapse can be traced to strategic inertia which gave rise to several internal problems, such as the overheating of the Soviet economy and the suppression of ethnic and political minorities. External problems included the rise of ethnonationalism in places like the former Yugoslavia, Hungary, Chechnya, Georgia and Poland, all of which had been deftly subsumed with a grander ideological narrative of Communism. Yet, it was Soviet imperial overstretch that perhaps contributed most to the end of 'actually existing' state socialism in Eastern Europe. As a consequence of the collapse of the old order the once indefatigable dialectic of Communism versus Capitalism gave way to a new dispensation of 'order versus disorder'.[50]

It was not only in Eastern Europe that old power hubs began to crumble and give rise to power differentials. In Africa the winds of change blowing across the continent from the 1950s onwards finally claimed one of its most significant casualties as Apartheid in South Africa finally came to an end. Elsewhere the story was not so positive. In Somalia, Rwanda and the Democratic Republic of Congo several generations after decolonisation the scourge of inter-ethnic tension and violence precipitated the collapse of state order. In West Africa, Sierra Leone, once a thriving British colony, became the happy hunting ground of irregular warriors who saw an opportunity emerging from the ruins of United Nations missions.[51]

In the years immediately following the US-led Coalition's intervention in Iraq after 2003, the spiralling death toll of troops and Iraqi civilians presaged a radical reinterpretation of Coalition strategy. Out went the emphasis on military force protection (i.e., preserving the lives of troops) and in came the aspiration to protect the lives of Iraqi civilians. In the short term, American political leaders accepted a 'surge' in troop numbers, which ultimately paid strategic dividends in the long term by stabilising this highly combustible Middle Eastern state. Iraq is rarely spoken about as a glowing military success. However, it did lead to considerable soul-searching amongst senior military commanders afterwards as they sought to make sense of their contribution to support for Iraq's fledgling government after 2004. Analysts who claim to be able to pull through lessons from past conflicts for utilisation in completely different contexts should resist the temptation. Finding a useable Polaroid snapshot upon which to base future military operations is futile and should be avoided at all costs. That is not to say that militaries have not done so. In the British case, the ability of soldiers to interact with people at a human level, assessing their needs and providing security while the political narrative finds its way to organising things at a higher level, became a lost art. A recently declassified report on lessons learned in Iraq, written by former senior British commander Lieutenant General Chris Brown, looked at what Britain's military did, and why, during the occupation of Iraq. It is now possible to see that, from a military perspective, there was a total absence of any British government strategy for Iraq, which 'hindered the UK's ability to provide support to the emerging Iraqi government'.[52] If that was not bad enough, the military's long experience of dealing with complex interventions had been ignored. The long awaited Iraq Inquiry has confirmed the extent of this strategic malaise. Although not risking passing judgement on whether the war was illegal, it clearly concluded that the evidence for going to war was flimsy at best. It presented a negative view of Britain's second Iraq War.

In Afghanistan, a recalibration of the ISAF mission by General Stanley McChrystal in 2009 emphasised the need for a new, 'integrated and properly resourced civil-military strategy'. Reflecting much later on the strategic assessment, General McChrystal revealed how he used a 'car-mechanic analogy' to focus the minds of his assembled team:

> We were to avoid becoming emotionally tied to any particular course of action or outcome. As 'car-mechanics,' we would diagnose what was wrong with the car and recommend what actions and resources we would need to fix it. It was up to the car owner to decide whether they wanted the car fixed, whether they wanted only limited repairs, or, indeed, whether the car was worth fixing at all. Our role was to conduct an accurate diagnosis and offer effective fixes.[53]

Of course, this may have been the approach to the strategic assessment taken by McChrystal and his team but it was driven by a multiplicity of complex factors ranging from US policy towards Afghanistan to the lessons being learned from past experience. It was no accident that the General had assembled a diverse team of experts, which included civilian and military experts.

As McChrystal and his team travelled throughout the country they soon realised that the military had become fixated on force protection, a largely defensive strategy that brought with it so many problems in Iraq and for the British when they deployed south into Helmand in 2006–7. There they would simply adapt a version of the so-called 'ink spot' strategy that the British had employed half a century earlier in Malaya, but which had a longer gestation in French military circles when it was used in Morocco and Madagascar by General Lyautey. It was a deceptively simple strategy and one that ensured free zones would be established amongst the population that had to be secured and cleared of insurgents. 'Success in counter-insurgency was less dependent upon the brilliance of the strategy – the concept is not hard to understand – than it was on the execution,' wrote McChrystal. 'Counterinsurgency is easy to prescribe, difficult to perform.'[54] By learning the lessons of Iraq, notably working to a 'unified vision', 'protecting the population' and 'neutralising the insurgent', American military leaders believed that they were thinking strategically about how to best use force in the service of their policy goals. The truth was, as Colonel Gian Gentile has argued persuasively, they were simply applying antiquated tactical procedures to solve twenty-first century problems.[55]

The Enemy gets a Vote

We should not overlook the propensity of the enemy to impact on one's plans in war. This might seem like an obvious point to make to the point of absurdity, yet it is worth reiterating the truism that the enemy gets a vote in strategy and war. As Clausewitz reminds us, war is a duel on a larger scale, with the enemy's ability to think and act independently a sign of friction in war. In this respect belligerents are locked in a grip like two wrestlers who must try and throw each other in order to win the contest. Behaving as if the aim is not to throw the enemy into submission misses the point. In his essay *A Long Short War: The Postponed Liberation of Iraq* (2003), renowned journalist Christopher Hitchens observed how al-Qaeda's 'means, its ends, and its ideology all consist of the application of fanatical violence and violent fanaticism, and of no other things. It's "terrorist," all right.' Hitchens was of the opinion that al-Qaeda was 'partly a corrupt multinational corporation, partly a crime family, partly a surrogate for the Saudi oligarchy and the Pakistani secret police, partly a sectarian religious cult, and partly a fascist organization'.[56] Given that *Daesh* declared in June 2014 that it had come to 'liberate' the people of Mosul we now know that it is also partly a guerrilla outfit capable of taking and holding ground while striking fear into the hearts and minds of the Iraqi people more than a decade on from the Western intervention in Iraq. As of late 2015 the Iraqi state seemed incapable of throwing its opponent. The surest sign of this came when Mosul's governor and his security forces fled the battlefield, having hardly fired a shot in anger, and enabled *Daesh* to fill a vacuum by championing the cause of the Sunni dispossessed. The net result was to be starkly illustrated by scenes of internally displaced peoples streaming towards the Kurdish north of Iraq. In the summer months of 2014 one-third of Mosul's population (some 1.5 million people) were forcibly removed from their homes.

Daesh's strategy has been to blend the most effective aspects of terrorism and insurgency, which has utilised the means and methods of war in ways that challenge the categorisation of war. Lieutenant Colonel Frank Hoffman informs us that this type of warfare is hybrid in character and cherry-picks its tactics and strategy from a range of state and non-state adversaries. Hybrid warfare has come to define the violence unleashed by *Daesh* in Iraq and Syria. The killing of twelve people in Paris in the offices of satirical magazine *Charlie Hebdo* in January 2015 and the return of *Daesh* terrorists to the city in November 2015, when 132 people were gunned down, sent shockwaves throughout the West. The Paris attacks demonstrated that *Daesh* is capable of combining the worst features of al-Qaeda in Iraq – that is, a sociopathic commitment to spilling the blood of non-Sunnis – with a new strategy aimed at disrupting the Western way of life, which is, by and large, settled and peaceful. Outwardly *Daesh* resembles a death cult, while giving all the inward appearance of a pseudo-state operating under the jackboot of fascist rule (arguably, it enjoys neither internal or external sovereignty). Yet, to think of *Daesh* as Islamofascist – even with its clear corporate identity, an aversion to enforcing strict Sharia law via its blackshirt-wearing stormtroopers, not to mention the callous extermination of minority ethno-religious groups, and the observance of blind obedience to its leader – perhaps obscures more than it reveals.

The The reality is that *Daesh* is a parasitic organism and in order to survive must latch onto its host (in this case, the modern sovereign states of Iraq and Syria) in order to ensure it can survive the natural antibodies that protect pre-Islamic tribal structures. Our consideration of the attempts by commanders in state-based armies to grapple with the difficult problems of terrorism and insurgency, especially in those places far from their own homeland, means that the issue of applying force in the service of policy goals will continue to remain a challenge. It will also remain a challenge for those in-theatre commanders close to the action, who will continue to see the unfolding drama of war in a very different light from their superiors and their political masters back home in capital cities.

Conclusion

Despite claims that force has lost its utility in the post-Cold War era, there are plenty of individuals, groups and states that are prepared to employ it as an instrument of policy. The truth is that these political entities are attempting to get their way in the world by using whatever resources they have at their disposal. As we have seen, this was certainly the case when the British beat a retreat from their colonial territories in the middle of the twentieth century. Then, the priority was in ensuring the preservation of order as well as saving face and ensuring the orderly transition of power from one form of government to another. As US grand strategy in the Cold War also demonstrates, the overriding desire of all Great Powers at this time was in the preservation of the balance of power on the geopolitical level. However, that is not to say that the West or East were above seeking the diminution of power and resources of their opponents. Clearly, any attempt to sap the power or legitimacy of their rivals was good news indeed and ensured that propaganda and other resources were directed towards the ultimate goal of seizing and maintaining the upper hand in Great Power politics. Grand strategy, therefore, offered states an effective way to connect their policy of maintaining their place at the top of the pecking order with the tactics of military posturing (including deterrence, coercion and, occasionally, brute force), subversion, alliance-building, espionage and 'proxy wars'. Nowadays, of course, states and non-state actors use the same levers of power in different ways. Like their predecessors, they will continue to use force for as long as it is believed that it may offer a more decisive outcome than less lethal means.

Key Questions

1. How effective has force been in securing the political object of war?
2. What role did the threat of force play in the Cold War?
3. How effective were the British in applying strategy during their wars of decolonisation?
4. Why have states continued to use force in the post-Cold War period?
5. What do the actions of non-state actors, such as terrorists and insurgents, tell us about the future role of armed force in international relations?

Further Reading

Bennett, Huw, *Fighting the Mau Mau: The British Army and Counter-insurgency in the Kenyan Emergency* (Cambridge: Cambridge University Press, 2012).

Cesarini, David, *Major Farran's Hat: Murder, Scandal and Britain's War against Jewish Terrorism, 1945–1948* (London: Vintage, 2010).

Edwards, Aaron, *Defending the Realm? The Politics of Britain's Small Wars since 1945* (Manchester: Manchester University Press, 2012, 2014).

Elliott, Christopher L., *High Command: British Military Leadership in the Iraq and Afghanistan Wars* (London: Hurst, 2015).

French, David, *The British Way in Counterinsurgency* (Oxford: Oxford University Press, 2011).

Gentile, Colonel Gian, *Wrong Turn: America's Deadly Embrace of Counter-insurgency* (New York: Free Press, 2011).

Hammes, Colonel Thomas, *The Sling and the Stone: On War in the 21st Century* (St Paul, MN: Zenith Press, 2004).

McChrystal, General Stanley, *My Share of the Task: A Memoir* (London: Portfolio Penguin, 2013).

Nagl, Lieutenant Colonel John A., *Knife Fights: A Memoir of Modern War in Theory and Practice* (London: Penguin, 2014).

Nye Jr., Joseph S., *Is the American Century Over?* (Cambridge: Polity, 2015).

Porch, Douglas, *Counterinsurgency: Exposing the Myths of the New Way of War* (Cambridge: Cambridge University Press, 2013).

Stone, John, *Military Strategy: The Politics and Technique of War* (London: Continuum, 2011).

Urban, Mark, *The Edge: Is the Military Dominance of the West Coming to an End?* (London: Little Brown, 2015).

Waltz, Kenneth N., *Man, the State and War: A Theoretical Analysis* (New York: Columbia University Press, [1959] 2001).

Weiss, Michael and Hassan Hassan, *ISIS: Inside the Army of Terror* (New York: Regan Arts, 2015).

6   The Role of Strategy in Ending Wars and Building Peace

Scope

Strategy has become synonymous with war, though it also has considerable purchase on the peace that may precede or follow organised violence. As this chapter makes clear, strategy is well-suited to help us to understand the criss-crossing between war and peace and crisis and confrontation that has occurred throughout history. Before we move towards formulating an analysis of how the military means of fighting wars interact with political ends, and may even be thought of in terms of preventing bloodshed, we must reassess our understanding of what peace is. In this respect, the chapter invites readers to consider the proposition that peace is a compromise in the uneven equilibrium between belligerents who are forever locked in a perpetual conflict that, at times of confrontation, may boil over into bloodshed. According to some strategists, war follows whenever belligerents seek a more decisive resolution to their dispute. By elucidating how strategy has been used in ending wars and building peace, it is possible to understand how it might be used in the future to manage or control wars, and, perhaps, to prevent confrontation from spilling over into violent conflict.

Introduction

The remarkable feature of the Cold War world, despite the dominance of nuclear weapons, was the stability of the international system. Observing the bipolar order in the early 1980s, political scientist Kenneth Waltz believed that the 'prevalence of peace, together with the fighting of circumscribed wars, indicates a high ability of the post-war international system to absorb changes and to contain conflicts and hostility'.[1] In considering whether the proliferation of nuclear weapons beyond the Western and Eastern bloc countries would lead to greater or lesser instability, Waltz believed it could only further stabilise the international system. This was a point echoed by his contemporary, Hedley Bull, who felt that both the US and the Soviet Union became more responsible actors in the years after the Cuban missile crisis of 1961. Moreover, Bull argued, their behaviour, even amidst war in the Middle East in 1967 and 1973, 'seemed more predictable'. In his opinion, the world 'came to sense that some of the tension had lessened in the relationship between the superpowers, that the danger of nuclear war was less immediate, that the perils of the nuclear age might after all be surmounted, at least in the short run'.[2]

If we accept Professor Colin S. Gray's contention that strategy 'is all about the consequences of the threat and the use of force'[3] then it is possible to broadly agree that the Cold War contributed in some way to the stability of the international system, for the consequences of not doing so could be horrendous, so that any rational person would be dissuaded from contemplating them. What made the two rival power blocs so strong, to echo Waltz's earlier point, was 'not simply because they have nuclear weapons but also because their immense resources enable them to generate and maintain power of all types, military and other, at strategic and tactical levels'. The ability to move with relative ease between different levels of war is a distinguishing feature of Great Powers and it is vital, therefore, that they understand the nature of the wars they fight and also why they engage in bloodshed in the first place.

One of the anticipated consequences of war, according to Sir Basil Liddell Hart, is peace. As he wrote convincingly in *Strategy: An Indirect Approach*, 'The object in war is a better state of peace – even if only from your own point of view. Hence it is essential to conduct war with constant regard to the peace you desire.'[4] However, peace is by no means an unproblematic concept. Peace, like war, remains contested throughout the social sciences. Peace is not simply the reverse of war, nor is it the natural order of things.[5] Arguably, peace is merely another stage in the clash of wills between parties in conflict played out in a peaceful political context. This may well appear a cynical interpretation of that most innocuous of concepts. How we obtain peace is *always* a strategic question, which involves the continual interaction of parties in conflict until the armed forces of one completely disappears.

The Role of Strategy in Armed Conflict

Though strategy is fundamentally concerned with matching ends with means in war, it remained foremost in Clausewitz's mind that '[t]he main lines along which military events progress, and to which they are restricted, are political lines that continue throughout the war into the subsequent peace'.[6] And so, strategic engagement between belligerents was born out of the necessity of resolving violent conflicts in a manner that was politically acceptable to all sides. Liddell Hart, a veteran of the First World War, gassed and wounded on the battlefield of the Somme, later came to offer a deeply cynical view of Field Marshal Douglas Haig's military strategy, which would put thousands of soldiers to death. His cynicism followed him through to the Second World War, when he criticised the lack of consideration given to the peace which must always follow war. 'No peace', he assured us, 'ever brought so little security.' The Cyprus conflict, the 'troubles' in Northern Ireland and the South African transition away from apartheid, are all examples where the strategies of coercion, deterrence and dialogue have been exploited as ways to end wars and build peace. This chapter will examine how 'win–lose' and 'win–win' strategies have been used to manage these conflicts.

While other variables, such as the transformation in the relations between warring factions, the intervention of third parties or, indeed, the acceptance that political ends cannot be reached by military means alone, are important, it is the positioning of belligerents emerging from conflict that makes all the difference. Some armed conflicts, such as the case of the Tamil Tiger insurgent group, which prosecuted a twenty-six-year campaign of terror against the

Sri Lankan government, demonstrates how brute force, rather than negotiation, has been used successfully in effecting an end to terrorism. However, this is very much the exception to the rule and only came after various other methods were tried in order to end the conflict, including third party intervention, negotiation and reconciliation between the ethnic Sinhalese and Tamil communities, all of which failed. In the end, a hammer blow from the Sri Lankan armed forces annihilated the Tamil Tigers, marking a decisive end to the long-running armed conflict. In the massive retaliation against Tamil Tiger forces, the Sri Lankan military felt unburdened by liberal democratic notions of applying force according to international rules and norms. For Gordon Weiss, the former UN official in Sri Lanka, this was to prove vital in the prosecution of the war. 'States in which accountability is subordinate to ideology, and to oligarchs, simply do not recognise such limits or choices', he wrote. 'Theirs is a strategy largely or sometimes completely comprised of terror.'[7] In the case of Sri Lanka, like countless other cases, once the balance of terror tipped in the favour of the state, a war of annihilation was deemed necessary and expedient. This should not surprise us, argues Philip Bobbitt, for:

> WAR IS NOT a pathology that, with proper hygiene and treatment, can be wholly prevented. War is a natural condition of the State, which was organized in order to be an effective instrument of violence on behalf of society. Wars are like deaths, which, while they can be postponed, will come when they will come and cannot be fully avoided.[8]

Wars, in other words, are naturally occurring phenomena that are unavoidably part and parcel of the human experience. The reason why war continues is that it simply cannot be wished out of existence. That is the bad news. The good news, according to historian Ian Morris, is that 'the average person is twenty times less likely to die violently than the average person was in the Stone Age'.[9] To take Morris's reasoning further, however, we need to ask why war still has currency in the relationships between human beings.

In Michael Howard's phraseology, the predominance of the use of force in the international system is directly attributable to two factors: (1) the instability of the actors themselves and (2) the function of the state as a guardian of certain value systems. In the case of the former, war is regarded as a rational way of obtaining an object, while in the latter it is the state that must safeguard its political community from attack.[10] If we consider the first point on the instability between the actors (both state and non-state), it is obvious that power relations and differentials mean that there will always be those who perceive themselves to be in constant competition with others. For Realists, this is reducible to the quest for the further accumulation of power and glory. Consequently, states, as the primary political units in the international system, will always be predisposed to moving to consolidate their power while preserving the balance that may ensure their survival in the face of challenges. In order to flesh out these two hypotheses, it is necessary to examine these variables in relation to the termination of war and the coming of peace.

Is War Declining?

It is in this respect that we must bring into sharper focus the words of George Santayana, who, writing in the aftermath of the First World War, lamented how young men singing 'Tipperary' in an Oxford bar could be so sure that they had seen the end of war. 'You suppose that this war has been a criminal blunder and an exceptional horror', he asks in his famous meditation on war; 'you imagine that before long reason will prevail, and all those inferior people that govern the world will be swept aside, and your own party will reform everything and remain always in office.' Santayana thought this attitude mistaken. 'This war has given you your first glimpse of the ancient, fundamental, normal state of the world, your first taste of reality', he informs his fellow punters.[11]

In his influential book *The Better Angels of Our Nature* (2011), Professor Steven Pinker makes the compelling case that war – and violence generally – is on the wane, reassuring us that, 'optimism requires a touch of arrogance, because it extrapolates the past to an uncertain future'.[12] It is evident that war has been an integral part of human life since man first made an appearance on earth. All of those directly affected by war – whether combatants or non-combatants, war's victims or survivors – have experienced something that has had a profound effect on them. If we take into account Pinker's conclusion that violence is on the decline, then there has been a definite reduction in the body count of those killed in organized armed conflict. However, that does not mean this decline will continue. Since the publication of Pinker's book in 2011 the numbers killed in internal civil wars has remained constant, with some 90 per cent of civil wars today being reoccurrences of earlier conflicts.

Yet, historian Ian Morris concurs with Pinker's analysis, arguing not only that violence is declining but that there are grounds for further optimism, especially since, in 2012, violence only killed about one person in every 4,375. Statistically the declinist argument is even more encouraging when comparing the second decade of the twenty-first century with earlier periods in history. Only 0.7 per cent of people alive today will die violently, contrasted with 1–2 per cent of those in the twentieth century, 2–5 per cent in ancient empires, 5–10 per cent in Eurasia in the age of Steppe migrations and a startling 10–20 per cent in the Stone Age.[13] Professor John Gray has challenged the declinist position, making a strong case that while it is 'true that warfare has changed, it has not become less destructive'.[14]

Ending Wars

Strategists, no more than non-strategists, do not hold the conceptual master key when it comes to understanding how wars might effectively be brought to an end. Nonetheless, there remains an almost insatiable appetite within states to bring crises and confrontations to a speedy conclusion in the hope of reaching a more decisive resolution of a dispute with another state, or, as is more likely in the post-Cold War world, with a non-state actor. As we will see in the next chapter, this has often led to the over-fetishisation of military technique and a belief in the superiority of force and new technologies. Certainly in Clausewitz's *On War*, it was understood that fighting was 'the central military act' and that all other activities 'merely support it'. However, Clausewitz was well aware of the political purpose that gave fighting its rationale, which was aimed primarily at 'the destruction or defeat of the enemy'.[15] It follows, therefore, that once this military effect is accomplished, events would move in a more peaceful direction. War, in Clausewitz's time, as in our own, consisted of several engagements and all of these were to be knitted together in a strategic narrative that proved the defeat of the enemy. In some industrial wars this has been signalled by the signing of a formal armistice between states. In other wars, though, it was less likely, in large part because the sorts of conflicts typically took place not in stark black and white terms but in a world of grey where such defeats were not as readily apparent or accepted by one side or the other. Classic examples of 'unfinished business' include the Korean War (the Democratic People's Republic of Korea in the north still believes it ended in a ceasefire) and the occupation of northern Cyprus by Turkey (which is considered illegal by the international community).

Debate over the definition of war is unlikely to be resolved by the application of the intellectual propensity to theorise about something that ultimately comes down to a dispute between two or more parties being settled by bloodshed. The idea that fighting might actually become a necessity in war is such an abhorrent thought to many people that any sign of being prepared to ponder its physical and philosophical dimensions might well lead to accusations of jingoism. But ponder its real meaning we must. In particular, we must investigate not what causes wars or what prolongs them necessarily (covered elsewhere in this book), but what brings this most violent of activities to a close and what, if anything, arising from war itself, contributes to the building of peace in the aftermath of such destruction and human suffering.

Victory and Defeat

Wars rarely end decisively. Where they do, as a consequence of invasion and subjugation, as in the fall of France in 1940, they are swift and devastating. We know from the analysis of Germany's *Blitzkrieg* in Chapter 2 that much depends on mobility, surprise and coordinated firepower to precipitate an overwhelming feeling of shock and surprise. The effectiveness of German military operations at this time depended also on the fact that the German Army was 'better equipped, better trained and led, with immediate signals communication between armoured units and sub-units together with unchallenged airborne artillery supplied by dive-bombers all working together, with soldiers confident in and motivated by the Nazi regime'.[16] Undoubtedly, the speed and aggression displayed by the German troops proved decisive in inflicting the trauma on an entire country. Whether or not its political class were divided or its military commanders intellectually weak and unimaginative created a chain reaction that reached right down into the lower ranks who were doing the fighting and dying.

All this operational prowess amounted to very little as the war progressed and German strategy became entangled in Hitler's own personal hubris. By 1944 the Allies had inflicted severe battlefield defeats on the Germans in north-west Europe, which was to contribute ultimately to their defeat in May 1945. Of the big three powers that met to decide the fate of the world in July 1945, it was the US that emerged as one of the strongest states. Confident that it could end the Second World War decisively, which it did within weeks by dropping atomic bombs on Japan in August 1945, the US soon eclipsed Great Britain and Soviet Russia in power terms. Writing about the dimensions of US power in the middle of the twentieth century, Hedley Bull observed how:

> Its power, at least in the first two decades after 1945, was overwhelming: indeed, if in this period there was any 'threat' to the general balance of power, in the sense of a distribution of power throughout the system such that no one state was preponderant, it was from the United States rather than from the Soviet Union that this came. Flushed with victory and supremely confident of its own values, it

sought, sometimes unilaterally and sometimes through the medium of the United Nations and a host of associated international organizations in which at that time it had a commanding position, to promote its own preferred vision of international order.[17]

As we know from events in the Vietnam War, the US has not always been able to channel that enormous power in the direction of victory over a weaker opponent. Vietnam demonstrated that despite commanding the best armed forces in the world powerful states still face uncertainty when they decide to use force to contain or roll back insurgents determined to fight for the liberation of their country. With the loss of almost 60,000 American lives and nearly ten times as many Vietnamese lives, the intervention is generally regarded as having ended in strategic defeat for the US.

In the closing stages of the war the North Vietnamese were buoyed up by the apparent inability of the US to follow a coherent strategy. As a senior NVA general put it in his memoirs:

> Our victory in the Tay Nguyen was tremendous, not only implementing but surpassing our plans. And we still had good conditions to exploit our victory. The enemy were in confusion and disorder, with us in close pursuit. Our forces were maturing increasingly through the fighting, their spirits many times stronger. Our logistics operations guaranteed that we had the amount of ammunition estimated in the plan, and that we could take a great deal more from the enemy. The strategic roads allowed our vehicles to run farther and faster than before. There was still about a month and a half of dry season weather for us to continue our activities. On all the battlefields throughout the South we had coordinated actions well.[18]

There is evidence to suggest that the North Vietnamese approached what would become the final stages of the war confident that they would win against a much more powerful adversary, one that had crippled its cities with a massive strategic bombing campaign aimed at preventing the continuing supply of weapons, equipment and troops to the resistance forces in the South. As the arch-critic of US intervention overseas, Noam Chomsky, observed after his return from a fact-finding mission to Hanoi in 1970, 'There will be a long struggle: the reactionary forces against the popular forces in

Asia. But the feeling of nationalism runs very high, and the reactionary forces cannot win'.[19] He was proven right. The North Vietnamese did not buckle under the pressure exerted by the powerful US military in the two Vietnams.

Writing some time after the war, Robert McNamara, the US Secretary of State responsible for introducing troops into Vietnam in the 1960s, felt that the intervention had been disastrously foolhardy:

> We failed then – as we have since – to recognize the limitations of modern, high-technology military equipment, forces, and doctrine in confronting unconventional, highly motivated people's movements. We failed as well to adapt our military tactics to the task of winning the hearts and minds of a people from a totally different culture.[20]

The idea that Americans were ignorant of the history, culture and politics of foreign peoples is prevalent in McNamara's retrospective lessons from Vietnam. However, is it really the case that powerful states can expect to intervene in the internal affairs of other states without experiencing friction? Moreover, is it actually the case that those who make war should know how to fight it? These are important strategic questions.

Retreat, desertion and defeat in the face of superior numbers is nothing new in war. Machiavelli made mention of it in his *Art of War* (1521): 'For it sometimes happens that when soldiers see a war protracted and a battle put off from time to time, they lose their ardor and become so weary of the hardships that they grow mutinous and desert their colors'.[21] Moreover, if an enemy is determined to fight then there is little likelihood, according to Machiavelli, that the engagement can be avoided.

> It may also happen that necessity may force you – or opportunity may invite you – to fight, but you find your soldiers dispirited and averse to it; in the one case, it is necessary to repress their ardor, and in the other, to excite it.[22]

Machiavelli was in favour of giving men little option than to seize victory through fighting. 'Whoever engages in war must use every means to put himself in a position of facing his enemy in the field, and beating him there if possible.'[23] The insertion of the clause 'if possible' is revealing, for it highlights the uncertainty of war that can make even the most robust strategies crumble in the face of a determined enemy. As the Allied retreat from Burma in the Second World War attests, even the best laid plans can come unstuck when faced with a highly motivated enemy with a better plan. Field Marshal Lord Slim recalled in his memoirs how:

> I had now an opportunity for a few days to sit down and think out what had happened during the last crowded months and why it had happened. The outstanding and incontrovertible fact was that we had taken a thorough beating. We, the Allies, had been outmanoeuvred, outfought, and outgeneralled. It was easy, of course, as it always is, to find excuses for failure, but excuses are no use for next time; what is wanted are causes and remedies.[24]

The ability to ask honest and probing questions rather than bury past experience alongside crushing defeats did not survive the Second World War. In Britain, a succession of small wars across a frail empire meant that politicians had much more say in the conduct of campaigns and could exercise real influence over these by way of the enduring civilian leadership provided by the proverbial 'man on the spot' who was the senior representative of the government in colonial theatres. In the eyes of many of these men, for they were always men, conflict had to end in ordered transition from empire to independence without recourse to humiliating defeat on either side. By playing up what went right, states like Britain avoided having to perform a post-mortem on bad strategic decisions that happened principally due to human error or the unanticipated tenacity of one's adversaries.

Not all wars end in the acceptance by the losing side that they have been defeated in the arena of armed force. Some losers have attempted to camouflage the fact of their own demise by appearing magnanimous in their commitment to seeing in the breaking dawn of peace. However, the reality is that they have been beaten. The point, as Clausewitz reminds us, is not to humiliate the enemy so as to undermine their ability to sell a deal to their support base. For, without the ability to bring their supporters along with them, the basis of any peace deal will be eroded very quickly. Even in today's world where intervention to arrest the fighting between two or more belligerents is still possible, it is no guarantee it will terminate hostilities. In Paul Diehl's opinion:

> Peace operations are not magic wands that wipe away what has gone before, and therefore it may not be surprising that conflicts with a long history of militarized disputes – what have often been labelled as enduring rivalries – are more prone to renewed fighting even with the presence of peacekeepers.[25]

The UN has come to realise that these 'new wars' are more complex and harder to end. Civil wars like those that have raged in Africa, Asia and the Middle East are often recurrences of those that went before. Old enmities die hard and can intoxicate the ensuing peace that may come in the aftermath of violent conflict.

Negotiation

If we accept that states can utilise a range of assets at their disposal to achieve what they want, it stands to reason that the political and diplomatic instruments may be more amenable to this than force, especially where force has been denied utility because of the inability of governments to articulate the policy objectives which they seek. The turn to negotiation and the peaceful settlement of disputes was not only the direct consequence of the formation of the United Nations in 1945 but also the desire amongst the great powers to place a premium on the 'pacific settlement of disputes' so as to ensure the continuing preparation of plans for defence against the possible aggression or armed attack of other states. After the bloody war over East Pakistan in 1972 Pakistan and India would come to prioritise the planning of attack and defence over and above the armed challenge posed by insurgents and terrorists, most recently in relation to the contested Kashmir region and the continuing conflict in neighbouring Afghanistan.

As we saw in Chapter 5, negotiation with terrorists and insurgents has been a common occurrence in Britain's small wars since 1945. Commanders have often pursued contact with the enemy through clandestine channels, even amidst the high tempo of military operations. This has almost always been from a position of strength rather than weakness and is designed to ensure the extraction of favourable terms and conditions. In the heat of battle there has been an almost universal drive to reach a longer-term political settlement for ending conflict. The medium of dialogue has not always curried favour amongst those at the tactical and operational levels who have soldiered in the frontline against terrorism, whether in Palestine, Malaya, Kenya, Cyprus, Aden, Northern Ireland, Iraq or Afghanistan. Nonetheless, at a strategic level, it has meant that Britain has been able to sustain the high tempo of military engagements in order to secure overall policy goals.

In the Northern Ireland conflict, ongoing since 1969, Britain has gone through a number of strategic options for ensuring the Irish question is kept at arm's length, from supporting a unionist dominated government at Stormont to the imposition of Direct Rule from 1972 (with several exceptions after the signing of the 1998 Belfast Agreement between the rival unionist and nationalist parties) to the return of power-sharing between unionists and republicans at Stormont in May 2007. Between the outbreak of the 'Troubles' between 1969 and the decommissioning of republican and loyalist terrorist weapons in 2005 and 2009, respectively, the British pursued a sophisticated security policy aimed at deterring, disrupting and arresting terrorists.[26] Occasionally, the British state reserved the right to resort to more forceful resolution of terrorist violence, particularly in the 1970s and 1980s. As one of the British Army's leading authorities on colonial warfare, Frank Kitson, put it at the time:

> As insurgency de-escalates from heavy rioting and a high level of violence, it is often helpful to pass as much of the offensive operations as possible to special forces as their activities tend to be less obvious and provide less opportunities for enemy propaganda.[27]

The failure of a number of security responses and peace initiatives in the 1970s meant that the British government had to rethink its strategy to reduce the levels of violence and the threat to stability in this peripheral part of the United Kingdom. One of the key tenets pursued was known as police primacy in which the Royal Ulster Constabulary took the lead in combatting terrorism and the British Army would take a supporting role after 1976. By the 1980s this had developed to a certain extent that the security response relied on the prosecution of terrorist suspects through the courts, based on an evidential approach to detecting, pursuing and prosecuting terrorism like any other form of unlawful activity.

Provisional IRA Ceasefire Statement, 31 August 1994

Recognising the potential of the current situation and in order to enhance the democratic process and underlying our definitive commitment to its success, the leadership of the IRA have decided that as of midnight, August 31, there will be a complete cessation of military operations. All our units have been instructed accordingly.

At this crossroads the leadership of the IRA salutes and commends our volunteers, other activists, our supporters and the political prisoners who have sustained the struggle against all odds for the past 25 years. Your courage, determination and sacrifice have demonstrated that the freedom and the desire for peace based on a just and lasting settlement cannot be crushed. We remember all those who have died for Irish freedom and we reiterate our commitment to our republican objectives. Our struggle has seen many gains and advances made by nationalists and for the democratic position.

We believe that an opportunity to secure a just and lasting settlement has been created. We are therefore entering into a new situation in a spirit of determination and confidence, determined that the injustices which created this conflict will be removed and confident in the strength and justice of our struggle to achieve this.

We note that the Downing Street Declaration is not a solution, nor was it presented as such by its authors. A solution will only be found as a result of inclusive negotiations. Others, not the least the British government have a duty to face up to their responsibilities. It is our desire to significantly contribute to the creation of a climate which will encourage this. We urge everyone to approach this new situation with energy, determination and patience.[28]

Although levels of violence had declined by the 1980s, there was still a considerable challenge to British political authority. In order to ensure a significant reduction in the security threat, the British leaned more heavily on its 'back channel' negotiations with terrorist representatives in the 1980s and 1990s to bargain with its adversaries as the principal means of resolving the conflict. One of the most senior figures in Sinn Fein at that time, Danny Morrison, said that republicans had chosen to enter into dialogue with the British from a position of strength:

> The republican view is quite simple. Britain has no right to be in Ireland. It didn't have any right yesterday; it doesn't have any today; and will not have any right tomorrow. But we have to deal with practicalities and pragmatics and the fact of the matter is that the armed struggle went a certain distance, and I would argue, as far as it could go without deteriorating into something unseemly and impossible to end. Ironically, in the 1990s the IRA was probably better armed than ever as a result of the delivery of the weapons from Libya – the ones that got through before the capture of the Eksund – and, for all we know, with other weapons that got through from other places. Yet both sides had reached a military stalemate. A military stalemate had developed where each side had, not necessarily brought the other to the point of exhaustion (and that's a relative term) – but had explored almost all means of conscionable confrontation. I remember a big story in the London *Independent* quoting anonymously several senior British army officers saying that they couldn't defeat the IRA.[29]

Presented with a means of permitting the IRA to back down honourably, the British decided not to request a formal surrender. This did not prevent the Conservative government from insisting that the organisation disarm before entering talks, a proviso that led to the breakdown in the IRA ceasefire and the explosion of a massive bomb in the Docklands area of London, the city's financial beating heart, on 9 February 1996.

The return of a new Labour government under Tony Blair in May 1997 meant that a softening of the political rhetoric would follow and Sinn Fein were permitted back into the multi-party talks, albeit with further assurances given to the unionist party that any Sinn Fein move towards government would have to be accompanied by decommissioning by the Provisional IRA. With the benefit of hindsight, however, it has now been established that IRA members involved in serious terrorist activities, including multiple murders, were to be given letters reassuring them that they would not be pursued after a peace agreement was signed ending the conflict. The British Labour government sought to provide guarantees to these terrorists in order to secure the resolution of the longest-running security problem in British history. While it was certainly in the state's national interests in the short term to end a sophisticated campaign of terror that had led to the deaths of almost 4,000 people and the injuring of ten times that number, it has, arguably, caused considerable detrimental harm to the process of reconciliation.

Extracts from the United Nations' *Handbook on the Peaceful Settlement of Disputes between States* (1992)

22. The Manila Declaration on the Peaceful Settlement of International Disputes highlights flexibility as one of the characteristics of direct negotiations as a means of peaceful settlement of disputes (sect. I, para. 10). Negotiation is a flexible means of peaceful settlement of disputes in several respects. It can be applied to all kinds of disputes, whether political, legal or technical. Because, unlike the other means listed in Article 33 of the Charter, it involves only the States parties to the dispute, those States can monitor all the phases of the process from its initiation to its conclusion and conduct it in the way they deem most appropriate.

68. When negotiations are successful, they normally lead to the issuance by the parties of an instrument reflecting the terms of the agreement arrived at. This document may be a comprehensive agreement. It may be a joint statement or communiqué. A memorandum or declaration defining broad points of agreement may precede the issuance of a more detailed agreement.

69. If the negotiations are unsuccessful, the parties may choose to adjourn the negotiation process sine die or to issue a communiqué recording the failure of the negotiations. If the dispute relates to the interpretation or application of a treaty, the failure of the negotiations may result in denunciation of the treaty by one of the parties.[30]

The ending of apartheid in 1994 heralded a transformation in South Africa. Apartheid legalised racial segregation between minority whites and majority blacks in the country between 1948 and 1990. Blacks were stripped of rights and in 1964 the African National Congress launched a campaign of violence designed to bring down apartheid rule. With the release from prison of ANC leader Nelson Mandela in 1990 the government and ANC entered into negotiations, which culminated in democratic elections in April 1994. The elections brought to power the first majority black government in the country's history, replacing rule that was once based on coercion with a new dispensation based on consent. Negotiations aimed at dismantling apartheid were based on the principles of inclusivity, the building of trust and an internal-based solution. This was a very different process from the one in Northern Ireland, which relied heavily on the British and Irish governments and the US to broker a deal between the warring factions. The basis of South Africa's democratic transition would actively promote F. W. De Clerk and Nelson Mandela as 'partners in peace' that became the centrepiece of the dialogue between former opponents. In many ways the outcome was win–win, unlike in Northern Ireland and Cyprus, with the South African people regarded as being the real winners in the negotiated settlement.

Mediation

In its *Handbook on the Peaceful Settlement of Disputes between States* (1992),[31] the United Nations defined mediation as 'a method of peaceful settlement of an international dispute where a third party intervenes to reconcile the claims of the contending parties and to advance his own proposals aimed at a mutually acceptable compromise solution'. One has to look no further than the Dayton Peace Talks in 1995, when it was decided by the major regional powers that violence would have to end in Bosnia. Peacebuilding expert Roland Paris suggests that the Dayton Accord 'explicitly ought to transform Bosnia into a liberal democracy on the assumption that doing so would reduce the likelihood of renewed fighting' between Bosnia Serbs, Muslims and Croats.[32] In other civil wars, such as those in the Democratic Republic of Congo, the intervention of peacekeeping forces has done little to hasten the end of the fighting and it is arguable that the deep-seated differences found in long-running European disputes, such as in Cyprus, have staved off a comprehensive peace deal between warring factions. In these circumstances two obvious options are available. First, the orthodox consensus appears to be that we intervene to keep the warring factions apart, or, second, as some strategists have argued, we leave the war to run its course, for 'it is not always wise for the world's peacemakers to freeze-frame a war that is far from concluded militarily'.[33] Though provocative, this view is borne out somewhat by the empirical evidence, which suggests that 90 per cent of all civil wars today are re-runs of earlier armed conflicts that were 'freeze-framed' in the past. Examples include Sudan, Eritrea, Georgia and other 'frozen conflicts' like Cyprus, as we will discover later in the chapter.

The idea of governments being in strong positions, where there is less of an incentive to negotiate with an armed opposition, can be seen in the Syrian civil war which began in 2011. The government of President Bashar al-Assad had been rocked by the same desire for reform that swept across the Middle East in the Arab Spring. Attempts by the US and UK to force the removal of Assad by peaceful means failed and a lack of appetite in the West for any kind of intervention beyond 'non-lethal aid' to civilians and 'moderate' opposition forces meant there was no prospect of direct intervention in the civil war that would take the lives over 250,000 people on all sides in its first four years. Although the prospect of further Western intervention failed to garner domestic public support, Russia was on hand to vehemently oppose any attempt in international political terms, a position that did not preclude the Russian Duma from supporting military deployments in support of Assad. In the first two years of the conflict the regime lost and then regained ground in key districts and cleared out oppositional positions. By January 2014 talks in Geneva saw the government and opposition come to the negotiating table in an attempt to resolve the conflict. These failed and a return to violent conflict in which the regime forces were literally fighting for their lives meant that the strategy became one of existential fear that the outcome of the war would decide not only the fate of the individuals and whole ethnic groups but the state itself. That *Daesh* was dedicated to the overthrow of the Syrian and Iraqi governments and the establishment of a new caliphate extending its reach from the Middle East to the Iberian Peninsula leaves the fate of the international state system hanging in the balance.

However, a negotiated settlement still remains the preferred option for ending civil wars. In 1992 the former UN Secretary General Boutros Boutros-Ghali published his *An Agenda for Peace*, an influential report that saw the promotion of liberalisation as a 'remedy for civil conflict' in the post-Cold War world.[34] As much about emphasising a new agenda for the UN, paralysed by decades of Cold War enmity, as it was in framing a new agenda for understanding the challenges still posed to international security, it was a remarkably clear-sighted document. Produced within a year of the dissolution of the Soviet Union, *An Agenda for Peace* was Boutros-Ghali's plan for ensuring that the 'pervasive and deep nature of conflict' in the international system could be tackled at its source. Although it focused on the concepts of preventive diplomacy, peacemaking and peacekeeping, Boutros-Ghali introduced a fourth concept, post-conflict peacebuilding, which offered profound insight into our understanding of the dynamics of war as it transitioned into peace. While the emerging post-Cold War order presented new challenges – assertions of nationalism and sovereignty prevailed – it would not be long before identity conflicts threatened ethnic, religious, social, cultural and linguistic conflagration.

Extract from *An Agenda for Peace* (1992)

With the end of the cold war there have been no such vetoes since 31 May 1990, and demands on the United Nations have surged. Its security arm, once disabled by circumstances it was not created or equipped to control, has emerged as a central instrument for the prevention and resolution of conflicts and for the preservation of peace. Our aims must be:

- To seek to identify at the earliest possible stage situations that could produce conflict, and to try through diplomacy to remove the sources of danger before violence results;
- Where conflict erupts, to engage in peacemaking aimed at resolving the issues that have led to conflict;
- Through peace-keeping, to work to preserve peace, however fragile, where fighting has been halted and to assist in implementing agreements achieved by the peacemakers;
- To stand ready to assist in peace-building in its differing contexts: rebuilding the institutions and infrastructures of nations torn by civil war and strife; and building bonds of peaceful mutual benefit among nations formerly at war;
- And in the largest sense, to address the deepest causes of conflict: economic despair, social injustice and political oppression. It is possible to discern an increasingly common moral perception that spans the world's nations and peoples, and which is finding expression in international laws, many owing their genesis to the work of this Organization.[35]

The Role of the Military in Building Peace

'Peacekeeping is not a job for soldiers', runs the phrase coined by former UN Secretary General Dag Hammarskjöld, 'but only soldiers can do it'. This is the motto adopted by the Bangladeshi International Peace Support Operations Training (BIPSOT) centre in Dhaka, Bangladesh, which trains the country's forces for deployment on UN peacekeeping missions around the world. For years Bangladesh has acted as the main troop contributing nation to UN Peace Support Operations. Between 1971 and 2008 they had lost 281 soldiers in a versatile mix of activities from monitoring ceasefires to keeping warring factions apart in many complex security environments. Bangladeshi peacekeepers would privately admit that they are motivated by the altruistic objective of making the world a safer and more secure place, which is moulded and shaped by their Islamic religious beliefs.[36]

In traditional Cold War peacekeeping UN forces were deployed to establish a buffer zone between two warring factions in the form of State A vs State B. Their main task was to keep the belligerents from engaging in fighting against each other while a long-term political solution was found to the crisis, conflict or confrontation. Monitoring ceasefires, disarming factions and building confidence were all activities attempted by UN peacekeepers. Cyprus is perhaps the quintessential case study of traditional Cold War peacekeeping. The island passed from Ottoman to British control in 1878 and became a formalised part of the British Empire under the Treaty of Lausanne in 1923 until independence in 1960. UN peacekeeping in Cyprus dates from 1964, although a counter-insurgency campaign was fought by the British Security Forces in 1955–9. In the wake of this it retreated to sovereign bases on the island, which continued to form a strategic interests for years to come. Britain had long supported the peacekeeping activities of the United Nations. It used its position as one of the five permanent members on the Security Council to support operations on the island. It has always been a priority of British foreign policy that the sovereign military bases would be retained, even in the event of a settlement between the two rival intercommunal groups on the island. As far back as 1965 the Foreign Secretary was suggesting that: 'It is clearly in our interest that peace should be maintained in Cyprus' and that the British 'should agree to continue to contribute our contingent at its present level of between 1,000 and 1,100 men and to meet all its costs'. Defence Secretary Denis Healey sent the following telegram to Prime Minister Harold Wilson:

> If we withheld our contribution UNFICYP [United Nations Peace-keeping Force in Cyprus] would wither. If it did, at worst there might

be an explosion on the island; at best, the situation would become so taut that we should have to consider withdrawal to the Sovereign Base Areas and military reinforcement of those. International considerations apart, therefore, it will pay us to keep UNFICYP in being while hope of a political settlement remains.[37]

Although the Treasury considered it unwarranted to support the airlift capabilities of other contributing nations, it still decided to continue its deployment in Nicosia. In a further Foreign Office communiqué to UN headquarters in New York it was pointed out that apart from the contingent of UK forces, only $1 million would be offered for the duration of the next mandate. In a meeting of the UNSC it was reported by the UK delegation that:

> Fedorenko (Soviet Union) spoke very briefly. He said that the Soviet Union supported the independence and territorial integrity of Cyprus, but this must be genuine independence and safety. All foreign troops and foreign bases must be removed. The Greeks and Turks in Cyprus must settle the problem between themselves without outside interference. The Soviet Union had no objection to the extension of UNFICYP until 26 June on the understanding that it carried out its task in accordance with the resolution of 4 March, 1964, with the same mandate and with the same financial arrangements.[38]

Cyprus, like Northern Ireland, may be representative of 'old wars', or, at the very least, of the prototype to Mary Kaldor's 'new wars', but the logic that underpins them all is one based on identity politics and the cold logic of zero-sum ethnonationalism. Unlike in South Africa, which was presented as win–win, these 'old new wars' are seen as win–lose by the belligerents. Thus, Northern Ireland is akin to the three-way ethno-national dispute in Bosnia between Serb, Muslim and Croat, who often held extremely divergent views and harboured ancient enmities that were frequently at odds with the international community's ideas for the resolution of civil conflict.

If we agree with Rupert Smith's characterisation of the early twenty-first century as being typified by 'wars amongst the people', it must follow that the strategic logic by which we understood 'old wars' is somewhat flawed when applied to the international security environment. In recognition of the complexities of building peace in today's world, there has emerged a much more nuanced consensus about how the termination of hostilities merely represents a waypoint, albeit an abrupt one, in the erratic transition from war to peace. Mary Kaldor has written that for human rights enforcement to work in future there is a requirement for the international community to make a more substantive contribution to peace operations that goes well beyond mere rhetoric:

> Humanitarian intervention perhaps needs to be reconceptualized as international presence in conflict-prone areas, a presence that represents a continuum from civil society actors to international agencies up to and including international peacekeeping troops on a march larger scale than seen so far. In part it means a change in outlook, especially the training, equipment, principles and tactics of peacekeeping troops. But above all it involves a genuine belief in the equality of all human beings; and this entails a readiness to risk the lives of peacekeeping troops to save the lives of others where this is necessary.[39]

Few would deny that strategy will be as important in this endeavour as tactics and principles. The movement away from seeing unilateral intervention by states as unlawful (unless it is in self-defence or as part of a UN mandated force) and illegitimate means that strategy will remain integral to the ending wars and the building of peace.

What implications does this have for modern militaries in building peace? There are competing perspectives on the utility of the military instrument. Revisiting the work of Galula we can discern several points worth exploring here. Galula articulated the need for the military to be prepared to adapt to perform functions other than war-fighting. In his words:

> To confine soldiers to purely military functions while urgent and vital tasks have to be done, and nobody else is available to undertake them, would be senseless. The soldier must then be prepared to become the propagandist, a social worker, a civil engineer, a schoolteacher, a nurse, a boy scout. But only for as long as he cannot be replaced, for it is better to entrust civilian tasks to civilians.[40]

Implied in this extract from Galula's influential book is the danger of allowing the military to colonise civilian tasks. Yet, in today's security environment one might argue that it is impossible for civilians to become solely responsible for these tasks when danger lurks around every corner. As with much of counter-insurgency and peacekeeping theory, perhaps the solution lies somewhere in between:

> That the political power is the undisputed boss is a matter of both principle and practicality. What is at stake is the country's political regime, and to defend it is a political affair. Even if this requires military action, the action is constantly directed toward a political goal. Essential though it is, the military action is secondary to the political one, its primary purpose being to afford the political power enough freedom to work safely with the population.[41]

Galula's work was based on his own personal experience in French military operations in Algeria in the 1950s and adhered to a particular understanding of counter-insurgency operations as pacification. This was considerably different from the British approach to fighting irregular adversaries, according to Lieutenant Colonel Peter McCutcheon, who described French *guerre revolutionnaire* as soldiers fighting 'a brutally efficient campaign . . . in a [political] vacuum'.[42] In post-war Britain, as we saw in Chapter 5, there was no such vacuum. Political leaders did know what their policy was and how force could be used to enable the accomplishment of those ends: withdrawal from empire by 1970 and an abandonment of the East of Suez role, a withdrawal, moreover, that depended on British military bayonets to ensure a peaceful transition. We must be very careful when bringing 'lessons' from the past into the present, especially when we are faced with entirely new security challenges. It is imperative that honest questions are asked of ourselves and that the agencies we expect to be employed for the purpose of policy be the right ones. As this chapter has demonstrated through a range of twentieth-century case studies, the resolution of confrontations and conflicts can only happen whenever it is recognised that one size does not fit all. Strategy must be flexible and adapt according to the context in which it is wielded.

Conclusion

This chapter has asked whether it is possible to control war by way of terminating hostilities through victory, defeat or dialogue or in the deployment of UN peacekeepers. The truism articulated by both Carl von Clausewitz and, much later, by Johan Galtung, that the political lines run throughout war and into peace has also been found to reinforce the rational purpose behind wars, even if they do not immediately appear to be fought according to any recognisable logic. With that in mind, we need to move away from an understanding of war and peace as part of a linear sequence of events. If war is complex, chaotic and dialectical in nature, then it is logical that peace be somewhat similar.

Key Questions

1. Why is war so difficult to bring to an end?
2. What strategies can be pursued to end wars?
3. How effective is the UN's approach to negotiation and mediation?
4. What is the best strategy for ending conflict in an era of crisis and confrontation?
5. Why do states find it more difficult to plan for peace than for war?

Further Reading

Bobbitt, Philip, *The Shield of Achilles: War, Peace and the Course of History* (London: Penguin, 2002).

Boutros-Ghali, Boutros, *An Agenda for Peace: Preventive Diplomacy, Peacemaking and Peacekeeping* (17 June 1992). Available at <http://www.unrol.org/files/A_47_277.pdf> (last accessed 21 November 2015).

Bull, Hedley, 'The great irresponsibles? The United States, the Soviet Union, and world order', *International Journal*, 35: 3, Summer 1980, pp. 437–47.

Clausewitz, Carl von, *On War*, edited and translated by Michael Howard and Peter Paret (Princeton, NJ: Princeton University Press, 1976).

Clayton, Anthony, *Defeat: When Nations Lose a War* (Ely: Melrose Books, 2010).

Diehl, Paul F., *Peace Operations* (Cambridge: Polity, 2008).

Gray, Colin S., *Another Bloody Century: Future War* (London: Weidenfeld and Nicolson, 2005).

Gray, Colin S., *Strategy and History: Essays in Theory and Practice* (Abingdon: Routledge, 2006).

Gallula, David, *Counter-insurgency Warfare: Theory and Practice* (London: Praeger Security International, [1964] 2006).

Galtung, Johan, *Twenty-Five Years of Peace Research: Ten Challenges and Some Responses* (Berlin: July 1984), p. 29. Available at <http://www.transcend.org/galtung/papers/Twenty%20Five%20Years%20of%20Peace%20Research-Ten%20Challenges%20and%20Some%20Responses.pdf> (last accessed 19 March 2013).

Howard, Michael, *The Causes of Wars and Other Essays* (London: Unwin Paperbacks, 1983).

Kaldor, Mary, *Human Security: Reflections on Globalization and Intervention* (Cambridge: Polity, 2006).

Kaldor, Mary, *New and Old Wars: Organized Violence in a Global Era*, 2nd edn (Cambridge: Polity, 2006).

Machiavelli, *The Art of War* (Indianapolis: Bobbs-Merrill Company, 1965).

McNamara, Robert S., *In Retrospect: The Tragedy and Lessons of Vietnam* (New York: Vintage, 1996).

Paris, Roland, *At War's End: Building Peace After Civil Conflict* (Cambridge: Cambridge University Press, 2004).

Slim, Field Marshal Sir William, *Defeat into Victory* (London: Cassell and Company, 1956).

Smith, General Sir Rupert, *The Utility of Force: The Art of War in the Modern World* (London: Penguin, 2005).

7 Strategy Redux?

Scope

This chapter details some of the major challenges in the international security environment today and asks whether strategy is equipped to help us deal with them. Previous chapters have focused on the ability of state actors to formulate and execute strategies and the steps that they have taken in war, peace, crisis and confrontation to attain the goals that they have set for themselves. Continuing with the theme of learning to adapt amidst fast-changing circumstances, this chapter suggests that fear, honour and interest continue to coalesce in ways that necessitate the improvement of strategic education for modern defence and security professionals. Although some prior competence in strategy is necessary to ensure the ends being pursued are appropriately balanced against the means at one's disposal, there is also a requirement to continually improve one's grasp of the universal theory of strategy. In this strategists can avail themselves of several millennia of strategic history to provide a suitable compass by which we can orientate ourselves to the future, for the detail may change, but not the nature of war, warfare and strategy. However, in order to be successfully applied, strategy relies on both a rigorous understanding of the past and a detailed appreciation of the different political and military contexts in which it may be practised.

Introduction

Strategy, like war, is a serious business. In wartime it can mean the difference between life and death. In peacetime it ensures that threats to peace and security can be deterred effectively or resolved without the need to resort to the use of force at all. For this reason understanding how to *do* strategy well is essential for those who wish to avoid the pitfalls faced by people in the past. Professor Colin S. Gray argues that most of what is 'presented in the twenty-first century as bold new strategic theory, innovative doctrine, and practice, that is a radical change from preceding behaviour, is really locatable in three classics and in the ever contestable historical record'.[1] The three classics in question – Thucydides' *A History of the Peloponnesian War*, Sun Tzu's *The Art of War* and Clausewitz's *On War* – have been consulted in preceding chapters. However, it is worth examining Gray's view that the three classics 'must be married to a study of strategic history' in order to avoid the pitfall of strategists ignorant of history, who remain 'marooned on a very small island of expertise'. As Gray and Johnson have argued, 'Since we cannot know anything in detail about the future, and the present is inherently transient, we need to extract whatever is extractable from our all too rich strategic history'.[2] This chapter, therefore, sets out to examine how strategic history might be mined in order to shine a light on many security problems that have a timeless quality to them.

In considering some of the key security challenges facing strategists in the world today it is worth keeping in mind three interrelated points in relation to the fine balance to be struck between investment in technology and investment in people, the increasing inability of states to influence the international security environment, and the success of non-state actors in challenging the basis of the international states system. Although it is sometimes said that irregular adversaries, such as al-Qaeda and *Daesh*, pose significant challenges to international security, it would be wrong to overlook the role played by strong states in fomenting instability around the world. In looking specifically at contextual factors, leading strategists have encouraged us to remain sceptical of orthodox narratives deployed to explain complex events, processes and outcomes, and to constantly reassess our understanding of the world around us. There is no better place to begin Chapter 7, therefore, than by looking at the balance between technological and human factors in strategy.

The Role of Technology in Strategy

We are constantly being told that the security challenges we face today are new and innovative and unlike anything we have faced in the past. This is a point echoed in many of the defence and security reviews undertaken by states in the West. As we can see from the assertions made in both the United States' *Quadrennial Defense Review* (2014) and the United Kingdom's *Global Strategic Trends – Out to 2045* (2014), there is a widely held view that technology has been a key driver in the transformation of the international security environment. It is obvious that developed nations have succeeded in utilising 'the advent of superior Information Technology (IT) and weapons of precision' in a way that has 'vastly enhanced the power of advanced military forces'.[3] To be sure, the onset of new technologies has enabled state-based armed forces to become far more networked on the battlefield and to project power further and faster – and in a more economical fashion – than ever before. And we know that we have arrived at this moment through a long process of adaptation and change that has accompanied the digital revolution, particularly since the invention of the Internet and its growth after the end of the Cold War.

The strong belief in the 1990s was that digitalisation was a key enabler of the so-called Revolution in Military Affairs (RMA), which could explain how superior technology would win the battle every time when faced with an adversary that possessed none or few of these advantages. And, to an extent, NATO operations in Kosovo in 1999 proved the case. Limited intervention by way of air operations against a far less militarily capable state did indeed prove the RMA thesis, though it did not take into account the ability of adversaries to adapt to the overwhelming firepower directed against them. Thus, after the initial invasion of Iraq in 2003 a vigorous insurgency grew up out of the miscalculation by the US-led Coalition to demobilise the Iraqi Army, while simultaneously failing to protect the Iraqi people. This strategic *faux pas* left behind an enormous pool of ready volunteers for the insurgency. As one of the foremost chroniclers of American military strategy Steven Metz would later observe:

As Americans grappled with these problems, the insurgents continued to evolve. They understood that combining regular, low-level violence with occasional large, high-profile attacks maximised fear and publicity. Humans can tolerate danger in constant and expected doses. Anticipation of a different kind or level of danger, though, increases anxiety, which, in turn, saps morale and will. Fear of the unknown is the most debilitating kind.[4]

In many respects what happened in Iraq was a harbinger for so much else that has since developed across the Middle East region. It also highlighted how an over-reliance on technology could not meet the very people-centric challenges thrown up by a complex security environment like Iraq.

In his book *The Direction of War* (2013), Professor Sir Hew Strachan makes the point that despite the proliferation of new technologies, states are still waging war 'without using the full range of their technological capabilities',[5] a restriction, he claims, which is not limited to nuclear weapons. As Professor Strachan argues, 'The conditioning influences in shaping strategy in Iraq and Afghanistan have been less technological and more social, political and historical.' It is easy to get carried away by the introduction of new technologies but perhaps it is not too trite a point to suggest that the invention of the television in the 1950s did not replace the radio and, indeed, as we were to witness much later, the Internet has led to an augmentation of existing technologies in an entirely new or 'hybrid' format. Amidst all of this technological innovation states still expect their adversaries to think like they do. There is a real danger that states that remain fixated on the means in warfare – instead of a more holistic analysis of strategy, which includes ends and ways – overlook the other strategic parts of the equation. If we accept Professor Strachan's hypothesis that 'it is patently absurd to deny that the impact of new technology can be strategically significant', how then do we square that with his other view that the wars currently being waged are 'still predominantly the products of national, religious and ethnic identity'[6] with the aims of 'governance and state formation'? In interrogating this conundrum, it is useful to turn our attention towards an example of how terrorist groups have presented a clear challenge to the authority of weaker states and to ask how they exploit strong sub-national identities and hostility towards external intervention in order to gain strategic advantage over governments.

How Non-State Actors use Strategy

On the morning of 12 October 2000, Hassan al Khamri and Ibrahim al-Thawar, two young Saudi nationals, washed themselves from head to toe, paying particular attention to their feet, then carefully laid out their prayer mats alongside one another and prepared themselves for their morning's activity that would lead directly to their deaths. After prayer they sat cross-legged on the floor, with towels wrapped round their waists, eating a meal, before dressing themselves. They left their safe house in Aden, Yemen's second city, shortly before 10 a.m., for a short trip by car to the quayside. There they launched a small white boat, laden with explosives, which included trinitrotoluene TNT and RDX, from a nearby jetty. As the dinghy slipped into the calm waters of the Indian Ocean, the two men gazed across to the bulky outline of the USS *Cole*, a 8,300 tonne, 293-man crew billion dollar frigate and pride of America's vast navy. Paddling out to within a few hundred yards of the ship, Khamri and Thawar gave a friendly wave to a few sailors who had gathered on the port side of the ship to watch them. Beneath decks American servicemen went about their morning routine, some standing in line at the mess hall while others lay in their bunks reading or writing letters home to their loved ones. As Thawar and Khamri drifted closer to the ship, they promptly stood to attention and detonated their deadly cargo of explosives, ripping a huge gash in the side of the warship. Seventeen American sailors were killed and over forty injured in the bomb attack on the USS *Cole* that morning.

Thawar and Khamiri had not acted alone. They were aided and abetted by a small network of Yemenis, who were later apprehended, tried and convicted by Yemeni authorities for their part in the attack on the USS *Cole*. The facilitator for the attack would remain at the top of the FBI's Most Wanted list for many years after the attack, having evaded capture twice until his arrest and release from prison in a deal between Yemeni authorities and al-Qaeda militants in 2006. One of his co-conspirators, Abd al Rahim al Nashiri, subsequently became the terrorist group's commander in the Arabian Peninsula. Prior to the attack on the USS *Cole* he had flown to Afghanistan to meet with the leader of al-Qaeda, Osama bin Laden, and settle the details of the operation. Intelligence later suggested that bin Laden had personally selected the location and target for the attack. There is little doubt that the orders for the attack on the USS *Cole* came directly from al-Qaeda's 'General Command' and that the training in handling and preparing the explosives was undertaken in the back streets of Kandahar in Afghanistan. The attack on the USS *Cole* was the latest in the long line of plots by terrorists in southern Yemen. The plan was a re-run of an earlier failed attempt by the same conspirators in January 2000, when they tried to sink another US warship, the USS *Sullivan*. On that occasion the dinghy carrying the explosives sank because of the weight of its cargo. Other attacks, dating back to the early 1990s, included the murder of two US Marines on shore leave in Aden's Goldmore Hotel.

Al-Qaeda in the Arabian Peninsula (AQAP) was able to lay firm roots in Yemen for a number of reasons, not least that it exploited hostility between those living in the south-west of the country who believed they were being 'colonised' by those from the north. The primitive development of the south and the disparity with the more prosperous and secure north provided AQAP with a fertile recruiting and training ground in places like Abyan and Shabwa provinces in southern Yemen. The evidence for inequality throughout the country is compelling. Yemen is one of the poorest countries in the world. In demographic terms, of the 25,408,288 people who live there, almost half are women and 42 per cent are under the age of fourteen. With a young population there is considerable stress on resources, with some 45.2 per cent of people living under the poverty line and a further 35 per cent unemployed. For every dollar that is ploughed into the country from international aid, $2.4 dollars leaves it illicitly. A recent report by the Yemen Forum at Chatham House in London has talked about how the drones-led counter-terrorism under President Abd-Rabbu Mansour Hadi (who won presidential elections in February 2012, a southerner from the Fadhli tribe) risks undermining Yemen's stability in the longer term, something that would come to pass when the Houthi militias from the northern border with Saudi Arabia marched on Sana'a in September 2014. The Chatham House report found that financial assistance to the Hadi government (and to Saleh before him) dwarfed development aid and, therefore, did much to distort the centralising powers of government.

Apart from the fundamental socio-economic problems and the unfinished political transition from the old guard of Ali Abdullah Saleh to a new political dispensation, experts generally agree that the threat posed by AQAP to Yemeni national security has destabilised the country even further. On 27 September 2013, for instance, *The Economist* ran a feature which appeared to ask if drones in Yemen, the Westgate Siege in Nairobi, piracy off the Gulf of Aden and ongoing violence in Iraq are part and parcel of 'the new face of terror'. Dr David Kilcullen, doyen of Western counter-insurgency studies, was interviewed by *The Economist* about the findings from his new book, *Out of the Mountains*, which posits a similar hypothesis: that the old way of understanding war – within the conceptual framework of inter-state war or, more boldly perhaps, the 'global war on terror' – is outmoded. But is this actually the case? If anything, *The Economist* and Dr Kilcullen seem to merely be re-stating the 'new wars' thesis familiar to those who have been closely observing this 'new face of terror' since the attacks on the United States on 9/11.

The truth is that jihadism in the Arabian Peninsula predates 9/11 and can be traced back to the return of Yemeni fighters from the war against the Soviets in Afghanistan in the early 1990s. Indeed, there seems to be a consensus amongst experts on Yemen that we should not treat AQAP and the surrounding socio-political context in isolation. Clearly there is much more going on in Yemen that is not specifically tied to the tiny group of jihadis who are threatening national, regional and international security. The dangers posed by Yemen becoming a 'failed state' due to reoccurring civil wars are, arguably, much more far-reaching than the transient threat posed by AQAP. Rather than seeing what is happening in Yemen as a new challenge – and, therefore, a break with the past – we should see it as a continuation of the uneven development of political economy in the country, the prevalence of conditions conducive to terrorism and a crisis over the legitimacy of the state that triggered an insurgency in 2014 and the effective toppling of the Western-backed government by early 2015. According to Alastair Harris, Yemen is neither a failing state nor a failed one. Having only been united in 1990, when the Marxist-dominated Peoples Democratic Republic of South Yemen joined the north, it descended into a brief civil war in 1994, when the northern government defeated the southern rebels and set about consolidating their support in the south. In order to ensure that the south remained subservient, Saleh not only made a Faustian pact with returning jihadis, he also staffed the southern regional governates with his loyal supporters and those from his own tribe.

Counter-terrorism experts, no matter how jingoistic, must acknowledge that attritional strategies alone rarely bring success and instead breed deep-seated failure to contest the loyalty of the population as they are pushed and pulled between the state and its irregular challenger. As Human Rights Watch correctly surmised in a report: 'Should the United States continue targeted killings in Yemen without addressing the consequences of killing civilians and taking responsibility for unlawful deaths, it risks further angering many Yemenis and handing another recruiting card to AQAP'.[7] For what it is worth, AQAP may be damaged by drone strikes but we know that the use of tactics such as targeted assassination in irregular warfare rarely, if ever, brings an end to terrorism and insurgency. AQAP's operations in and around Abyan and Shabwah are not an aberration and have their genesis in the group's seizure of the Abyan provincial capital of Zingibar – which it held for several months – which demonstrates that the new face of terrorism is capable of holding ground. As we now know, AQAP and its ideological kinsmen from the extremist group Ansar al-Sharia (AAS), an ISIS-style group that has since reared its ugly head in other parts of the Middle East and North Africa, such as Tunisia, Egypt and Libya, have been learning the mistakes of jihadi groups elsewhere. Indeed, AQAP and AAS have the advantage of having been operating in the southern Yemeni provinces for some time.

By May 2011 the latter had actually established a mini-caliphate in the small cities of Ja'ar and Zingibar in Abyan Province, where they committed numerous atrocities, including decapitations and amputations for, amongst other things, those accused of witchcraft. In a report published by Amnesty International in 2012, human rights workers found that governing bodies set up by AAS 'committed human rights abuses ranging from curbing freedom of expression to ordering cruel, inhuman and degrading punishments and summary killings'. According to Amnesty, 'Some of these abuses also violated IHL and may have constituted war crimes'. Fourteen months later the emirate had been destroyed in a concerted effort by Yemeni troops backed by US special operations forces and UAVs. More than three years later, however, there is evidence that AAS have returned and are simply biding their time before making another bid to take control of those southern towns and cities where they are strong.

Three years after the tumultuous events of 9/11, Osama bin Laden made public the al-Qaeda strategy of 'bleeding the West dry'. By erecting the black flag of his organisation in disparate regions, from Mali to Nigeria and Iraq to Yemen, his decision caused the United States to spend more than $3 trillion protecting its citizens by combating a range of al-Qaeda affiliates in America, Europe, North and Sub-Saharan Africa, the Middle East and South-East Asia. Costly interventions in Afghanistan may have failed to weaken Western powers in the way that Osama bin Laden had hoped, but the global economic downturn has since forced them to recalibrate and downsize their strategic ambitions in even more far-reaching ways. In entering into armed competition, however, there is every possibility that the deep divisions that already exist between north and south – especially as military forces reflect pre-Islamic tribal boundaries – will become even more pronounced. It is the prospect of a split into two separate states that appears to be an even greater danger to Yemen's stability than the wanton barbarism exhibited in the deeds of AQAP, AAS or for that matter *Daesh*.

State-Based Challenges to International Order

As the case study of AQAP reveals, even terrorists are capable of viewing strategy as the umbilical cord that joins policy to tactics.

In simple terms it provides the plan by which political entities orientate themselves to the political and military environment around them. The recent Western interventions in Afghanistan, Iraq and Libya all threw up considerable challenges for Western strategy-making. In the haste to grapple with some of the complex problems these environments posed, policymakers, government officials and military commanders turned to civilian advisors to offer theories that could be worked into their strategies for dealing with terrorists and insurgents. Interestingly, many of these military and civilian experts were prone to cherry-pick lessons from the past to add weight to their gut instinct on how they thought these wars should be fought. This was to prove problematic for a range of reasons, not least in their lack of formal education or training in history, which meant that they were prone to offering little more than Polaroid snapshots of the past in a rush to backfill government analytical capability.[8] One of the most well-known examples of this was in Afghanistan where parallels were drawn in relation to British military involvement, not in earlier colonial engagements in Afghanistan but in the completely different context of 1950s Malaya.[9] Some experts believed that the application of the concept of 'ink-spots' of development and security was enough to resolve what was fast becoming a resilient set of insurgent, terrorist and criminal enemies. Although the plan might well have worked, it was not supported by the deployment of forces.

What was also lost on those advocating rummaging through the past for 'lessons' from other parts of the world was a basic understanding of the principles of war, which emphasised the concentration (not the dispersal) of force on enemies, whether regular or irregular. Ironically, a greater understanding of the nuances of history would have pointed to the fact that whenever the Chief of the Imperial General Staff, Sir John Harding, sought to apply his 'Malaya Plan' to Kenya it had only mixed results. When he applied the same template to Cyprus in 1955–7 it proved incapable of providing a winning formula and the fight between British Security Forces and George Grivas's EOKA group ended in a stalemate in 1960. By the time British strategists got to the problem of growing insurgencies in Aden (1963–7) and Northern Ireland (1969–2007), any parallels were completely irrelevant, even if they were constantly harped back to. This proved that the British did not always take seriously their assertion that every context should be looked upon as unique.[10]

Arguably, decisions which explicitly draw on the historical record for inspiration should not be left to amateurs, no matter how gifted or talented they are. The introduction to this book made the case that the theory of strategy, like the theory of history, was too important to be left to theorists alone. And so with theorists, historians of strategy should be consulted by practitioners, for all good strategists, argues Colin Gray, ought to be shrewd historians.[11] In this sense, senior defence and security practitioners would be wise to turn to professional historians for advice or guidance on the past. After all, one would not turn to an oncologist for advice on gynaecology, no matter how skilled in general medicine they might appear. In considering the uses and abuses of the past we must also be wary of drawing too many pertinent comparisons in the fight against terrorism and insurgency, primarily because most of the historic cases did not see the application of templates in the countering of irregular adversaries.

As we have also discovered above, strategy is the process that links politics to action.[12] In the Libya crisis in 2011, there were clear trade-offs made by UN member states for explicit reasons of national interest. Germany, for instance, abstained from the UN Security Council vote on Resolution 1973, not because of a reaffirmation that they had returned to restraint in military matters but because Germans needed time to debate the matter at home.[13] Since reunification in the early 1990s, Germany's foreign policy has sought to closely integrate its security decisions with other Western European states, a legacy perhaps of the Cold War. On the other hand, the German government has cited their more entrenched belief in the limited utility of armed force. As the German Ambassador to the UN informed the Security Council on 17 March 2011, if the steps authorised by the UN:

> turn out to be ineffective, we see the danger of being drawn into a protracted military conflict that would affect the wider region. We should not enter a military confrontation on the optimistic assumption that quick results with few casualties will be achieved.[14]

This stance was problematic for two main reasons. First, Germany had significant economic interests in the North African region and, second, the rhetoric emanating from Foreign Minister Guido Westermede about the Arab Spring elsewhere, such as Egypt and Syria, seemed to jar with Germany's more cautious position on Libya. It was widely reported in the spring of 2011 that Westermede and Chancellor Angela Merkel risked alienating the political class in their own country, including many within their own Christian Democratic Union party,[15] in taking this gamble. As a permanent member of the UN Security Council, Britain was, perhaps, less inhibited, precisely because intervention to avert a pressing humanitarian disaster has become a key component of its national rules of engagement since 2004.

Nevertheless, although the major parties in Britain had come to reject the notion of liberal intervention with the arrival of the Conservative–Liberal Democrat government in Downing Street in May 2010, this was not a rejection of intervention per se, but rather of the idea that it could only be delivered by the West alone. As Foreign Secretary William Hague made clear in his first statement on Libya:

> In all the countries witnessing great change it is important that the solutions are owned by the people . . . I am sure that Libyans are determined, as we should be, that they also own the solution to this. At the same time, the whole world has humanitarian responsibilities – the United Nations has, of course, a responsibility to protect – so we have to balance those against the consideration that he rightly points to.[16]

The decision by British ministers to remain within the parameters of the UN Charter on the issue of Libya was a direct by-product of the Iraq intervention, which lacked lawful authority. However, it still lacked endorsement from regional actors, who continued to hold out for a purely diplomatic resolution. Since its formation in 2004, the African Union has cautioned against making rash decisions to use violence, calling on all parties to respect Libya's 'unity and territorial integrity',[17] while emphasising respect for international humanitarian law and international efforts to find a diplomatic solution.[18]

191

Britain's role in securing the crucial UN Security Council vote on 'preclusive intervention', which ultimately culminated in the forcible removal (and death) of Colonel Gaddafi at the hands of the armed opposition, is worth considering as an illustrative example of how states must make strategic trade-offs between their foreign policy 'ends' and the 'ways' and 'means' at their disposal.[19] Voting in favour of intervention in Libya for human protection purposes, the British Ambassador to the UN at the time, Sir Mark Lyall Grant, informed the Security Council that: 'The central purpose of this resolution is clear: to end the violence, to protect civilians, and to allow the people of Libya to determine their own future, free from the tyranny of the Qadhafi regime'.[20] This was entirely consistent with the UK's 'national interest', argued Prime Minister David Cameron, which he attributed to a three-fold justification: First, if Libya lapsed into further internal conflict, it would spread, ultimately putting pressure on Britain. Second, that helping Libya become a democracy guaranteed that it was much 'more likely to adhere to the international rule of law and be good, friendly neighbours'. And, third, 'they are less likely to fight wars of aggression and commit violence against their own people', thus reducing the risk to British security.[21] Despite being consistent with UK national interests it was not entirely free of criticism as the influential Defence Select Committee noted in a report:

> When committing to undertake new operations, such as Libya, the Government should state from the outset where that operation fits in the Defence Planning Assumptions and which of the military tasks it is meeting. This should not be limited to the numbers of Armed Forces personnel required, but also the capabilities that will be deployed and the consequences that this may have for other operations or wider defence-related matters, such as the defence budget and defence industry priorities. We can only conclude that the Government has postponed the sensible aspiration of bringing commitments and resources into line, in that it has taken on the new commitment of Libya while reducing the resources available to the MoD.[22]

It has been argued by those close to the prime minister that Britain had little choice in committing to the Libyan intervention. If nothing else it gave the military an opportunity to test its commitment to the new Anglo-French Defence Treaty signed at Lancaster House in London in 2010. Nevertheless, for journalist John Kampfner, there was no excuse for not having a clearly articulated strategy. That the questions faced by British strategists over the past 20 years of 'when, how and whether to intervene in sovereign countries to prevent or stem mass abuses – remain as acute as ever', in Kampfner's view, invited further meditation than they had been given up to that point.[23] Nevertheless, it is possible to make the case that the risk taken by Britain was couched in more power-related terms. For instance, there were frequent reports in the press at the time that military chiefs were complaining of 'huge demands' being placed on both the Royal Air Force and the Royal Navy and that, consequently, morale was 'fragile'.[24] Unusually, given their predilection for complaining when force is not considered by politicians, retired officers went further by arguing that at a time of austerity the government was foolhardy for engaging in another foreign adventure. In many respects it is not difficult to grasp Morgenthau's point that 'a nation may try to play the role of a great power without having the prerequisite for doing so', though this might well serve to 'court disaster'.[25] Britain risked much in its campaign in Libya.

Thomas G. Weiss has been one of the most consistent supporters of the Responsibility to Protect (R2P) doctrine, arguing at the outset of the Libya intervention that if it 'goes well, it might well put teeth into the fledgling R2P doctrine' and 'for the moment', he contended, 'spoilers are on the defensive'.[26] Weiss was wedded to the view that R2P had proven its worth. While David Chandler has queried the extent to which Western liberal states actually intervened in the traditional sense, he commended them for 'an intervention freed from liberal interventionist baggage'.[27] Taking a rather different vantage point, Philip Bobbitt claims that the West has learned the lessons of the Iraq intervention, in the sense that the deployment of foreign boots on the ground was avoided in Libya. The onus has been much more on regional organisations to take moral responsibility for threats to peace and security in their own back yard. Local elites have been co-opted and Libyans have effected do-it-yourself 'regime change', a phrase dropped for fear of unpalatable connotations with Iraq being drawn.

The issue of non-consensual intervention for the purposes of civilian protection guided the UK's responses to crises in the international system from the Kosovo War in 1999, despite Russian characterisation of the stance as a 'Trojan Horse' for 'regime change' by the West. In reality, the Western appetite for enduring missions was on the wane by 2011, making risky deployments unattractive for politicians and unpalatable for public opinion. Britain may no longer be a great power but the government in London has continually sought to indulge in what might well be characterised as 'grand strategy lite'.

At present, there is no evidence to suggest a declining belief in military power as one of the principal means of accomplishing policy objectives, as Britain's intervention in Libya in 2011 has underlined. While there are political and financial benefits from employing force to deliver quick results, such as intervening via proxies, there are also inherent limitations. Increasingly, as Major General Mungo Melvin has written, 'Political goals must reflect what is militarily possible'.[28] This has been reflected in how civilian and military leaders have since moved towards making a distinction between 'wars of choice' and 'wars of necessity', with the former increasingly defended on the same grounds as the latter. Consequently, 'small wars', in which the principal opponents of a state are non-state actors, such as terrorist or insurgent groups, are conflated by politicians with 'big wars', where one or more states opposes other states in a titanic struggle in which national survival dominates all strategic considerations. The question arising out of this is should defence and security planners place so much emphasis on change as opposed to continuity when responding to the myriad security challenges facing the UK?

Strategy and the Concept of Hybrid Warfare

The concept of a hybrid threat has become fashionable in recent years thanks to the work of Frank G. Hoffman. Originating from studies by the US Marines in Quantico in the 1990s, it rested on the prediction of Marine General Charles Krulak that wars of the future would represent 'the step-child of Chechnya rather than the son of Desert Storm'. This new form of warfare has come to serve as the central waypoint for modern militaries as they shrug off the trappings of Cold War 'certainties' and face the future with eager anticipation. As this book has already discussed, modern militaries have traditionally realised all too late in the day how an over-reliance on technology at the expense of understanding the human face of their adversaries has left them at a disadvantage. Notwithstanding this analytical deficit they have sought to acquire a greater depth of understanding of the places in which they are likely to operate and the enemies they are likely to face. This new-found situational awareness has been precipitated by the disappearance from view of the 'old certainties' of the Cold War and the advent of the 'age of uncertainty'. It is anticipated that in the future these 'new' irregular threats, like terrorism, insurgency and organised crime, will pose an even greater challenge to global, regional and state stability than 'old' state-based conventional threats. In attempting to grapple with the conceptual repercussions of this paradigm shift, from inter-state wars to 'wars amongst the people', military practitioners have looked to a handful of innovative thinkers in their own ranks – as well as some civilian academics – to help them make sense of these profound changes in the global security environment. Militaries have arrived at the realisation that in order to mitigate present and future challenges, they must be prepared to outsmart their adversaries mentally as well as physically.

Since 2010 the British government has characterised a myriad of complex challenges under the rubric of a Future Character of Conflict (known in military circles by the mnemonic F/COC), in which it is argued that technology no longer provides the agile edge in complex, modern conflicts. 'Responding to this will require an agile acquisition and support network capable of responding to changing operational needs', they argue. 'There is a sense that the West is currently too equipment-focused; in the future we may have to rely more on our people to provide an edge; this will require far greater investment in selection, training and education.'[29] As the British Strategy Defence and Security Review of 2010 subsequently went on to claim a few months later, 'We will need highly capable and motivated personnel with specialist skills, including cultural understanding; strategic communications to influence and persuade; and the agility, training and education to operate effectively in an increasingly complex environment'.[30]

It is interesting that the British military places training and education at the forefront of its attempts to out-think its adversaries, given that a British parliamentary committee found that much of what passes for strategic thinking had by now atrophied. 'We have failed to maintain the education of strategic thinkers, both in academia and in governmental institutions', it concluded.

> The UK lacks a body of knowledge on strategy. Our processes for making strategy have become weakened and the ability of the military and the Civil Service to identify those people who are able to operate and think at the strategic level is poor.[31]

As developments in Iraq and Ukraine were to prove, this was not something addressed with great urgency. Arguably, in making the case that the future is 'uncertain' in their National Security Strategy (2010) and SDSR the British simply reinforced the sophistry that because much had changed, over 2,500 years of strategic history could offer little help in facing the future with confidence.

That 9/11, the financial crisis of 2007–8, Russian intervention in Ukraine and Syria, and the revitalisation of Islamist terrorism and insurgency have all presaged the need to think strategically is self-evident. What is unclear though is just how a strategic culture can be encouraged at a national and international level. In a report published in 2010, entitled *Who Does UK National Strategy?*, British parliamentarians observed how: 'If we now have a renewed need for National Strategy, we have all but lost the capacity to think strategically. We have simply fallen out of the habit, and have lost the culture of strategy making.'[32] This is curious given Britain's long and illustrious imperial past and its demonstrable ability to do 'grand strategy'. Yet, for much of the twentieth century, it has been the US, not Britain, which has chosen to deal with global threats and risks in a more methodical way. This was underlined by the formation of the National Security Council in 1947 and its imitation in many other countries ever since. However, the past decade's strategic shocks in the UK – 9/11, military interventions in Afghanistan and Iraq, and 'home-grown' Islamist terrorist attacks in London on 7 July 2005 (which became known as 7/7) or in Glasgow on 30 June 2007 – have furnished politicians with convenient way-points in knitting together a grand narrative of the contemporary security landscape. In other words, these attacks, though infrequent, are subsumed in a grand narrative that confirms the enormous challenges facing the British people, while at the same time reassuring them that the government is doing something about them. As such, 9/11 and 7/7 are harbingers for the major security challenges that affect the current generation of politicians and policymakers, for whom the memory of the Cold War has faded.

The British government's response to the global economic crisis has further accelerated the transformation of the UK's strategic position, leaving its military capable of undertaking 'contingency operations' in the main after withdrawing combat troops from Afghanistan in 2014. Due principally to a bulging deficit, the UK has been forced to balance more frugally its goals in the international system with the ways and means at its disposal. Britain was forced to rethink how it resourced fundamental commitments, such as defence and security, amidst cuts to the defence budget of 8 per cent and a reduction to the Army of 20 per cent. With Russia talking up the need to respect international norms while intervening in the internal affairs of sovereign states in its 'near abroad', one would be forgiven for believing that international law has been abandoned in favour of the continuation of realpolitik. The presence of power as the lubricant by which the wheels of international relations turns is the single greatest fact of life in today's security environment. States still matter but they are finding it increasingly difficult to get their way amidst a crowded international system that has seen non-state actors – from transnational organised criminal gangs to terrorist and insurgent groups and multinational corporations – becoming so powerful that they are challenging the foundations of the state. The world looks very different now than it did on 9/11, never mind the end of the Cold War.

The 9/11 Wars have become a superficially attractive starting point for the analysis of Britain's security challenges. Moreover, there has been an added tendency to conflate their significance with threats like Soviet Communism. In terms of lethality, journalist Jason Burke has calculated that the total deaths linked to the 9/11 Wars, including British and American troops, private security contractors, civilians, terrorists and insurgents, could be as high as 250,000. Although nowhere near the body counts amassed by more conventional armed conflicts, these wars have been mainly asymmetrical affairs (i.e., where the more powerful state has been pitted against a less powerful, non-state opponent such as a terrorist or insurgent group), and have had far-reaching repercussions for the West.

The crumbling of the Sykes–Picot line dividing Iraq's border with Syria in 2014 triggered one of the greatest security challenges to Iraq since it was granted independence from the British in 1932. Although many might point to the Ba'athist coup that eventually brought Saddam Hussein to power in the 1970s or the invasion of Iraq in 2003 as crossroads in the state's development, the truth is that the integrity of the state was not threatened until the acquiescence by the US to Prime Minister Nouri al-Maliki's insistence that they drop any prospect of a Status of Forces Agreement upon withdrawal in 2011. This offered a strategic opportunity for *Daesh*, which emerged out of the margins of inequality where Maliki had forced the Sunnis since 2011. Journalist Andrew Hosken informs us that:

> On paper, it seemed impossible that Baghdad could fall to Islamic State. After all, some thirty thousand jihadis could surely not be a match for more than four million Shia who lived in Baghdad alone? No man is an island and neither are nation states, even if they are islands. Iraq's tragedy had long been a cause of deep anxiety to its neighbours. The key question is: in their concern and cynicism and insecurity had Iraq's neighbours, both Shia and Sunni, contributed to the rise of ISIS and the calamity that had befallen their region. The answer is assuredly 'yes'. Iraq had contributed to its own disaster, but it had been aided and abetted by the states on its borders.[33]

Daesh has proven that, with a little consideration given to strategy, even the smallest band of irregular adversaries can capitalise on the inability of state opponents to out-think and outmanoeuvre those they have come to underestimate. While it took a little over a year to wrest back key provincial towns in Yemen from AAS and AQAP, taking back physical and human terrain in Iraq and Syria may take considerably longer.

Conclusion

This chapter has suggested that both states and non-state actors have recognised that sooner or later they will have to think more strategically about how they get what they want. There can be no question that states remain the most important political actors in the world today. Nevertheless, we must also accept that non-state actors continue to have real impact on state policies and will continue to pose significant challenges in the international security environment for many years to come. The delicate balance between technology and human factors in strategy is important for it shows that irregular adversaries may turn the strength of their opponents to their advantage. As a direct consequence of these new challenges, war (understood here as the clash of wills between two opponents and the application of force to achieve their stated policy ends) is changing radically and modern militaries are still finding themselves increasingly deployed by governments as the primary instrument to defend states against the maelstrom of global ethnic, religious and tribal turmoil. From the rugged mountain ranges of Tora Bora, to the lush and fertile (but no less deadly) landscape of Helmand Province, to the hot and humid, arid desert of Yemen, modern militaries are operating in theatres of war populated by people who have embraced traditional and non-traditional methods of war. The challenge in combating these threats is therefore complex and will continue to have profound repercussions for the future.

Key Questions

1. Why is there a need to balance technology and human factors in strategy?
2. What does the activity of AQAP in the southern parts of Yemen reveal about the use of strategy by non-state armed groups?
3. What does the Libya intervention of 2011 tell us about how states use force in the international system?
4. What are the hybrid challenges to international security and how can strategy help us to understand these?
5. Why is it so important to understand the importance of human factors in strategy-making?

Further Reading

Cohen, Eliot A., 'Change and transformation in military affairs', *Journal of Strategic Studies*, 27: 3, September 2004, pp. 395–407.

Edwards, Aaron, *Defending the Realm? The Politics of Britain's Small Wars since 1945* (Manchester: Manchester University Press, 2012).

Freedman, Lawrence, *Strategy: A History* (Oxford: Oxford University Press, 2013).

Gray, Colin S., 'Clausewitz rules, OK? The future is the past – with GPS', *Review of International Studies*, 5: 5, December 1999, pp. 161–82.

Gray, Colin S., *Another Bloody Century: Future Warfare* (London: Weidenfeld and Nicolson, 2005).

Gray, Colin S., 'War – continuity in change, and change in continuity', *Parameters: The US Army's Senior Professional Journal*, 40: 1, Summer 2010, pp. 5–13.

Kaldor, Mary, *New and Old Wars: Organized Violence in a Global Era*, 2nd edn (Cambridge: Polity, 2006).

Kilcullen, David, *The Accidental Guerrilla: Fighting Small Wars amidst a Big One* (London: Hurst, 2009).

Kilcullen, David, *Out of the Mountains: The Coming Age of the Urban Guerrilla* (London: Hurst, 2013).

King, Anthony, 'Understanding the Helmand campaign', *International Affairs*, 86: 2, March 2010, pp. 311–32.

Ledwidge, Frank, *Losing Small Wars: British Military Failure in Iraq and Afghanistan* (London: Yale, 2011).

Metz, Steven, *Iraq and the Evolution of American Strategy* (Washington DC: Potomac Books, 2008).

Mills, Greg, 'Calibrating ink spots: filling Afghanistan's ungoverned spaces', *RUSI Journal*, 151: 4, August 2006, pp. 16–25.

Mockaitis, Thomas R., *British Counterinsurgency in the Post-Imperial Era* (Manchester: Manchester University Press, 1995).

Newton, Paul, Paul Colley and Andrew Sharpe, 'Reclaiming the art of British strategic thinking', *RUSI Journal*, 155: 1, February 2010, pp. 44–50.

Porch, Douglas, 'The dangerous myths and dubious promise of COIN', *Small Wars and Insurgencies*, 22: 2, May 2011, pp. 39–57.

Porch, Douglas, *Counterinsurgency: Exposing the Myths of the New Way of War* (Cambridge: Cambridge University Press, 2013).

Strachan, Hew, *The Direction of War: Contemporary Strategy in Historical Perspective* (Cambridge: Cambridge University Press, 2013).

Conclusion

'Field Marshal Slim – Master of Strategy' reads the epigraph on a huge statue to one of Britain's most famous generals. Situated outside the Ministry of Defence Main Building in Whitehall, London, the 'big three' statues erected in memory of Field Marshals Bernard Montgomery, Alan Brooke and Bill Slim line the western boulevard. All three were towering figures in twentieth century military history for they had all cut their teeth on the battlefields of the First World War, Monty as a Captain, Brook as a Major and Slim as a young subaltern. All three were leaders in junior command positions along the Western Front and all three were wounded in action. During the inter-war period all three rose through the ranks of the British Army and were to command huge armies in the Second World War, with Brooke serving as the Chief of the Imperial General Staff in 1941–6, Montgomery in 1946–8 and Slim in 1948–52. It is often forgotten, however, that the armies these men controlled had little institutional memory of earlier wars and, indeed, the vast majority of those who served in the Second World War had not seen action before, with the exception of senior non-commissioned officers and some officers. Nevertheless, the armies they presided over were to be crucial to the winning of the war. While some of this may be attributed to passion, chance or interest, much of it was directly connected to their skill as strategists.

As Chapter 7 made clear, strategy is both a universal body of theory that can guide practitioners in their exercise of power and also a way to understand history from a strategic point of view. For Professor Colin S. Gray, it is difficult to exaggerate the importance of the 'so what?' question, as the North Star of an education in strategy'.[1] In the practice of strategy it is necessary to keep in mind the bigger picture so as to prevent an over-obsession with the tactical minutiae from clouding our judgement. As we have discovered throughout this book, good strategy can win wars while poor strategy can get people killed. Strategy is a practical activity that issues a challenge to those who engage in it to manage the ends–means relationship as skilfully as possible. Much of the time the main preoccupation of strategists in international security is with the use, or threat, of force to attain political objectives. However, as I have argued, it has much to say about the phases that lead into and away from war, including peace, crisis, confrontation and resolution. As we have seen, the tendency to think about war and peace as a dichotomy in some kind of two-step process has been found to be somewhat outmoded. Therefore, we have an urgent responsibility to reappraise the strategic process by which policy and tactics are linked to political choices, processes and events that do not conform to neat sequential phases.

Our understanding of strategy has developed considerably in the quarter of a century since the end of the Cold War. The expectations placed upon strategists have increased as the 'age of uncertainty' has itself grown as a metaphor for a lack of confidence about the international security environment. The shift in the balance of power in the international system away from unipolarity (probably) towards multipolarity (possibly) continues and may well lead to the relative decline of the United States as the world's predominant great power. Whether one is prepared to accept the Russian and Chinese narrative of this imminent transition in power, influence and wealth from the West to the East is a moot point. The failed state-building projects in Afghanistan and Iraq proved that not only were the Middle Eastern and South-West Asian regions inimical to Western attempts to intravenously introduce liberal democracy into their body politic, but also that even strong states could no longer bend their non-state opponents to their will, or, for that matter, defeat them as decisively as they wished. What the decline in Western dominance in the international system has illustrated, above all, is that the character of war may well be changing but its fundamental nature remains the same. Interest, passion and chance play a huge role in driving

forward strategic choices as much today as they did three millennia ago. Of course there are many people who harbour the
comforting belief that war will simply go out of fashion; that it
will become obsolete. This is a noble position to take. However,
it is also lost in a moral maze that bears little resemblance to the
empirical evidence provided by the historical record.

From the 'golden age of strategy' at the height of the Cold War,
civilian strategists have performed important functions for governments in the business of national security and defence planning.
They have been derided by some critics for their close symbiotic
relationship with the practitioners of strategy. However, while the
apron strings might well stretch further than those critics allow
into realms of business and international organisations, there
nonetheless remains a keenness by states to think the unthinkable.
As long as this remains the case, there will be a necessity for strategists to say the unsayable in challenging group think and half-life
notions of 'loyal contrarianism'.

As *Strategy in War and Peace* has made clear from the outset, one of the most important skills that strategic thinkers must
covet is the ability to draw on strategic history as a way to aid our
comprehension of future challenges. Because history permits us
an insight into previous strategic events, episodes, and processes,
students of strategy should also, ultimately, be students of history.
There may be very few strategies that have not been utilised in the
past; however, there is an urgent need for historians to ensure strategists are well aware of how advances in scholarship can improve
our understanding of complex social, political, economic and military phenomena. As Professor Gray has so illuminatingly put it,
'What has happened is that we are ever revisiting a stable core of
ideas and pressing them in terms comfortable for our times and
circumstances'. In reality, those who 'till the field of strategy for
the purpose of producing a healthy crop of general theory, must
always plough, and plough again, the same field'.[2] If we accept this
challenge, then we might well be in a better position to rise to the
interconnected challenge of facing the future international security
environment with confidence.

Notes

Preface

1. Bernard Brodie, *Strategy in the Missile Age* (Princeton, NJ: Princeton University Press, 1959), p. 386.
2. Ibid. p. 386.
3. Baron Antoine-Henri de Jomini, *The Art of War* (London: Greenhill Books, [1862] 1992), p. 337.
4. Captain A. T. Mahan, *The Influence of Sea Power upon History, 1660–1783* (London: Sampson Low, Marston, Searle and Rivington, 1889), p. 7.
5. Basil Liddell Hart, *Strategy: The Indirect Approach* (London: Faber and Faber, 1941), p. 369.
6. J. C. Wylie, *Military Strategy: A General Theory of Power Control* (Annapolis, MD: Naval Institute Press, [1967] 2014), p. 12.
7. Ibid. p. 13.
8. Pioneered by political scientist John J. Mearsheimer, in his book *The Tragedy of Great Power Politics*, updated edition (New York: W. W. Norton, 2014), 'offensive realism' suggests that 'the basic structure of the international system forces states concerned about their security to compete with each other for power. The ultimate goal of every great power is to maximize its share of world power and eventually to dominate the system' (p. 363). In maximising this power, states rely upon grand strategies by which to mobilise the vast resources at their disposal.

Introduction

1. Steven Pinker, *The Better Angels of Our Nature: The Decline of Violence in History and its Causes* (London: Allen Lane, 2011); Ian

Morris, *War – What is it Good For? The Role of Conflict in Civilisation, from Primates to Robots* (London: Profile Books, 2014). For an alternative view, see John Gray, 'Steven Pinker is wrong about violence and war', *The Guardian*, 13 March 2015, available at <http://www.theguardian.com/books/2015/mar/13/john-gray-steven-pinker-wrong-violence-war-declining> (last accessed 15 March 2015). See the reply by Pinker, 'Guess what? More people are living at peace now. Just look at the numbers', *The Guardian*, 20 March 2015, available at <http://www.theguardian.com/commentisfree/2015/mar/20/wars-john-gray-conflict-peace> (last accessed 25 July 2016). For a more up-to-date analysis see data contained in IISS, *Armed Conflict Survey 2015* (Abingdon: Routledge, 2015).

2. See, for instance, *The United States National Security Strategy* (Washington, DC: The White House, 2015), available at <https://www.whitehouse.gov/sites/default/files/docs/2015_national_security_strategy.pdf> (last accessed 14 July 2015), and Ministry of Foreign Affairs, *Concept of the Foreign Policy of the Russian Federation* (12 February 2013), available at <http://archive.mid.ru//brp_4.nsf/0/76389FEC168189ED44257B2E0039B16D> (last accessed 14 July 2015).

3. The involvement of civilian strategists was by no means uncontroversial. Professor John Baylis made the case that while it may have been morally repugnant, the strategy of nuclear deterrence was nevertheless justifiable: 'Nuclear deterrence therefore is acceptable in moral terms as long as one intends (in private at least) never to use such weapons in practice and as long as they are never used as a result of one's strategy.' John Baylis, 'How valid are the criticisms of nuclear deterrence', in Ken Booth and John Baylis, *Britain, NATO and Nuclear Weapons: Alternative Defence versus Alliance Reform* (Basingstoke: Macmillan, 1989), p. 250.

4. The first president of the Russian Federation, Boris Yeltsin, accused NATO of 'sowing the seeds of mistrust' and warned that Europe was in danger of plunging into a 'Cold Peace'. Elaine Sciolino, 'Yeltsin says NATO is trying to split the continent again', *New York Times*, 6 December 1994.

5. Kenneth N. Waltz, 'The Spread of Nuclear Weapons: More May be Better', *Adelphi Papers*, 1981, 21: 171, p. 386.

6. Joseph S. Nye, *Is the American Century Over?* (Cambridge: Polity, 2015), p. 94.

7. Lawrence Freedman, *Strategy: A History* (Oxford: Oxford University Press, 2013), p. 512.

8. Ibid. p. 509.
9. Lawrence Freedman, 'Does Strategy Studies have a future?', in John Baylis, James J. Wirtz and Colin S. Gray, *Strategy in the Contemporary World*, 4th edn (Oxford: Oxford University Press, 2013), p. 382.
10. Ibid. p. 389.
11. Carl von Clausewitz, *On War*, translated and edited by Michael Howard and Peter Paret (Princeton, NJ: Princeton University Press, 1976), p. 260.
12. Colin S. Gray, *Strategy and History: Essays on Theory and Practice* (Abingdon: Routledge, 2006), p. 2.
13. Basil H. Liddell Hart, *Strategy: The Indirect Approach* (London: Faber, 1945), p. 13.
14. A state's 'soft power' assets include three key ingredients, according to political scientist Joseph S. Nye Jnr – its culture, its political values and its foreign policies. See his *Soft Power: The Means to Success in World Politics* (New York: PublicAffairs, 2004), p. 11.
15. Paul Kennedy, *Grand Strategies in War and Peace* (London: Yale University Press, 1991), p. 5.
16. Dwight D. Eisenhower, *The Whitehouse Years: Waging Peace, 1956–1961* (London: Heinemann, 1966), p. 621.
17. Ibid. p. 622.
18. Colin Powell, *My American Journey* (London: Robert Beard Books, 1995).
19. Hew Strachan, *The Direction of War: Contemporary Strategy in Historical Perspective* (Cambridge: Cambridge University Press, 2013), p. 19.
20. Robert D. Kaplan, 'The coming anarchy', *The Atlantic*, February 1994, available at <http://www.theatlantic.com/magazine/archive/1994/02/the-coming-anarchy/304670/> (last accessed 14 July 2015).
21. Samuel P. Huntington, *The Clash of Civilizations and the Remaking of World Order* (London: Simon and Schuster, 1996), p. 29.
22. Francis Fukuyama, 'History and September 11', in Ken Booth and Tim Dunne (eds), *Worlds in Collision: Terror and the Future of Global Order* (Basingstoke: Palgrave Macmillan, 2002), p. 34.
23. George W. Bush, State of the Union Address, 29 January 2002, available at <http://georgewbush-whitehouse.archives.gov/news/releases/2002/01/20020129-11.html> (last accessed 13 June 2015).
24, Stephen Biddle and Peter D. Feaver, 'Assessing strategic choices in the war on terror', in James Burk (ed.), *How 9/11 Changed our Ways of War* (Stanford, CA: Stanford University Press, 2013), p. 30.
25. Ibid. p. 48.

26. Caspar W. Weinberger, 'The Uses of Military Force', remarks prepared for delivery by the Secretary of Defense , National Press Club, Washington DC, 28 November 1984, available at <http://www.pbs.org/wgbh/pages/frontline/shows/military/force/weinberger.html> (last accessed 10 June 2015).
27. Sun Tzu, *The Art of War*, translated and with an introduction by Samuel B. Griffith (Oxford: Oxford University Press, 1963), p. 77.
28. Strachan, *The Direction of War*, p. 12.
29. For more on this point see World Bank, *World Development Report 2011: Conflict, Security, and Development* (Washington, DC: World Bank, 2011).
30. John Mackinlay, *The Insurgent Archipelago* (London: Hurst, 2009), pp. 23–5.
31. Mary Kaldor, *New and Old Wars: Organized Violence in a Global Era*, 2nd edn (Cambridge: Polity, 2006).
32. Hew Strachan, 'Strategy and the limitation of war', *Survival*, 2008, 50: 1 (February–March), p. 32.
33. Liddell Hart, *Strategy*, p. 351.
34. Clausewitz, *On War*, p. 178.
35. So far the only empirically based study of this uprising against the Taliban is Howard Gambrill Clark, 'Lions of Marjah', unpublished PhD thesis, King's College London, 2014.
36. Freedman, 'Does Strategy Studies have a future?', p. 386.

Chapter I

1. Peter Paret, *Clausewitz and the State: The Man, His Theories and His Times* (Princeton, NJ: Princeton University Press, 2007).
2. Basil H. Liddell Hart, *Strategy: The Indirect Approach* (London: Faber, [1932] 1945), p. 351.
3. Hew Strachan, *The Direction of War: Contemporary Strategy in Historical Perspective* (Cambridge: Cambridge University Press, 2013), p. 63.
4. Beatrice Heuser, *Reading Clausewitz* (London: Pimlico, 2002), p. 194. Emphasis in original.
5. Thomas Waldman, 'Politics and war: Clausewitz's paradoxical equation', *Parameters*, 40: 3, Autumn 2010, p. 9.
6. Colin S. Gray, 'War – continuity in change, and change in continuity', *Parameters*, 40: Summer 2010, p. 9.

7. Stanley Hoffman, *The State of War: Essays on the Theory and Practice of International Politics* (London: Pall Mall Press, 1965), p. 135.
8. Paul Kennedy, *The Rise and Fall of the Great Powers: Economic Change and Military Conflict from 1500 to 2000* (London: Fontana Press, 1988), p. 390.
9. H. P. Willmott, *The Great Crusade: A New Complete History of the Second World War* (London: Pimlico, 1989), p. 167.
10. Tim Bean argues that the Japanese attack on Pearl Harbor was 'probably unnecessary, and it was definitely counter-productive ... [T]he operation was a disaster because it stirred up intense anger in the American population: a far more lethal force than five obsolescent battleships.' Tim Bean, 'Naval warfare in the Pacific, 1941–5', in Simon Trew and Gary Sheffield (eds), *100 Years of Conflict, 1900–2000* (Stroud: Sutton Publishing Limited, 2000), p. 194.
11. Carl von Clausewitz, *On War*, edited and translated by M. Howard and P. Paret (Princeton, NJ: Princeton University Press, 1976), p. 605.
12. Aleksandr A. Svechin, *Strategy*, edited by Kent D. Lee (Minneapolis, MN: East View Publications, [1927] 1991), p. 69.
13. Professor Hervé Couteau-Bégarie, quoting Jacques Laurent, 'Un outil pour la pensée militaire soviétique', *Stratégique*, 23: 1984–3, p. 46, in Hervé,Couteau-Bégarie, *Traité de Stratégie* (Paris: Economica, 2006), p. 29. I am indebted to Lieutenant Colonel (Retired) Peter McCutcheon MBE for translating this extract from the original French language source.
14. Sudanese Armed Forces definition of 'Strategy' translated by the author at the Higher Military Academy, Khartoum, December 2014.
15. MoD, *British Defence Doctrine*, 5th edn (Swindon: DCDC, November 2014), pp. 7–8.
16. Hoffman, *The State of War*, p. 262.
17. Kennedy, *The Rise and Fall of the Great Powers*, p. 695.
18. Michael Howard, *The Invention of Peace: Reflections on War and International Order* (London: Profile Books, 2000), p. 102.
19. Stephen Biddle, 'Strategy in war', *PS, Political Science and Politics*, 40: 3, July 2007, pp. 461–6.
20. Liddell Hart, *Strategy*, p. 336.
21. Colin Gray, *The Strategy Bridge: Theory for Practice* (Oxford: Oxford University Press, 2010), p. 18.
22. Frank Ledwidge, *Losing Small Wars: British Military Failure in Iraq and Afghanistan* (London: Yale University Press, 2011), p. 73.
23. General Stanley McChrystal, *My Share of the Task: A Memoir* (London: Portfolio, 2013), p. 295.

24. Paddy Griffith, *Forward into Battle: Fighting Tactics from Waterloo to the Near Future* (Swindon: Crowood Press, [1981] 1990), p. 166.
25. 'J. Robert Oppenheimer, Atom Bomb Pioneer, Dies', obituary, *New York Times*, 19 February 1967. Available at <http://www.nytimes.com/learning/general/onthisday/bday/0422.html> (last accessed 17 June 2015).
26. Lawrence Freedman, *Strategy: A History* (New York: Oxford University Press, 2013), p. 147.
27. Hoffman, *The State of War*, p. 267.
28. Herman Kahn, *On Escalation: Metaphors and Scenarios* (London: Pall Mall Press, 1965), p. 12.
29. Ibid. p. 13.
30. Ibid. p. 231.
31. See John Baylis and James Wirtz, 'Introduction', in John Baylis, James J. Wirtz and Colin S. Gray (eds), *Strategy in the Contemporary World: An Introduction to Strategic Studies*, 3rd edn (Oxford: Oxford University Press, 2010).
32. Michael Cox, 'Hans J. Morgenthau, Realism, and the rise and fall of the Cold War', in Michael C. Williams, *Realism Reconsidered: The Legacy of Hans Morgenthau in International Relations* (Oxford: Oxford University Press, 2007), p. 186.
33. Hans J. Morgenthau, *Politics Among Nations: The Struggle for Power and Peace*, brief edition, edited by Kenneth W. Thompson (Boston, MA: McGraw-Hill, [1948] 1993), p. 14.
34. Cox, 'Morgenthau', p. 184.
35. Hans. J. Morgenthau, 'To intervene or not to intervene', *Foreign Affairs*, 45: 1–4, October 1966–July 1967, p. 425.
36. Hans J. Morgenthau, 'U.S. misadventure in Vietnam', *Current History*, 88: 534, January 1989, p. 32.
37. For more on this point see Douglas B. Klusmeyer, 'Morgenthau and Republicanism', *International Relations*, 24: 4, 2010, p. 407.
38. Morgenthau, 'To intervene or not to intervene', p. 430.
39. John J. Mearsheimer, *The Tragedy of Great Power Politics*, updated edn (New York: W. W. Norton, 2014) p. 19.
40. Morgenthau, 'To intervene or not to intervene', p. 429.
41. Morgenthau, *Politics Among Nations*, pp. 159–60; Morgenthau, 'To intervene or not to intervene', p. 436.
42. Morgenthau, *Politics Among Nations*, p. 159.
43. Ibid. p. 80.
44. Mearsheimer, *The Tragedy of Great Power Politics*, p. 419.

45. Kenneth N. Waltz, *Theory of International Politics* (New York: McGraw-Hill, 1979), p. 65.
46. Margot Light, *The Soviet Theory of International Relations* (Brighton: Wheatsheaf Books, 1988), p. 9.
47. Ibid. p. 213.
48. Heuser, *Reading Clausewitz*, p. 144.
49. Cyril Falls, *Ordeal by Battle* (London: Methuen, 1943), p. 67.
50. J. C. Wylie, *Military Strategy: A General Theory of Power Control* (Annapolis, MD: Naval Institute Press, [1967] 2014), p. 31.
51. Mary Kaldor, *New and Old Wars: Organised Violence in a Global Era*, 2nd edn (Cambridge: Polity, 2006).
52. Mary Kaldor, 'In defence of new wars', *Stability*, 2: 1, 2013, pp. 1–16.
53. Clausewitz, *On War*, p. 77.
54. Major General J. F. C. Fuller, *War and Western Civilisation, 1832–1932: A Study of War as a Political Instrument and the Expression of Mass Democracy* (London: Duckworth, 1932), p. 252.
55. Paul Collier, *The Bottom Billion: Why the Poorest Countries are Failing and What Can be Done About it* (Oxford: Oxford University Press, 2008).
56. Martin Van Creveld, *The Transformation of War: The Most Radical Reinterpretation of Armed Conflict since Clausewitz* (New York: Free Press, 1991).
57. Christopher Daase, 'Clausewitz and small wars', in Hew Strachan and Andreas Herberg-Rothe (eds), *Clausewitz in the Twenty-First Century* (Oxford: Oxford University Press, 2007), p. 183.
58. General Sir Rupert Smith, *The Utility of Force: The Art of War in the Modern World* (London: Penguin, 2005), p. 181.
59. MoD, *Strategic Trends Programme: Global Strategic Trends – Out to 2040*, 4th edn (Shrivenham: DCDC, 2010), p. 70.
60. Michael Rose, 'Afghanistan: some recent observations', *RUSI Journal*, 153: 5, October 2008, p. 9.
61. General Sir Richard Dannatt, *The Military Today as a Force for Good – A Contradiction in Terms?* Available at <http://www.progressonline.org.uk/magazine/article.asp?a=3058> (last accessed 12 June 2009).
62. David Kilcullen, *The Accidental Guerrilla: Fighting Small Wars Amidst a Big One* (London: Hurst and Company, 2009), p. 301.
63. Ibid. p. 292.
64. Frank Hoffman, 'Hybrid warfare and challenges', *Joint Force Quarterly*, 52, First Quarter 2009, p. 37. Available at <http://www.

potomacinstitute.org/media/mediaclips/2009/Hoffman_JFQ_109. pdf> (last accessed 4 June 2009).

65. Kilcullen, *The Accidental Guerrilla*, p. 292.
66. Wylie, *Military Strategy*, p. 14.
67. Qiao Liang and Wang Xiangsui, *Unrestricted Warfare* (Beijing: PLA Literature and Arts Publishing House, February 1999). Available at <http://www.terrorism.com/documents/unrestricted.pdf> (last accessed 22 June 2015).
68. Major-General Peng Guang Qian, 'The twenty-first century war: Chinese perspectives', in Julian Lindley-French and Yves Boyer (eds), *The Oxford Handbook of War* (Oxford: Oxford University Press, 2012), p. 300.
69. PRC, *Defense White Paper 2014*. Available at <http://eng.mod.gov. cn/Database/WhitePapers/2015-05/26/content_4586711.htm> (last accessed 15 June 2015).
70. Mearsheimer, *The Tragedy of Great Power Politics*, p. 361.
71. World Bank, *World Development Report 2011* (Washington, DC: World Bank, 2011), p. 52.
72. Mao Tse-Tung, *Selected Military Writings of Mao Tse-Tung* (Peking: Foreign Languages Press, 1963), p. 218.
73. Vladimir Putin, *Presidential Address to the Federal Assembly*, 4 December 2014. Available at <http://en.kremlin.ru/events/president/ transcripts/statements/47173> (last accessed 10 June 2015).
74. Russian Ministry of Foreign Affairs, *The Foreign Policy Concept of the Russian Federation*, 12 February 2013. Available at <http:// archive.mid.ru//brp_4.nsf/0/76389FEC168189ED44257B2E0039B 16D> (last accessed 21 November 2015).
75. Richard Sakwa, 'The deep roots of the Ukraine crisis', *The Nation*, 15 April 2015. Available at <http://www.thenation.com/article/204449/ deep-roots-ukraine-crisis> (last accessed 12 June 2015).
76. Mark Urban, *The Edge: Is the Military Dominance of the West Coming to an End?* (London: Little, Brown, 2015), p. 51.
77. Thomas C. Schelling, *The Strategy of Conflict* (Cambridge, MA: Harvard University Press, [1960] 1980), p. 5.
78. Colin S. Gray, *Another Bloody Century: Future Warfare* (London: Weidenfeld and Nicolson, 2005), p. 248.
79. Hew Strachan, 'The lost meaning of strategy', *Survival*, 47: 3, 2005, p. 34.
80. Hew Strachan, 'Strategy and war', in Julian Lindley-French and Yves Boyer (eds), *The Oxford Handbook of War* (Oxford: Oxford University Press, 2012), p. 30.
81. Falls, *Ordeal by Battle*, p. 78.

Chapter 2

1. Thucydides, *History of the Peloponnesian War* (London: Penguin, 1972), p. 122.
2. Machiavelli, Niccolò, *The Prince*, translated with an introduction by George Bull (London: Penguin Books, 1961), p. 48.
3. Carl von Clausewitz, *On War*, edited and translated by M. Howard and P. Paret (Princeton, NJ: Princeton University Press, [1832] 1976), p. 178.
4. Ibid. p. 178.
5. Paul Kennedy, 'American grand strategy, today and tomorrow: learning from the European experience', in Paul Kennedy (ed.), *Grand Strategies in War and Peace* (New Haven, CT: Yale University Press, 1991), p. 168.
6. Sebastian Junger, *War* (London: Fourth Estate, 2010), p. 239.
7. General Stanley McChrystal, *My Share of the Task: A Memoir* (London: Portfolio, 2013), p. 310.
8. Clausewitz, *On War*, p. 142.
9. Ibid. p. 143.
10. Basil Liddell Hart, *Strategy: Thoughts on War* (Staplehurst: Spellmount, [1944] 1999), p. 336.
11. Notes from General Wall's lecture on 'Values Based Leadership', 7 May 2014.
12. Christopher L. Elliott, *High Command: British Military Leadership in the Iraq and Afghanistan Wars* (London: C. Hurst and Co., 2015), p. 193.
13. Eliot A. Cohen, *Supreme Command: Soldiers, Statesmen, and Leadership in Wartime* (New York: Free Press, 2002), p. 99.
14. Ibid. p. 100.
15. Ibid. p. 132.
16. Julian Corbett, *Some Principles of Maritime Strategy* (London: Longmans, Green and Co., [1911] 1938), p. 4.
17. Peter Stothard, *30 Days: A Month at the Heart of Blair's War* (London: HarperCollins, 2003), p. 186.
18. Iraq Inquiry, Oral Evidence of Rt Hon General the Lord Walker of Aldringham, 1 February 2010, pp. 4–5. Available at <http://www.iraq-inquiry.org.uk/media/45534/100201-walker-final.pdf> (last accessed 10 March 2014).
19. Ibid.
20. Basil Liddell Hart, *Strategy: Thoughts on War* (Staplehurst: Spellmount, [1944] 1999), p. 152.

21. Thucydides, *History of the Peloponnesian War*, p. 404.
22. Donald Kagan, *The Peloponnesian War: Athens and Sparta in Savage Conflict, 431–404* BC (London: HarperCollins, 2003), p. 249.
23. Antony Beevor, *The Second World War* (London: Weidenfeld and Nicolson, 2012), p. 634.
24. LHCMA, Alanbrooke Papers, 6/3/1, Montgomery to Alanbrooke, 17 November 1944.
25. LHCMA, Alanbrooke Papers, 6/3/1, Montgomery to Alanbrooke, 17 November 1944.
26. LHCMA, Alanbrooke, 6/3/1, Alanbrooke to Montgomery, 24 November 1944.
27. LHCMA, Alanbrooke, 6/3/1, Alanbrooke to Montgomery, 24 November 1944.
28. Beevor, *The Second World War*, p. 655.
29. LHCMA, Alanbrooke, 6/3/1, Montgomery to Alanbrooke, 29 November 1944.
30. Beevor, *The Second World War*, p. 634.
31. LHCMA, Alanbrooke, 6/3/1, Prime Minister's Personal Minute to CIGS, 2 December 1944.
32. LHCMA, Alanbrooke, 6/3/1, Strategy in North West Europe, 18 December 1944.
33. LHCMA, Alanbrooke, 6/3/2, Eisenhower to Montgomery, 1 December 1944.
34. LHCMA, Deane-Drummond Papers, Op Vector, Orders, dated 19 November 1958.
35. LHCMA, Deane-Drummond Papers, letter from John Watts to Deane-Drummond, 2 December 1958.
36. LHCMA, Deane-Drummond Papers, signal from D Squadron SAS Muscat to 22 SAS Regiment Malaya, dated 9 December 1958.
37. LHCMA, Deane-Drummond Papers, letter from John Watts to Deane-Drummond, 9 December 1958.
38. LHCMA, Deane-Drummond Papers, Deane-Drummond to Hamilton, dated 30 October 1958.
39. Peter McCutcheon, 'Breaking the camel's back: the departure from the philosophy of cultured force – the French counterinsurgency campaign in Algeria, 1954–62', in Gregory Fremont-Barnes (ed.), *A History of Counterinsurgency: Volume 1: From South Africa to Algeria, 1900 to 1954* (Santa Barbara, CA: Praeger, 2015), p. 212.
40. Ibid. p. 212.
41. Ibid. p. 224.

42. TNA, DEFE 13/838, Lieutenant-General Sir Frank King to Merlyn Rees MP, 16 April 1974.
43. Bodleian Library Special Collection, University of Oxford (BLSC), Harold Wilson Papers, MS. Wilson, C. 845, Albert Murray to Mrs. D. Bickett [sic], 16 May 1974.
44. House of Commons Debates (Hansard), Vol. 967, Col. 1206, 24 May 1979.
45. Etain Tannam, 'Explaining British-Irish cooperation', *Review of International Studies*, 37: 2011, p. 1199.
46. Bruce Hoffman, 'Al-Qaeda's uncertain future', *Studies in Conflict and Terrorism*, 36: 8, 2013, pp. 635–53, p. 639.
47. *The Guardian*, 11 June 2014.

Chapter 3

1. Field Marshal Lord Alanbrooke, 'Diary Entry for 19 August 1943', in Alex Danchev and Dan Todman (eds), *War Diaries, 1939–1945: Field Marshal Lord Alanbrooke* (London: Weidenfeld and Nicholson: 2001), p. 444.
2. Richard Overy, *Why the Allies Won* (London: Pimlico, 1996), p. 265.
3. Colin Gray, *The Strategy Bridge: Theory for Practice* (Oxford: Oxford University Press, 2010).
4. Samuel P. Huntingdon, *The Soldier and the State: The Theory and Politics of Civil-Military Relations* (Cambridge, MA: Harvard University Press, 1957), pp. 71–2.
5. Gordon A. Craig, 'The political leader as strategist', in Peter Paret (ed.), *Makers of Modern Strategy: From Machiavelli to the Nuclear Age* (Oxford: Oxford University Press, 1986), p. 482.
6. Leon Trotsky, 'Marxism and military knowledge, 8 May 1922', in Leon Trotsky, *Military Writings* (New York: Pathfinder Press, 1971), p. 141.
7. Leon Trotsky, 'The Military Academy: Speech delivered on 8 November 1918', in Leon Trotsky, *The Military Writings and Speeches of Leon Trotsky* (London: Pathfinder Press, 1969), p. 211.
8. Trotsky, 'Our current basic military tasks, 1 April 1922', in Trotsky, *Military Writings*, p. 89.
9. Trotsky, 'Marxism and military knowledge, 8 May 1922', in Trotsky, *Military Writings*, p. 140.

10. Isaac Deutscher, *The Prophet Armed: Trotsky, 1879–1921* (London: Verso, 1953), p. 401.
11. Trotsky, 'The Military Academy: Speech delivered on 8 November 1918', in Trotsky, *Military Writings*, p. 216.
12. Clausewitz, Carl von, *On War*, edited and translated by M. Howard and P. Paret (Princeton, NJ: Princeton University Press, 1976), p. 77.
13. General Sir Rupert Smith, *The Utility of Force: The Art of War in the Modern World* (London: Penguin, 2006), p. 58.
14. Ibid. p. 169.
15. Clausewitz, *On War*, p. 608.
16. Ibid. p. 59.
17. Ibid. p. 254.
18. Ibid. p. 149.
19. Deutscher, *The Prophet Armed*, p. 288.
20. Thatcher, Ian D. *Leon Trotsky and World War One, August 1914-February 1917* (Basingstoke: Palgrave Macmillan, 2000), p. 210.
21. Deutscher, *The Prophet Armed*, p. 400.
22. Leon Trotsky, 'The military specialists and the Red Army, 31 December 1918', in Leon Trotsky, *The Military Writings and Speeches of Leon Trotsky: How the Revolution Armed, Vol. 1: The Year 1918*, translated and annotated by Brian Pearce (London: New Park Publications, 1979), p. 200.
23. Trotsky, 'The military specialists and the Red Army: The non-commissioned officers', in Trotsky, *Military Writings*, p. 230.
24. Ibid. pp. 230–1.
25. Karl Radek, 'The Organizer of Victory', in Leon Trotsky, *Military Writings* (New York: Pathfinder Press, 1971), p. 22.
26. Leon Trotsky, *My Life: The Rise and Fall of a Dictator* (London: Thornton Butterworth Limited, 1930), p. 385.
27. David M. Glantz and Jonathan M. House, *When Titans Clashed: How the Red Army Stopped Hitler* (Kansas: University Press of Kansas), p. 6.
28. Isaac Deutscher, *The Prophet Armed: Trotsky: 1879–1921* (London: Verso, 2003), p. 336.
29. Francesco Benvenuti, *The Bolsheviks and the Red Army, 1918–1922* (Cambridge: Cambridge University Press, 1988), p. 218.
30. Peter S. Wells, *The Battle that Stopped Rome: Emperor Augustus, Arminius, and the Slaughter of the Legions in the Teutoburg Forest* (New York: W. W. Norton, 2003), p. 216.
31. *The Times*, 20 May 1935. Lawrence died on 19 May 1935, one day prior to Liddell Hart's obituary.

32. Frank Kitson, *Low Intensity Operations: Subversion, Insurgency, Peace-keeping* (London: Faber and Faber, 1971), p. 67.
33. David Galula, *Counter-insurgency Warfare: Theory and Practice* (London: Praeger Security International, [1964] 2006), p. 62.
34. Ibid. p. 63.
35. Guenter Lewy, *America in Vietnam* (New York: Oxford University Press, 1978), p. 418.
36. AWM, PR84/178, Citation by Province Chief to General Jackson, dated 3 January 1967.
37. AWM 347, Directorate of Military Intelligence, 'Report on visit by CGS to Vietnam and Cambodia – 23/30 November 70', 8 December 1970.
38. Lewy, *America in Vietnam*, pp. 165–6.
39. For more on this point see Jeffrey Race, *War Comes to Long An: Revolutionary Conflict in a Vietnamese Village*, updated and expanded (Oakland, CA: University of California Press, [1972] 2010).
40. AWM, PR86/033, Brigadier P. Davies, Australian Military Forces HQ 1 AFT, Nui Dat, September 1967.
41. AWM 347, Directorate of Military Intelligence, 'Report on visit by CGS to Vietnam and Cambodia – 23/30 November 70', 8 December 1970.
42. AWM, PR86/033, Lecture of Australian Army Staff College Intelligence in Vietnam by Major B. W. Parnell – Australian Intelligence Corps.
43. One of the most significant books to be published on the birth of the Omani state is James Worrall, *Statebuilding and Counterinsurgency in Oman: Political, Military and Diplomatic Relations at the End of Empire* (London: I. B. Tauris, 2014), pp. 103–5.
44. St Antony's College, Oxford, Middle East Centre Archive (hereafter MEC), GB165-0327, John Graham Collection, Box 2/1, Secret: Appreciation of the Dhofar Situation, Feb '71.
45. MEC, GB165-0327, John Graham Collection, Box 2/1, Dhofar Background by Colonel M. G. Harvey, Commander Dhofar, HQ Salalah, 27 June 1971.
46. MEC, GB165-0327, John Graham Collection, Box 1/3, J. D. C. Graham, 'A Paper on the Persian Gulf: Security after British withdrawal' (dated 1973), p. 12.
47. MEC, GB165-0327, John Graham Collection, Box 1/3, The Persian Gulf: Security after British withdrawal, 1973, p. 10.
48. David Kilcullen, *The Accidental Guerrilla: Fighting a Big War amidst Small Wars* (London: Hurst and Company, 2009), p. 297.
49. DoD, *Field Manual 3-24*, p. 54.

50. Gian Gentile, 'The conceit of American counter-insurgency', in Celeste Ward Gventer, David Martin Jones and M. L. R. Smith (eds), *The New Counter-insurgency Era in Critical Perspective* (Basingstoke: Palgrave Macmillan, 2014), pp. 240–56.
51. Jason Burke, *The New Threat from Islamic Militancy* (London: Bodley Head, 2015), p. 81.
52. Gilles Kepel, *Jihad: The Trail of Political Islam* (London: I. B. Tauris, 2003), p. 303.
53. Christopher Hitchens, 'Londonistan calling', *Vanity Fair*, June 2007. Available at <http://www.vanityfair.com/news/2007/06/hitchens 200706> (last accessed 20 June 2015).
54. Cabinet Office, *Tackling Extremism in the UK: Report from the Prime Minister's Task Force on Tackling Radicalisation and Extremism* (London: Cabinet Office, 2013), p. 1. Available at <https:// www.gov.uk/government/uploads/system/uploads/attachment_data/ file/263181/ETF_FINAL.pdf> (last accessed 20 November 2015).
55. Home Office, *Proscribed Terrorist Organisations* (London: Home Office, 2014), p. 11. Available at <https://www.gov.uk/government/ uploads/system/uploads/attachment_data/file/472956/Proscription-update-20151030.pdf (last accessed 20 November 2015).
56. Christoph Reuter, 'The terror strategist: secret files reveal the structure of Islamic State, *Der Spiegel*, 18 April 2015. Available at <http://www.spiegel.de/international/world/islamic-state-files-show-structure-of-islamist-terror-group-a-1029274.html (last accessed 2 September 2015).
57. Interview with a senior PSNI counter-terrorism officer, 2013.
58. Clausewitz, *On War*, p. 608.
59. Sun Tzu, *The Art of War*, translated and with an introduction by Samuel B. Griffith (Oxford: Oxford University Press, 1963), p. 83.

Chapter 4

1. National Archives (Kew, London), AIR40/1494, Extracts from an Air Ministry Directorate of Intelligence report on 'Allied Air Attacks and German Morale', dated 2 April 1944.
2. Colin S. Gray, 'Moral advantage, strategic advantage?', *Journal of Strategic Studies*, 33: 3, 2010, p. 335.
3. UN, *Report of the High-level Panel on Threats, Challenges and Change* (New York: UN, 2004), p. 56.

4. Carl von Clausewitz, *On War* (Princeton, NJ: Princeton University Press, 1976), p. 87.
5. Carsten Stahn, '"Jus ad bellum", "jus in bello" . . . "jus post bellum"? Rethinking the conception of the law of armed force', *European Journal of International Law*, 17: 5, 2007, p. 927.
6. Richard Glover, 'English warfare in 1066', *English Historical Review*, 67: 262, January 1952, p. 15.
7. Bernard Brodie, *War and Politics* (London: Cassell, 1973), p. 226.
8. Clausewitz, *On War*, p. 260.
9. White House, *US National Security Strategy* (Washington DC: The White House, September 2002), p. 15.
10. Thucydides, *History of the Peloponnesian War* (London: Penguin, [1954] 1972), p. 405.
11. Gray, 'Moral advantage, strategic advantage?', p. 338.
12. Thucydides, *History of the Peloponnesian War*, p. 392.
13. Sigmund Freud, 'Why War? An Exchange of Letters between Albert Einstein and Sigmund Freud', Letter from Freud to Einstein, dated September 1932. Available at <http://www.freud.org.uk/file-uploads/files/WHY%20WAR.pdf> (last accessed 20 June 2015).
14. Erich Fromm, *The Anatomy of Human Destructiveness* (London: Penguin, 1973), p. 25.
15. Stanley Milgram, *Obedience to Authority: An Experimental View* (London: Pinter and Martin, 2013).
16. Judith Butler, *Precarious Life: The Powers of Mourning and Violence* (London: Verso, 2004), p. 150.
17. Ibid. p. 29.
18. Michael Waltzer, *Just and Unjust Wars: A Moral Argument with Historical Illustrations* (New York: Basic Books, [1977] 2000), pp. 32–3.
19. Leslie C. Green, *The Contemporary Law of Armed Conflict*, 3rd edn (Manchester: Manchester University Press, 2008), p. 49.
20. Ian Speller and Christopher Tuck, 'Introduction', in David Jordan et al., *Understanding Modern Warfare* (Cambridge: Cambridge University Press, 2008), p. 1.
21. Colin S. Gray, *The Strategy Bridge: Theory for Practice* (Oxford: Oxford University Press, 2010), p. 59.
22. ICRC, *Customary International Law: Rule 145*. Available at <https://www.icrc.org/customary-ihl/eng/docs/v1_rul_rule145> (last accessed 30 June 2015).
23. Michael Ignatieff, *The Lesser Evil: Political Ethics in an Age of Terror* (Edinburgh: Edinburgh University Press, 2005), p. 144.

24. Oliver Bullough, 'Inside Chechnya: Putin's reign of terror', *New Statesman*, 29 August 2012.
25. 'Islamists in Russia', *The Economist*, 27 April 2013.
26. HRW, *Country Summary: Russia*, January 2012.
27. HRW, *Attacks on Ghouta: Analysis of Alleged Use of Chemical Weapons in Syria*. Available at <http://www.hrw.org/sites/default/files/reports/syria_cw0913_web_1.pdf> (last accessed 28 August 2016).
28. For more on the fighting see Clive Jones, *Britain and the Yemen Civil War, 1962–1965* (Brighton: Sussex Academic Press, 2004).
29. Stahn, '"Jus ad bellum", "jus in bello" . . . "jus post bellum"?', pp. 921–43.
30. Clausewitz, *On War*, p. 88.
31. Mark J. Osiel, *The End of Reciprocity: Terror, Torture and the Law of War* (Cambridge: Cambridge University Press, 2009), p. 325.
32. David Kennedy, *Of War and Law* (Princeton, NJ: Princeton University Press, 2006), p. 113.

Chapter 5

1. Raymond Aron, *On War: Atomic Weapons and Global Diplomacy* (London: Secker and Warburg, 1958), p. 56.
2. Joe Nye, *Soft Power: The Means to Success in World Politics* (New York: Public Affairs, 2005).
3. Kenneth N. Waltz, *Man, the State and War: A Theoretical Analysis* (New York: Columbia University Press, [1959] 2001), p. 160.
4. Tony Judt, *Reappraisals: Reflections on the Forgotten Twentieth Century* (London: Vintage, 2009), p. 185.
5. Major General J. F. C. Fuller, *The Conduct of War, 1789–1961* (London: Eyre and Spottiswoode, 1961), p. 256.
6. General Sir Rupert Smith, *The Utility of Force: The Art of War in the Modern World* (London: Penguin, 2005), p. 181.
7. Carl von Clausewitz, *On War* (Princeton, NJ: Princeton University Press, 1976), p. 605.
8. Baron Antoine-Henri de Jomini, *The Art of War* (London: Greenhill Books, 1992), p. 321.
9. Leon Trotsky, 'Our current basic military tasks, 1 April 1922', in Leon Trotsky, *Military Writings* (New York: Pathfinder Press, 1971), p. 90.
10. Sigmund Freud, 'Why War? An Exchange of Letters between Albert Einstein and Sigmund Freud', letter from Freud to Einstein, dated

September 1932. Available at <http://www.freud.org.uk/file-uploads/files/WHY%20WAR.pdf> (last accessed 20 June 2015).

11. Smith, *The Utility of Force*, p. 1.
12. Waltz, *Man, the State and War*, p. 238.
13. X (later unmasked as George F. Kennan), 'The sources of Soviet conduct', *Foreign Affairs*, 25: July 1947, p. 576.
14. Thomas C. Schelling, *The Strategy of Conflict* (Cambridge, MA: Harvard University Press, [1960] 1980), p. 35.
15. Hedley Bull, 'The theory of international politics, 1919–1969', in Brian Porter (ed.), *The Aberystwyth Papers: International Politics, 1919–1969* (London: Oxford University Press, 1972), p. 346.
16. Lawrence Freedman, 'The first two generations of nuclear strategists' in Peter Paret (ed.), *Makers of Modern Strategy: From Machiavelli to the Nuclear Age* (Oxford: Oxford University Press, 1986), p. 764.
17. Herman Kahn, *On Thermonuclear War* (Princeton, NJ: Princeton University Press, 1961), p. 559.
18. Patricia Lewis, 'Things will never be the same again', *World Today*, 71: 3, June and July 2015, pp. 18–19.
19. Herman Kahn, *On Escalation: Metaphors and Scenarios* (London: Pall Mall Press, 1965), p. 12.
20. Ibid. p. 13.
21. Ibid. p. 231.
22. For more on the 'special relationship' see John Dumbrell, *A Special Relationship: Anglo-American Relations in the Cold War and After*, 2nd edn (Basingstoke: Palgrave Macmillan, 2006).
23. Dean Acheson, *Power and Diplomacy: The William L. Clayton Lectures on International Economic Affairs and Foreign Policy* (Cambridge, MA: Harvard University Press, 1958), p. 40.
24. Christopher Andrew, 'Intelligence in the Cold War', in Melvyn P. Leffler and Odd Arne Westad (eds), *The Cambridge History of the Cold War: Volume II – Crises and Détente* (Cambridge: Cambridge University Press, 2010), p. 417.
25. Henry A. Kissinger, *The Necessity of Choice: Prospects of American Foreign Policy* (London: Chatto and Windus, 1960), p. 358.
26. LHCMA, General Stockwell Papers, 6/2, Letter from General Miles Dempsey to Lieutenant General Sir Evelyn Barker, 24 January 1947.
27. David Cesarini, *Major Farran's Hat: Murder, Scandal and Britain's War against Jewish Terrorism, 1945–1948* (London: Vintage, 2010).
28. Montgomery of Alamein, Viscount Bernard Law, *The Memoirs of Field-Marshal the Viscount Montgomery of Alamein, KG* (London: Collins, 1958), pp. 39–40.

29. IWM, Colonel C R W Norman Papers, 87/57/2, Letter from Richard Norman to his mother, 29 February 1948.

30. KCL LHASC, General Stockwell Papers, 6/2, 'Top Secret Communiqué from Chief of Staff Brigadier Kirkman, 29 March 1948'.

31. LHCMA, General Stockwell Papers, 6/2, 'Top Secret Communiqué from Chief of Staff Brigadier Kirkman'.

32. Cited in Aaron Edwards, *Defending the Realm? The Politics of Britain's Small Wars since 1945* (Manchester: Manchester University Press, 2012, 2014), p. 75.

33. IWM, Field Marshal Lord Harding Papers, Letter from High Commissioner Sir Henry Gurney to General Sir John Harding, 10 May 1951.

34. Cited in Edwards, *Defending the Realm?*, p. 77.

35. John Nagl, *Learning to Eat Soup with a Knife: Counterinsurgency Lessons from Malaya and Vietnam* (Chicago, IL: University of Chicago Press, 2005).

36. For more on Stockwell see Jonathan Riley, *The Life and Campaigns of General Hughie Stockwell: From Normandy through Burma to Suez* (Barnsley: Pen and Sword, 2006).

37. *The Times*, 22 October 1953.

38. TNA, CO 822/693, Personal Reports by General Sir George Erskine on the Situation in Kenya, 'Top Secret Report from General Erskine to the CIGS, Field Marshall Harding, dated 7 July 1953'.

39. For example, see the unsubstantiated conjecture informing Mark Curtis's critique of Britain's 'real intentions': 'Britain's real foreign policy and the failure of British academia', *International Relations*, 18: 3, pp. 275–87. Curtis approaches his subject matter from an antagonistic, anti-establishment perspective, which attacks the tendency amongst some academics to 'maintain British elites' standing in the world', while seemingly unconcerned with observing the scholarly protocols of referencing sources.

40. David French, 'Nasty not nice: British counter-insurgency doctrine and practice, 1945–1967', *Small Wars and Insurgencies*, 23: 4–5, 2012, p. 757.

41. IWM, Erskine Papers, Secret: Emergency Directive No. 14: Operations after Hammer, dated 6 December 1954.

42. Frank Kitson, *Bunch of Five* (London: Faber, 1977), p. 13.

43. TNA, CO 822/693, Personal Reports by General Sir George Erskine on the Situation in Kenya, 'Top Secret Report from General Erskine to the CIGS, Field Marshall Harding, dated 7 July 1953'.

44. *East Anglian Daily Times*, 24 August 1953.

45. IWM, Erskine Papers, 75/134/1, General Erskine to Lady Erskine, 3 March 1954.
46. Ibid.
47. French, 'Nasty not nice', p. 757.
48. John Lewis Gaddis, 'Toward the post-Cold War world', *Foreign Affairs*, 70: 2, Spring 1991, p. 113.
49. House of Commons Debates (Hansard), Vol. 183, Col. 979, 17 January 1991.
50. Lawrence Freedman, 'Order and disorder in the New World', *Foreign Affairs*, 71: 1, 1992, pp. 20–37.
51. Robert D. Kaplan, 'The coming anarchy', *The Atlantic*, February 1994. Available at <http://www.theatlantic.com/magazine/archive/1994/02/the-coming-anarchy/304670/> (last accessed 14 July 2015).
52. Lieutenant General Chris Brown, *Operation Telic Lessons Compendium* (London: MoD, 2011). Available at <https://www.gov.uk/government/uploads/system/uploads/attachment_data/file/16787/operation_telic_lessons_compendium.pdf> (last accessed 20 November 2015).
53. General Stanley McChrystal, *My Share of the Task: A Memoir* (London: Portfolio, 2013), p. 317.
54. Ibid. p. 321.
55. Colonel Gian Gentile, *Wrong Turn: America's Deadly Embrace of Counterinsurgency* (New York: Free Press, 2013).
56. Christopher Hitchens, *A Long Short War: The Postponed Liberation of Iraq* (New York: Plume, 2003), p. 25.

Chapter 6

1. Kenneth Waltz, *The Spread of Nuclear Weapons: More May be Better*, Adelphi Papers, no. 171 (London: International Institute for Strategic Studies, 1981), p. 384. Waltz had made the case that bipolarity enhanced the stability of the international system much earlier than this. See Kenneth Waltz, 'The stability of a bipolar world', *Daedalus*, 93: 1964, pp. 881–909. For an explanation of aspects of the structure of the international system see Martin Hollis and Steve Smith, *Explaining and Understanding International Relations* (Oxford: Clarendon Press, 1991), pp. 101–4.
2. Hedley Bull, 'The great irresponsibles? The United States, the Soviet Union, and world order', *International Journal*, 35: 3, Summer, 1980, p. 446.

3. Colin S. Gray, *Strategy and History: Essays on Theory and Practice* (Abingdon: Routledge, 2006), p. 12.
4. Captain Sir Basil Liddell Hart, *Strategy: The Indirect Approach* (London: Faber, [1932] 1945), p. 351.
5. For more on this perspective see Michael Howard, *The Invention of Peace: Reflections on War and International Order* (London: Yale University Press, 2001).
6. Carl von Clausewitz, *On War*, edited and translated by M. Howard and P. Paret (Princeton, NJ: Princeton University Press, 1976), p. 605.
7. Gordon Weiss, *The Cage: The Fight for Sri Lanka and the Last Days of the Tamil Tigers* (London: Vintage, 2011), p. 258.
8. Philip Bobbitt, *The Shield of Achilles: War, Peace and the Course of History* (London: Penguin, 2002), p. 819.
9. Ian Morris, *War: What is it Good For? The Role of Conflict in Civilisation, from Primates to Robots* (London: Profile Books, 2014), p. 391.
10. See his essay 'The strategic approach to international relations' in his book: Michael Howard, *The Causes of Wars and Other Essays* (London: Unwin Paperbacks, 1983), pp. 36–48.
11. George Santayana, *Soliloquies in England and Later Soliloquies* (London: Constable and Company, 1922), p. 103.
12. Steven Pinker, *The Better Angels of Our Nature: The Decline of Violence in History and its Causes* (London: Allen Lane, 2011), p. 671.
13. Morris, *War*, p. 333.
14. See the exchange between John Gray and Steven Pinker in *The Guardian* newspaper: John Gray, 'Steven Pinker is wrong about violence and war', *The Guardian*, 13 March 2015. Available at <http://www.theguardian.com/books/2015/mar/13/john-gray-steven-pinker-wrong-violence-war-declining> (last accessed 15 March 2015). See the reply by Pinker, 'Guess what? More people are living at peace now. Just look at the numbers', *The Guardian*, 20 March 2015. Available at <http://www.theguardian.com/commentisfree/2015/mar/20/wars-john-gray-conflict-peace> (last accessed 2 September 2016).
15. Clausewitz, *On War*, p. 227.
16. Anthony Clayton, *Defeat: When Nations Lose a War* (Ely: Melrose Books, 2010), p. 32.
17. Bull, 'The great irresponsibles?', p. 440.

18. General Van Tien Dung, *Our Great Spring Victory: An Account of the Liberation of South Vietnam* (New York: Monthly Review Press, 1977), p. 112.
19. Noam Chomsky, 'A Special Supplement: In North Vietnam', *New York Review of Books*, 13 August 1970. Available at <http://www.nybooks.com/articles/archives/1970/aug/13/a-special-supplement-in-north-vietnam/> (last accessed 22 June 2015).
20. Robert S. McNamara, *In Retrospect: The Tragedy and Lessons of Vietnam* (New York: Vintage, 1996), p. 322.
21. Machiavelli *The Art of War* (Indianapolis: Bobbs-Merrill Company, 1965), p. 124.
22. Ibid. p. 126.
23. Ibid. p. 24.
24. Field Marshal Sir William Slim, *Defeat into Victory* (London: Cassell and Company, 1956), p. 115.
25. Paul F. Diehl, *Peace Operations* (Cambridge: Polity, 2008), p. 137.
26. Christopher Bass and M. L. R. Smith, 'The dynamic of Irwin's forgotten army: a strategic understanding of the British Army's role in Northern Ireland after 1998', *Small Wars and Insurgencies*, 15: 3, 2004, pp. 1–27.
27. Frank Kitson, *Directing Operations* (London: Faber, 1989), pp. 60–1.
28. *Irish Republican Army Ceasefire Statement, 31 August 1994*. Available at <http://cain.ulst.ac.uk/events/peace/docs/ira31894.htm> (last accessed 30 October 2015).
29. Interview with Danny Morrison, 23 November 2010, cited in Aaron Edwards, 'Deterrence, coercion and brute force in asymmetric conflict: the role of the military instrument in resolving the Northern Ireland "Troubles"', *Dynamics of Asymmetric Conflict*, 4: 3, December 2011, p. 232. Morrison is the former director of publicity for Sinn Fein.
30. United Nations, *Handbook on the Peaceful Settlement of Disputes between States* (New York: United Nations, 1992). Available at <http://www.un.org/law/books/HandbookOnPSD.pdf> (last accessed 22 June 2015).
31. Ibid.
32. Roland Paris, *At War's End: Building Peace After Civil Conflict* (Cambridge: Cambridge University Press, 2004), p. 99.
33. Colin S. Gray, *Another Bloody Century: Future War* (London: Weidenfeld and Nicolson, 2005), p. 339.
34. Paris, *At War's End*, p. 19.

35. Boutros Boutros-Ghali, *An Agenda for Peace: Preventive Diplomacy, Peacemaking and Peacekeeping* (17 June 1992). Available at <http://www.unrol.org/files/A_47_277.pdf> (last accessed 21 November 2015).
36. From observations and interactions with Bangladeshi peacekeepers at BIPSOT, Bangladesh, in July/August 2012.
37. TNA, PREM 13, 1992, 'Confidential Correspondence from Secretary of State for Defence to Prime Minister, 'Renewal of the Mandate for UNFICYP', 11 March 1965.
38. TNA, PREM 13, 1992, 'Confidential Telegram from UK Mission to the UN to the Foreign Office, 18 March 1965'.
39. Mary Kaldor, *Human Security: Reflections on Globalization and Intervention* (Cambridge: Polity, 2006), p. 71.
40. David Galula, *Counter-insurgency Warfare: Theory and Practice* (London: Praeger Security International, [1964] 2006), p. 62.
41. Ibid. p. 63.
42. Peter McCutcheon, 'Breaking the camel's back: the departure from the philosophy of cultured force – the French counterinsurgency campaign in Algeria, 1954–62', in Gregory Fremont-Barnes (ed.), *A History of Counterinsurgency: Volume 1: From South Africa to Algeria, 1900 to 1954* (Santa Barbara, CA: Praeger, 2015), p. 241.

Chapter 7

1. Colin S. Gray, *The Strategy Bridge: Theory for Practice* (Oxford: Oxford University Press, 2010), p. 2.
2. Colin S. Gray and Jeannie L. Johnson, 'The practice of strategy' in John Baylis, James J. Wirtz and Colin S. Gray (eds), *Strategy in the Contemporary World: An Introduction to Strategic Studies*, 4th edn (Oxford: Oxford University Press, 2013), p. 361.
3. Eliot A. Cohen, 'Change and transformation in military affairs', *Journal of Strategic Studies*, 27: 3, September 2004, p. 395.
4. Steven Metz, *Iraq and the Evolution of American Strategy* (Washington DC: Potomac Books, 2008), p. 160.
5. Hew Strachan, *The Direction of War: Contemporary Strategy in Historical Perspective* (Cambridge: Cambridge University Press, 2013), p. 167.
6. Ibid. p. 282.
7. Human Rights Watch, *'Between a Drone and Al-Qaeda': The Civilian Cost of US Targeted Killings in Yemen* (New York, 22 October 2013).

Available at <https://www.hrw.org/report/2013/10/22/between-drone-and-al-qaeda/civilian-cost-us-targeted-killings-yemen> (last accessed 20 November 2015).

8. For more on this point see Aaron Edwards, *Defending the Realm? The Politics of Britain's Small Wars since 1945* (Manchester: Manchester University Press, 2012).

9. Greg Mills, 'Calibrating ink spots: filling Afghanistan's ungoverned spaces', *RUSI Journal*, 151: 4, August 2006, pp. 16–25.

10. Douglas Porch, *Counterinsurgency: Exposing the Myths of the New Way of War* (Cambridge: Cambridge University Press, 2013).

11. Gray and Johnson 'The practice of strategy', p. 361.

12. Gray, *The Strategy Bridge*, p. 15.

13. For an excellent analysis on Germany's abstention in the UN Security Council on the use of force against Libya see Sarah Brockmeier, 'Germany and the intervention in Libya', *Survival*, 55: 6, 2013, pp. 63–90.

14. Explanation of vote by Ambassador Wittig on the Security Council resolution on Libya. Available at <http://www.new-york-un.diplo.de/Vertretung/newyorkvn/en/__pr/speeches-statements/2011/20110 317_20Explanation_20of_20vote_20-_20Libya.html> (last accessed 29 October 2015).

15. Spiegel Staff, '"A serious mistake of historic dimensions": Libya crisis leaves Berlin isolated', *Der Spiegel*, 28 March 2011. Available at <http://www.spiegel.de/international/germany/0,1518,753498,00.html> (last accessed 15 September 2015).

16. William Hague, 'Statement on Libya', House of Commons Debates (Hansard), 7 March 2011, Vol. 524, Col. 650.

17. African Union, *Peace and Security Council Communiqué*, issued at its 275th Meeting, Addis Ababa, 26 April 2011. Available at http://www.peaceau.org/uploads/communiquelibyaeng.pdf<http://au.int/en/dp/ps/sites/default/files/PSC%20Communique%20-%20 Libya%20_Eng%20_.pdf> (last accessed 3 January 2015).

18. Eliot A. Cohen, 'Change and transformation in military affairs', *Journal of Strategic Studies*, 27: 3, September 2004, p. 395.

19. Steven Metz, *Iraq and the Evolution of American Strategy* (Washington DC: Potomac Books, 2008), p. 160.

20. Sir Mark Lyall Grant, 'Explanation of vote on Libya', News – United Nations Security Council resolution on Libya No-Fly Zone has been approved. Available at <http://ukun.fco.gov.uk/en/news/?view=News&id=568282782> (last accessed 20 December 2011).

21. David Cameron, '"Foreign Policy in the National Interest": Speech to the Lord Mayor's Banquet', 14 November 2011. Available at <http://www.number10.gov.uk/news/lord-mayors-banquet/> (last accessed 10 December 2011).

22. House of Commons Defence Select Committee, *The Strategic Defence and Security Review and the National Security Strategy*. Sixth Report of Session, 2010–12, Vol. 1, 20 July 2011, HC 761 (London: TSO, 3 August 2011). Available at <http://www.publications.parliament.uk/pa/cm201012/cmselect/cmdfence/761/761.pdf> (last accessed 20 December 2011).

23. John Kampfner, 'If we want to punch above our weight, we'll have to pay for it', *The Independent*, 5 August 2011.

24. BBC, UK News, 'Cameron irritated over military chiefs' Libya comments'. BBC News website, 21 June 2011. Available at <http://www.bbc.co.uk/news/uk-13857733> (last accessed 4 September 2016).

25. Hans J. Morgenthau, *Politics Among Nations: The Struggle for Power and Peace*, brief edition, edited by Kenneth W. Thompson (Boston, MA: McGraw-Hill, [1948] 1993), p. 159.

26. Thomas G. Weiss, 'RtoP alive and well after Libya', *Ethics in International Affairs*, 25: 3, September 2011, pp. 1–6.

27. David Chandler, 'Libya: The End of Intervention?' *e-International Relations*, 17 November 2011. Available at <http://www.e-ir.info/?p=15325> (last accessed 4 January 2011).

28. Mungo Melvin, 'Soldiers, statesmen and strategy', *RUSI Journal*, 157: 1, February/March 2012, pp. 20–7.

29. MoD, *The Future Character of Conflict* (Shrivenham: DCDC, 2010), pp. 11–12.

30. HMG, *Strategic Defence and Security Review*, p. 16.

31. House of Commons Public Affairs Committee, *Who Does UK National Strategy?* First Report of Session, 2010–11, HC 435 (London: TSO, 18 October 2010), pp. 15, 28.

32. Ibid.

33. Andrew Hosken, *Empire of Fear: Inside the Islamic State* (London: Oneworld, 2015), pp. 188–9.

Conclusion

1. Colin S. Gray, *Perspectives on Strategy* (Oxford: Oxford University Press, 2013), p. 158.

2. Colin S. Gray, *The Strategy Bridge: Theory for Practice* (Oxford: Oxford University Press, 2010), p. 97.

Bibliography

Official Papers

House of Commons Public Affairs Committee, *Who Does UK National Strategy?*, First Report of Session, 2010–11, HC 435 (London: TSO, 18 October 2010).

MoD, *Land Operations: Volume I – The Fundamentals, Part 2 – Command and Control*, Army Code No. 70458, Part 2 (London: MoD, 28 April 1969).

MoD, *Land Operations: Volume III – Counter-Revolutionary Operations, Part 1 – Principles and General Aspects*, Army Code No. 70516, Part 1 (London: HMSO, 29 August 1969).

MoD, *Land Operations: Volume III – Counter-Revolutionary Operations, Part 2 – Internal Security*, Army Code No. 70516, Part 2 (London: HMSO, 26 November 1969).

MoD, *Land Operations: Volume III – Counter-Revolutionary Operations, Part 3 – Counter Insurgency*, Army Code No. 70516, Part 3 (London: HMSO, 5 January 1970).

MoD, *Land Operations: Volume III – Counter-Revolutionary Operations, Part 1 – General Principles*, Army Code No. 70516, Part 1 (London: HMSO, August 1977).

MoD, *Land Operations: Volume III – Counter-Revolutionary Operations, Part 2 – Procedures and Techniques*, Army Code No. 70516, Part 2 (London: HMSO, 1977).

MoD, *Strategic Defence Review*, Cm. 3999 (London: MoD, 1998).

MoD, *The Strategic Defence Review: A New Chapter* (London: MoD: July 2002).

MoD, *Operation Banner: An Analysis of Military Operations in Northern Ireland*, Army Code No. 71842 (London: MoD, July 2006).

MoD, Joint Defence Publication (JDP), 2/07, *Countering Irregular Activity within a Comprehensive Approach* (Shrivenham: DCDC, 2007).

MoD, *Joint Defence Publication 0-01: British Defence Doctrine*, (Shrivenham: DCDC: August 2008).

MoD, *Strategic Trends Programme: Future Character of Conflict* (Shrivenham: DCDC, February 2010).

MoD/Stabilisation Unit, Joint Doctrine Note 6/10, *Security Transitions: The Military Contribution* (Shrivenham: DCDC, November 2010).

Books and Articles

Acheson, Dean, *Power and Diplomacy: The William L. Clayton Lectures on International Economic Affairs and Foreign Policy* (Cambridge, MA: Harvard University Press, 1958).

Alderson, Colonel Alexander, 'Revising the British Army's counter-insurgency doctrine', *Royal United Services Institute Journal*, 152: 4, August 2007, pp. 6–11.

Alderson, Colonel Alexander, *The Validity of British Army Counterinsurgency Doctrine after the War in Iraq 2003–2009*, unpublished PhD thesis, Cranfield, November 2009.

Alderson, Colonel Alex, 'The Army's 'brain': a historical perspective on doctrine and development', *British Army Review*, 150, Winter 2010/11, pp. 60–4.

Aldrich, Richard J. and John Zametica, 'The rise and decline of a strategic concept: the Middle East, 1945–51', in Richard J. Aldrich (ed.), *British Intelligence, Strategy and the Cold War, 1945–51* (London: Routledge, 1992).

Allawi, Ali A., *The Occupation of Iraq: Winning the War, Losing the Peace* (New Haven: Yale University Press, 2007).

Anderson, David, *Histories of the Hanged: Britain's Dirty War in Kenya* (London: Phoenix, 2006).

Andrew, Christopher, *The Defence of the Realm: The Authorized History of MI5* (London: Allen Lane, 2009).

Angstrom, Jan and Isabelle Duyvesteyn (eds), *Understanding Victory and Defeat in Contemporary War* (Abingdon: Routledge, 2007).

Arendt, Hannah, *On Violence* (Orlando, FA: Harcourt Books, 1970).

Arendt, Hannah, *The Human Condition*, 2nd edn (Chicago: University of Chicago Press, 1999).

Aron, Raymond, *On War: Atomic Weapons and Global Diplomacy* (London: Secker and Warburg, 1958).

Aron, Raymond, *Democracy and Totalitarianism*, translated by Valence Ionescu (London: Weidenfeld and Nicolson, [1965] 1968).

Aron, Raymond, *The Imperial Republic: The United States and the World, 1945–1973*, translated by Frank Jellinek (London: Weidenfeld and Nicolson, 1973).

Barnett, Correlli, *Britain and Her Army, 1509–1970: A Military, Political and Social Survey* (London: Allen Lane, 1970).

Barnett, Correlli, *The Audit of War: The Illusion and Reality of Britain as a Great Nation* (London: Macmillan, 1986).

Barnett, Correlli, *The Lost Victory: British Dreams, British Realities, 1945–1950* (London: Macmillan, 1995).

Bass, Christopher and M. L. R. Smith, 'The dynamic of Irwin's forgotten army: a strategic understanding of the British Army's role in Northern Ireland after 1998', *Small Wars and Insurgencies*, 15: 3, 2004, pp. 1–24.

Baylis, John, Steve Smith and Patricia Owens (eds), *The Globalization of World Politics: An Introduction to International Relations*, 4th edn (Oxford: Oxford University Press, 2008).

Bayly, Christopher and Tim Harper, *Forgotten Armies: The Fall of British Asia, 1941–1945* (London: Allen Lane, 2004).

Bean, Tim, 'Naval warfare in the Pacific, 1941–5', in Simon Trew and Gary Sheffield (eds), *100 Years of Conflict, 1900–2000* (Stroud: Sutton Publishing, 2000), pp. 193–217.

Begin, Menachem, *The Revolt*, revised edition translated by Samuel Katz (London: W. H. Allen, 1983).

Bellamy, Chris, *Absolute War – Soviet Russia in the Second World War: A Modern History* (London: Macmillan, 2007).

Beevor, Antony, *The Second World War* (London: Weidenfeld and Nicolson, 2012).

Betz, David and Anthony Cormack, 'Iraq, Afghanistan and British strategy', *Orbis: A Journal of World Affairs*, 53: 2, Spring 2009, pp. 319–36.

Biddle, Stephen, 'Strategy in war', *PS: Political Science and Politics*, 40: 3, July 2007, pp. 461–6.

Bird, Tim and Alex Marshal, *Afghanistan: How the West Lost its Way* (London: Yale University Press, 2011).

Bourke, Joanna, *An Intimate History of Killing: Face to Face Killing in Twentieth Century Warfare* (London: Granta, 1999).

Braithwaite, Rodric, *Afghantsy: The Russians in Afghanistan, 1979–89* (London, Profile Books, [2011] 2012).

Brinkley, Douglas, 'Dean Acheson and the Special Relationship: The West Point speech of December 1962', *Historical Journal*, 33: 3, September 1990, pp. 599–608.

Brodie, Bernard and Fawn Brodie, *From Crossbow to H-Bomb*, revised and enlarged edition (London: Indiana University Press, [1962] 1973).

Brodie, Bernard, *War and Politics* (London: Cassell, 1973).

Broers, Michael, *Napoleon: Soldier of Destiny* (London: Faber, 2014).

Browning, Christopher, *Ordinary Men: Reserve Police Battalion 101 and the Final Solution in Poland* (London: Penguin, 2001).

Bull, Hedley, *The Anarchical Society: A Study of Order in World Politics*, 3rd edn (Basingstoke: Palgrave, [1977] 2002).

Burke, Jason, *Al-Qaeda: The True Story of Radical Islam* (London: Penguin Books, 2007).

Burke, Jason, *The New Threat from Islamic Militancy* (London: The Bodley Head, 2015).

Burleigh, Michael, *Moral Combat: A History of World War II* (London: Harper Press, 2010).

Bush, George W., *Decision Points* (London: Virgin Books, 2010).

Caesar, Julius, *The Conquest of Gaul* (London: Penguin, 1951).

Carr, E. H., *The Twenty Years' Crisis 1919–1939: An Introduction to the Study of International Relations* (London: Macmillan, [1939] 1970).

Cartledge, Paul, *Alexander the Great: The Truth Behind the Myth* (London: Pan Books, [2004] 2013).

Carver, Michael, *War since 1945* (London: Weidenfeld and Nicolson, 1980).

Castaneda, Jorge, *Companero: The Life and Death of Che Guevara* (London: Bloomsbury, 1997).

Castro, Fidel, *My Life* (London: Allen Lane, 2007).

Clark, Christopher, *The Sleepwalkers: How Europe Went to War in 1914* (London: Allen Lane, 2013).

Clark, General Wesley K., *Winning Modern Wars: Iraq, Terrorism, and the American Empire* (New York: Public Affairs, 2003).

Clausewitz, Carl von, *On War*, edited and translated by Michael Howard and Peter Paret (Princeton, NJ: Princeton University Press, 1976).

Cochrane, Feargal, *Ending Wars* (Cambridge: Polity, 2008).

Cohen, Eliot, *Supreme Command: Soldiers, Statesmen and Leadership in Wartime* (New York: Free Press, 2002).

Cole, Roger and Richard Belfield, *SAS Operation Storm: The SAS Under Siege, Nine Men against Four Hundred* (London: Hodder and Stoughton, 2011).

Coll, Steve, *Ghost Wars: The Secret History of the CIA, Afghanistan and Bin Laden, from the Soviet Invasion to September 10, 2001* (London: Penguin, 2004).

Collins, Michael, *The Path to Freedom* (Wales: Welsh Academic Press, [1922] 1996).

Collins, Randall, 'The micro-sociology of violence', *British Journal of Sociology*, 60: 3, 2009, pp. 566–76.

Corbett, Julian, *Some Principles of Maritime Strategy* (London: Longmans, Green and Co., [1911] 1938).

Cornish, Paul and Andrew M. Dorman, 'Dr Fox and the philosopher's stone: the alchemy of national defence in the age of austerity', *International Affairs*, 87: 2, 2011, pp. 335–53.

Dallaire, Lieutenant-General Roméo, *Shake Hands with the Devil: The Failure of Humanity in Rwanda* (London: Arrow Books, 2003).

Dannatt, General Sir Richard, *Leading from the Front: The Autobiography* (London: Bantam Press, 2010).

Dockrill, Michael, *British Defence Since 1945* (Oxford: Blackwell, 1989).

Dorman, Andrew M., *Blair's Successful War: Britain's Military Intervention in Sierra Leone* (Farnham: Ashgate, 2009).

Dorman, Andrew, 'Providing for defence in an age of austerity: future war, defence cuts and the 2010 Strategic (Security and) Defence (and Security) Review', *Political Quarterly*, 81: 3, July–September 2010, pp. 376–84.

Douchet, Giulio, *The Command of the Air* (London: Faber and Faber, 1943).

Dower, John W., *War Without Mercy: Race and Power in the Pacific War* (New York: Pantheon Books, 1986).

Downs, Frederick, *The Killing Zone: My Life in the Vietnam War* (London: W. W. Norton, [1978] 1993).

Doyle, Michael W., *Ways of War and Peace: Realism, Liberalism and Socialism* (New York: W. W. Norton, 1997).

Duffy, Christopher, *The Military Experience in the Age of Reason* (London: Routledge and Kegan Paul, 1987).

Edwards, Aaron, 'Abandoning armed resistance? The Ulster Volunteer Force as a case-study of strategic terrorism in Northern Ireland', *Studies in Conflict and Terrorism*, 32: 2, February 2009, pp. 146–66.

Edwards, Aaron, 'Misapplying lessons learned? Analysing the utility of British counter-insurgency strategy in Northern Ireland, 1971–76', *Small Wars and Insurgencies*, 21: 2, June 2010, pp. 303–30.

Edwards, Aaron, 'When terrorism as strategy fails: dissident Irish Republicans and the threat to British security', *Studies in Conflict and Terrorism*, 34: 4, April 2011, pp. 318–36.

Edwards, Aaron, *Dissident Irish Republican Terrorists and British Security* (Swindon: AHRC, September 2011). Available at <http://www.ahrc.ac.uk/News-and-Events/Publications/Documents/Lessons-Learnt-Dissident-Irish-Republicans.pdf> (last accessed 15 June 2015).

Edwards, Aaron, 'Deterrence, coercion and brute force in asymmetric conflict: the role of the military instrument in resolving the Northern Ireland "Troubles"', *Dynamics of Asymmetric Conflict*, Special Edition on Conflict and Post-conflict in Northern Ireland, 4: 3, December 2011, pp. 226–41.

Edwards, Aaron, *Defending the Realm? The Politics of Britain's Small Wars since 1945* (Manchester: Manchester University Press, 2012, 2014).

Edwards, Aaron, 'Britain's "9/11 Wars" in historical perspective: why change *and* continuity matter', *History and Policy*, 20 March 2013. <http://www.historyandpolicy.org/papers/policy-paper-143.html> (last accessed 5 September 2016).

Edwards, Aaron, *Mad Mitch's Tribal Law: Aden and the End of Empire* (London: Transworld, 2014, 2015).

Egnell, Robert, 'Lessons from Helmand, Afghanistan: what now for British counter-insurgency', *International Affairs*, 87: 2, 2011, pp. 297–315.

English, Richard, *Modern War: A Very Short Introduction* (Oxford: Oxford University Press, 2013).

Fairweather, Jack, *A War of Choice: The British in Iraq, 2003–2009* (London: Jonathan Cape, 2011).

Falls, Cyril, *The Nature of Modern Warfare* (London: Methuen, 1941).

Falls, Cyril, *Ordeal by Battle* (London: Methuen, 1943).

Falls, Cyril, *The Art of War: From the Age of Napoleon to the Present Day* (London: Oxford University Press, 1961).

Ferguson, Niall, *The Pity of War* (London: Allen Lane, 1998).

Ferguson, Niall, *Empire: How Britain Made the Modern World* (London: Penguin, 2003).

Ferguson, Niall, *The War of the World: History's Age of Hatred* (London: Allen Lane, 2006).

Ferguson, Niall, *Civilisation: The West and the Rest* (London: Allen Lane, 2011).

Fergusson, James, *A Million Bullets: The Real Story of the British Army in Afghanistan* (London: Bantam Press, 2008).

Fergusson, James, *Taliban: The True Story of the World's Most Feared Guerrilla Fighters* (London: Transworld, 2010).

Fitzgibbon, Spencer, *Not Mentioned in Dispatches: The History and Mythology of the Battle of Goose Green* (Cambridge: Lutterworth Press, 2001).

Freedman, Lawrence, 'Order and disorder in the New World', *Foreign Affairs*, 71: 1, 1992, pp. 20–37.

Freedman, Lawrence, *The Politics of British Defence, 1979–98* (Basingstoke: Macmillan, 1999).

Freedman, Lawrence, *The Official History of the Falklands Campaign, Vol. II: War and Diplomacy* (London: Routledge, 2005).

Freedman, Lawrence, *Strategy: A History* (Oxford: Oxford University Press, 2013).

Fremont-Barnes, Gregory, *Waterloo, 1815: The British Army's Day of Destiny* (Stroud: History Press, 2014).

Fremont-Barnes, Gregory (ed.), *A History of Counterinsurgency – Volume 1: From South Africa to Algeria, 1900–1954* (Santa Barbara, CA: Praeger, 2015).

Fremont-Barnes, Gregory (ed.), *A History of Counterinsurgency – Volume 2: From Kenya to Afghanistan, 1955–Present* (Santa Barbara, CA: Praeger, 2015).

Fuller, Colonel J. F. C., *The Reformation of War* (London: Hutchinson and Company, 1923).

Fuller, Colonel J. F. C., *The Dragon's Teeth: A Study of War and Peace* (London: Constable, 1932).

Fuller, Colonel J. F. C., *War and Western Civilisation, 1832–1932: A Study of War as a Political Instrument and the Expression of Mass Democracy* (London: Duckworth, 1932).

Gardiner, Ian, *The Yompers: With 45 Commando in the Falklands War* (Barnsley: Pen and Sword, 2012).

Gellhorn, Martha, *The Face of War* (London: Virago Press, [1936] 1986).

Gentile, Colonel Gian, *Wrong Turn: America's Deadly Embrace of Counterinsurgency* (New York: New Press, 2013).

Giustozzi, Antonio, *Koran, Kalashnikov and Laptop* (London: Hurst and Company, 2007).

Galula, David, *Counter-insurgency Warfare: Theory and Practice* (London: Praeger Security International, 1964, 2006).

Gray, Colin S., *Explorations in Strategy* (Westport, CT: Greenwood Press, 1996).

Gray, Colin S., 'Clausewitz rules, OK? The Future is the past – with GPS', *Review of International Studies*, 25: 5, December 1999, pp. 161–82.

Gray, Colin S., *Modern Strategy* (Oxford: Oxford University Press, 1999).

Gray, Colin S., *Another Bloody Century: Future Warfare* (London: Weidenfeld and Nicolson, 2005).

Gray, Colin S., *War, Peace and International Relations: An Introduction to Strategic History* (Abingdon: Routledge, 2007).

Gray, Colin S., 'War – continuity in change, and change in continuity', *Parameters: The US Army's Senior Professional Journal*, 40: 1, Summer 2010, pp. 5–13.

Griffith, Paddy, *Forward into Battle: Fighting Tactics from Waterloo to the Near Future*, revised and updated edition (Ramsbury: Crowood Press, 1990).

Grivas, George, *The Memoirs of General Grivas*, edited by Charles Foley (London: Longmans, 1964).

Guthrie, Charles and Michael Quinlan, *Just War: The Just War Tradition: Ethics in Modern Warfare* (New York: Walker and Company, 2007).

Gwynn, Charles, *Imperial Policing* (London: Macmillan, 1934).

Harnden, Toby, *Dead Men Risen: The Welsh Guards and the Real Story of Britain's War in Afghanistan* (London: Quercus, 2011).

Harris, J. P., *Men, Ideas and Tanks: British Military Thought and Armoured Forces, 1903–1939* (Manchester: Manchester University Press, 1995).

Harrison Place, Timothy, *Military Training in the British Army, 1940–1944: From Dunkirk to D-Day* (Abingdon: Routledge, 2000).

Hart, Russell A., *Clash of Arms: How the Allies Won in Normandy* (Oklahoma: University of Oklahoma Press, 2004).

Hashim, Ahmed S., *Iraq's Sunni Insurgency*, Adelphi Paper No. 402 (London: IISS, 2009).

Hastings, Max, *Overlord : D-Day and the Battle for Normandy* (London: Pan Books, 1984).

Hastings, Max, *The Korean War* (London: Michael Joseph, 1987).

Hauser, Beatrice, *Reading Clausewitz* (London: Pimlico, 2002).

Healey, Denis, *The Time of My Life* (London: Penguin, 1990).

Hemingway, Ernest, *Hemingway on War* (London: Vintage, 2014).

Hennessy, Brian, *The Sharp End: The Trauma of a War in Vietnam* (St Leonards, NSW: Allen and Unwin, 1997).

Herzog, Chaim, *The Arab-Israeli Wars: War and Peace in the Middle East* (Bath: Book Club Associates, 1982).

Heuser, Beatrice, *Reading Clausewitz* (London: Pimlico, 2002).

Hewitt, Steve, *The British War on Terror: Terrorism and Counter-Terrorism on the Home Front since 9/11* (London: Continuum, 2008).

Hill, Christopher, *God's Englishman: Oliver Cromwell and the English Revolution* (London: Weidenfeld and Nicolson, 1970).

Hitchens, Christopher, *Cyprus* (London: Quartet Books, 1984).

Hobbes, Thomas, *Leviathan* (London: Penguin Classics, [1651] 1987).